The Immigrant

The remarkable story of Philip Vampatella

By John Vampatella

To everyone who ever dreamed of a better life and who was willing to take a risk to pursue it.

Copyright © 2019 by John Vampatella

All Rights Reserved

ISBN: 9781670087126

Cover Photo: SS Napoli

Table of Contents

Chapter	Page
Introduction	5
Chapter 1 – Emancipation	9
Chapter 2 – Risorgimento	15
Chapter 3 – Lynching	22
Chapter 4 – Childhood	33
Chapter 5 – Crossing	42
Chapter 6 – Arrival	48
Chapter 7 – Beginnings	55
Chapter 8 – Rapuanos	61
Chapter 9 – The Great War	70
Chapter 10 – Enlistment	78
Chapter 11 – Reunions	88
Chapter 12 – Restrictions	97
Chapter 13 – Antoinette	105
Chapter 14 – Great River	111
Chapter 15 – The Klan and the Mafia	119
Chapter 16 – Prohibition	127
Chapter 17 – The Great Depression	135
Chapter 18 – Dreams	145
Chapter 19 – Recovery	154
Chapter 20 – Long Island Express	162
Chapter 21 – World War	172
Chapter 22 – Arkansas	182
Chapter 23 – Internment	195
Chapter 24 – Passeggiata	204
Chapter 25 – Fifties	210
Chapter 26 – Departure	219
Chapter 27 – Here and There	225
Chapter 28 – Flip	237
Chapter 29 – Endings	246
Afterword	255

Introduction

In the fall of 2017, I attended a conference with Athletes in Action, the organization I work with, called LENSES. The purpose of the conference was to help attendees see the world through the eyes of people who are different, who come from different circumstances, different backgrounds, who have different racial and cultural contexts. It was meant to engender empathy and give people tools to be able to have different perspective. It was, to be sure, an incredible, fun, challenging experience.

One thing the LENSES staff encouraged us with was that we all have our own ethnicity. Sometimes we make the mistake of thinking that there's "white" and there's "ethnic", as if "white" doesn't come with ethnicity or culture. Moreover, we were encouraged to look into our own cultural heritage, to learn more what it means to be…us. I took that to heart and have spent time reviewing my own family's roots and family tree and the cultures out of which we came.

That brought me to my paternal grandfather, Philip Vampatella.

In the summer of 2011, I took my family to New York City, and met my parents, Philip and Patricia Vampatella, there for several days of sightseeing. One place we visited was Ellis Island, where my father's father passed through in 1913 as a teenage boy, upon immigrating to the United States. There we learned about the process of immigration at that time and what an immigrant's journey looked like. Meanwhile, I was given a copy of my grandfather's memoirs, bound in a hardcover book with old-school typeface, complete with his notes in the margins (these were all photocopied pages, not the originals). He had put together a book about his life, pieced together in two parts. The first part read like a self-written biography, writing of himself in the third person. The second part began at the point where he obviously had, in real-time, actually started writing his personal biography, and this second part was a series of journal entries. He had transitioned at that point from historical biography to journal entries, because that's when he started writing this project. The journal entries ended before 1967, and he still had another 16 years to live. Unfortunately, there was no more after that.

The book was difficult to read, not because my grandfather did not have a mastery of the English language, but because the pages were faded and his hand-written edits and notes were not easy to decipher at times. As part of a family reunion in 2018, my cousin Cathy Gallagher and her husband Mark undertook to clean it up and bind it in a fresh volume. It is titled *"Passeggiata"* (my grandfather's original title), and can be found at Amazon.

As I dove into my grandfather's life, I found his story compelling and fascinating. Clearly, I had, and have, a personal stake in his journey. After all, without him, I simply would not exist. But his story reflected the very kind of cultural investigation I sought to undertake following my time at the LENSES conference. His story, in a sense, is my story.

I decided to put his story in a larger context. Scattered throughout his (auto)biography, he referenced larger events going on in the outside world, but I wanted to bring that to life in a deeper way. This isn't merely the story of Philip Vampatella. This is the story of Philip Vampatella set against the backdrop of a much larger world and culture, that helped shape the very experiences he would have. There are chapters in the book that are strictly about Philip and other people in his life, but there are chapters that are strictly about historical events that give context to what it was like to be an Italian-American in the early 20th century. In fact, the book opens up with several chapters that do not reference Philip at all, but set the table for his arrival to the United States in 1913.

So what kind of book is this? Well, it's not exactly a biography, though it is that. It's not exactly a history book, though it is that too. It would technically be considered "creative nonfiction". Because I want it to read as a story, not a history book or college textbook, it won't have any footnotes. There is a website for the book that contains all the sources I used for the history portions of the book. Some people who have put together sources that I ended up using may recognize their work; my list of sources represents my thank you for their contribution to this story. That website is: johnvampatella.com/theimmigrant.

The sole source for Philip's biography is his autobiography and journal notes that are found in the book *Passeggiata*. Obviously other people in Philip's life are mentioned, but I did not take the time to talk to them or, if they're deceased, their relatives, because I wanted this story told from Philip's perspective. This is how HE saw the world. This is HIS experience.

Chapter 18 is unique. Philip is deathly sick and recounts some vivid dreams he has while spending a month in the hospital. These dreams I have taken virtually word-for-word from *Passeggiata*, and here's why: I wanted the reader to see them exactly as Philip recalled. Moreover, this shows the reader a little bit of Philip's writing style and mastery of the language.

On occasion I make up an historical character, such as we come across in the very first chapter. Jacob is not an historical person but he represents the common slave at the time. Other times I make up dialogue that I think suits the scene. But whenever I use a story from *Passeggiata* where there's actual dialogue, I try to use it word-for-word.

During the process of working on this project, I asked for help from my father and a few other family members, helping me make sure I got an accurate understanding of various details. I wanted to make sure that my rendering of Philip's story was consistent with how they remembered him to be. But like I said, I did not go to them to give me another side of the story. I fully recognize that there's always another side to the story, and that Philip's recollection may not fully reflect the actual facts. That's okay. Again, the purpose is to tell *his* story from *his* recollection, not to provide a fully-researched biography that has been cross-referenced by interviews from other people in his life. Sometimes the portrayal of another person in the story is less than kind. I'm ok with that, not to disparage that person but rather to just give you a sense of what my grandfather thought, how HE viewed things. If anyone is offended, my apologies. You can take it up with Philip the next time you see him.

This has been a labor of love and in some respects represents my own life journey, as I have been interested in his story for most of my own life. At our family reunion in 2018, my cousin Jennifer played a tape recording (she had it digitized from the original cassette) from my grandfather. It was the first time I had heard his voice in nearly 35 years, and it was the first time my children had any contact with him. To hear his voice in that recording was special. I do not know if my grandfather was a remarkable man. In some respects I think he simply represents typical immigrants at the time and went through many of the same things other immigrants did. But to me he was quite remarkable, arriving in the U.S. as a teenager, having to find his own way in a new world, making a life for himself, raising a family, and leaving a legacy. He was far from perfect; he had many flaws, some of which are evident in this book. But to me, he was a great man, and it's a pleasure telling his story.

I'd like to thank my grandfather, for penning his personal memoirs as recorded in Passeggiata, my cousin Cathy Gallagher and her husband Mark, for putting Passeggiata in a more readable form and providing me with some crucial details, my cousin Jen Jones who answered a number of questions to help me fill in the blanks, my parents, Phil and Patricia Vampatella, who helped me get some stories straight, my wife Diane who encouraged me to pursue this project, and those that read it and gave me feedback.

To the reader, please understand that this is the story of my grandfather, told in the context of the larger story of Italian-Americans in the United States. In that light, his story is just a representation of what many Italian immigrants went through as they came to this country.

Chapter 1 – Emancipation

The slave, named Jacob, wiped the sweat from his dark brow. The July Charleston sun beat down with typical southern summer ferocity. Jacob looked out on the tobacco field owned by James Commerce, a sweeping plot of land with tobacco in row after row. For the Commerce family, tobacco was both a sign and a source of their wealth. But so was Jacob and his family, as well as the three dozen other slaves that worked on the Commerce plantation. The Commerce family had crossed the Atlantic from Liverpool, England, nearly 200 years before, and had established a home in Charleston. Tobacco quickly became the crop of choice and before long, they were engaged in a healthy business. A growing business required more workers, and fortunately for the Commerce family, there was a steady supply of labor coming over in slave ships from Africa. For five generations, the Commerce family had bought and sold slaves, and, like with any business enterprise, the number of slaves one owned indicated the level of one's wealth. The Commerce family was…wealthy.

Jacob was 28 years old, the son of Tom and Ruth Commerce, who had spent their entire lives on the Commerce plantation. They knew nothing about the outside world. Day after day, month after month, and year after year, Tom and Ruth had labored in the tobacco fields, providing their plantation owners with product to sell at the market. Generations ago, slaves on the Commerce plantation were given the last name of Commerce, a tradition that was common, though not universal, in the American south. The real names of Jacob's ancestors had long since passed out of record or memory, and like many slaves, their last name was the same as the plantation owner's.

Like Tom and Ruth, Jacob had known only one life. It was a life of sweat and toil and pain and hard, unrelenting labor. A life of forced servitude. A life of chains and commands and obedience and whips and blood, sweat, and tears. Many, many tears. From the moment he could first do any sort of work, Jacob had labored for the Commerce family. He had become an expert in tobacco, and an expert in dealing with the life of slavery.

Today, on September 22, 1862, though he was completely unaware of this fact, Jacob's life would change.

What Jacob did not know was that 530 miles away, President Abraham Lincoln declared Jacob to be a free man. Well, that is not strictly true. What Lincoln did was announce that any state engaged in war against the Union needed to cease hostilities and rejoin the union. In any state that did not end their rebellion, on January 1, 1863, every single slave in that state would be declared free. Lincoln's words were:

> "That on the first day of January in the year of our Lord, one thousand eight hundred and sixty-three, all persons held as slaves within any State, or designated part of a State, the people whereof shall then be in rebellion against the United States shall be then, thenceforward, and forever free; and the executive government of the United States, including the military and naval authority thereof, will recognize and maintain the freedom of such persons, and will do no act or acts to repress such persons, or any of them, in any efforts they may make for their actual freedom."

Jacob, of course, had no way of knowing what these words meant. He did not even know that they had been declared by President Lincoln. After all, he could not read, and it was unlikely that Mr. James Commerce himself would walk down the long row of tobacco leaves, gather Jacob and the other slaves, and let them hear the wonderful news of their emancipation. James Commerce, of course, did not even recognize the authority of Abraham Lincoln, being a loyal citizen of South Carolina, the first state to secede from the United States, more than a year and a half prior, in December of 1860. James Commerce was loyal to South Carolina and the Confederate States of America, not some slave-loving Republican in Washington.

And so Jacob went back to his backbreaking work, unaware that history had changed. It would take a formal proclamation on January 1, 1863, followed by two more years of brutal and bloody war between the North and the South before Jacob and his fellow slaves would realize this freedom.

. . . . .

The Emancipation Proclamation proved to be an enormous first step in the process of ending slavery in the United States, but it was far from the last. Lincoln faced two enormously difficult issues as President: (1) What to do about slavery, and (2) How to preserve the Union? The Civil War had not yet broken out, but there were signs of disunity and discontent raging across the nation. The 1860 Republican Party platform consisted of 17 points. Among them was a commitment to republicanism: a true national union, yet state sovereignty within that union. In point #3 of the party platform, the Republicans declared, "That to the Union of the States, this nation owes its unprecedented increase of population, its surprising development of material resources, its rapid augmentation of wealth, its happiness at home and its honor abroad; and we hold in abhorrence all schemes for Disunion, come from whatever source they may: And we congratulate the country that no Republican member of Congress has uttered or countenanced the threats of Disunion so often made by Democratic members, without rebuke and with applause from their political associates...."

Holding together the United States was of paramount importance for the Republicans and Lincoln in 1860. The slave states understood that history had begun to turn, that slavery was growing less and less tolerable as an institution. Yet the Southern economy – the massive cash crops of tobacco and cotton, for example – depended on the availability of cheap labor. As there was not yet mechanized farming, these crops were tended to by hand, and the enormous plantations that dotted the landscape in Alabama, Georgia, South Carolina, and Mississippi required millions of workers. The trans-Atlantic slave trade had been outlawed by Congress in 1807, but that did not eliminate slavery itself. In fact, the number of slaves in the United States grew dramatically in the early part of the 19th century, largely through the natural process of birth. From 1808 to 1860, the black population in the United States grew from 400,000 to 4.4 million, 3.9 million of whom were slaves.

There seemed to be an inexhaustible need for more slaves to work the Southern plantations. For decades, Democrats in Southern states called for a renewal of the slave trade. The 1860 Republican platform (point #9) strongly opposed this new trans-Atlantic slave trade, stating, "That we brand the recent re-opening of the African Slave Trade, under the cover of our national flag, aided by perversions of judicial power, as a crime against humanity and a burning shame to our country and age; and we call upon Congress to take prompt and efficient measures for the total and final suppression of that execrable traffic."

Republicans were committed to preserving the Union and to ending slavery. But how could this be done when half the nation was committed to preserving *slavery*? Mr. Commerce' livelihood and fortune required the services of slaves, and he was not alone. The entire Southern economy depended on slavery.

Lincoln's election, of course, only increased the cries for disunion – the very thing the Republican platform opposed. The harder the Republicans pushed to end slavery, the more they pushed the Southern states away. The only way to keep the Southern states in the Union was to grant the existence of the very inhumane institution that the Republicans opposed so greatly.

For Lincoln, these two enormous issues pulled at him in a vicious tug-of-war. On personal moral grounds, he was vehemently opposed to slavery. But as President, his first priority was the preservation of the Union.

Horace Greeley had been a crucial member of the movement to found the Republican party. His newspaper, the *New York Tribune*, served as the mouthpiece for Greeley's ideas for reform, which were deep and far-ranging. Greeley was perhaps most vocal about the subject of slavery, and he argued strongly for abolition, believing that the Union cause necessitated destroying the institution of slavery. In an editorial titled, "The Prayer of Twenty Millions", published on August 20, 1862, Greeley pushed Lincoln hard to free the slaves. Greeley wrote, "We complain that the Union cause has suffered, and is now suffering immensely, from mistaken deference to Rebel Slavery. Had you, Sir, in your Inaugural

Address, unmistakably given notice that, in case the Rebellion already commenced were persisted in, and your efforts to preserve the Union and enforce the laws should be resisted by armed force, you would recognize no loyal person as rightfully held in Slavery by a traitor, we believe the Rebellion would therein have received a staggering if not fatal blow."

Such a sharp criticism from a fellow Republican stung Lincoln, and he needed to reply. Two days later, the President sent Greeley a letter. In that letter, he explained his position more clearly. Lincoln said,

> *As to the policy I "seem to be pursuing" as you say, I have not meant to leave any one in doubt.*
>
> *I would save the Union. I would save it the shortest way under the Constitution. The sooner the national authority can be restored; the nearer the Union will be "the Union as it was." If there be those who would not save the Union, unless they could at the same time save slavery, I do not agree with them. If there be those who would not save the Union unless they could at the same time destroy slavery, I do not agree with them. My paramount object in this struggle is to save the Union, and is not either to save or to destroy slavery. If I could save the Union without freeing any slave I would do it, and if I could save it by freeing all the slaves I would do it; and if I could save it by freeing some and leaving others alone I would also do that. What I do about slavery, and the colored race, I do because I believe it helps to save the Union; and what I forbear, I forbear because I do not believe it would help to save the Union. I shall do less whenever I shall believe what I am doing hurts the cause, and I shall do more whenever I shall believe doing more will help the cause. I shall try to correct errors when shown to be errors; and I shall adopt new views so fast as they shall appear to be true views.*
>
> *I have here stated my purpose according to my view of official duty; and I intend no modification of my oft-expressed personal wish that all men every where could be free.*

Lincoln had established in few words both his official policy and personal preference, which he pursued together, but which had to come in some order of priority. And for Lincoln, the official Presidential purpose came first: the preservation of the Union. The freeing of the slaves would come second, and though he believed with all his heart that there should be no man in chains, his pursuit of emancipation would come only insofar as it served the purpose of preserving the Union.

Lincoln had written that letter while the Emancipation Proclamation sat in his desk drawer. He knew, having written those words to Greeley, that he would try to preserve the Union while freeing the slaves.

. . . . .

Jacob Commerce knew none of this. He did not know who Horace Greeley was. He did not read the New York Tribune. He did not know the tension that existed in Washington, DC, even among fellow Republicans. He did not know that Lincoln was explaining to a New York newspaper editor why he was pursuing the course of action that led to the Emancipation Proclamation.

All Commerce knew was that the tobacco fields needed tending to, and that it was his job to tend to them. And so with the sweat pouring off his forehead and humming a Negro spiritual, he strode through the rows of tobacco, completely unaware that he was soon to be a free man. Legally, anyway. The reality was, of course, quite different.

Chapter 2 – Risorgimento

The *Duomo* in Milan, Italy took some 430 years to build. The Milanese people like to say that the massive gothic cathedral is "ever being built". In order to get the marble to the piazza where the *Duomo* was being built, huge canals had to be dug to transport the stone from the quarries on barges to the city center. It took 30 years to dig the canals just to ship the stone used to build the *Duomo*.

Much more recently, another large and impressive building was built, right next to the *Duomo*. It is the *Galleria Vittorio Emanuele II*, designed in 1861 and built by Guiseppe Mengoni between 1865 and 1867. The cross-shaped building is four stories high and in the center, the arcade is covered by a spectacular glass dome. In the center are four mosaics portraying the coat of arms of Turin, Florence, and Rome, the three captials of the kingdom of Italy. Milan's own coat of arms is the fourth. On one side of the Galleria is the famous *Duomo*, and on the other is the equally famous *Teatro Alla Scala*, one of the world's premier opera houses.

It is, in fact, the oldest active shopping mall in Italy, named for the man who unified various Italian states into one nation: Vittorio Emanuele (Victor Emmanuel).

. . . . .

The Italian peninsula was a collection of independent tribes and cities, constantly at war with one another. In this way, it was not unlike many other parts of the world in the centuries and decades preceding the birth of Christ. The city of Rome rebelled against its Etruscan overlords in the mid 500s B.C., and a Roman monarchy was established. The Etruscans still held sway, however, and it wasn't until 509 B.C. that this monarchy, and the Etruscans, were finally defeated, and the Roman Republic was born.

Roman influence began to spread throughout the entire Italian peninsula. Rome fought wars with the Sabines, the Vientes, and with Tarquinii, Falerii, and Caere over the next two centuries. By the middle of the 400s B.C., Rome had conquered their Etruscan and Latin neighbors, and following a brief downturn following the sack of Rome by invading Celtic tribes from 390-387 B.C., resumed their expansion throughout the peninsula. Between 280-275 B.C., Rome fought what became known as the Pyrrhic wars. By this point in time, Rome had become the dominant force on the Italian peninsula, but had not yet truly been tested against the powers in Greece or North Africa. Conflict between Rome and the Greek kingdom of Epirus erupted and Pyrrhus, the ruler of this portion of Greece, launched an assault on Rome. Over five years, Pyrrhus battled the Romans up and down the peninsula, and even though the Greeks largely were victorious, Pyrrhus had lost so many men that his best course of action was to withdraw. The term "Pyrrhic victory" became attached to a victory won at such a great cost as to make the victory, effectively, a defeat. Following the Roman victory over Pyrrhus, Roman forces conquered Greek colonies in southern Italy, and by the mid 200s B.C., Rome was the dominant force in all of Italy.

For the next 180 years, Rome fought against its main Mediterranean rival, Carthage, in what became known as the Punic Wars. In the Second Punic War, the Carthaginian general Hannibal Barca led an incredible invasion of Italy, and defeated Rome at the Battle of Cannae. Under threat of annihilation from Hannibal, Rome employed a bold strategy of sending general Scipio Africanus to invade Carthage on African soil. Carthage recalled Hannibal to defend the capital, but in the Battle of Kama, Roman forces defeated Hannibal and the Carthaginians. In the Third Punic War, Rome completely annihilated Carthage and destroyed the city once and for all, and Rome's main Mediterranean enemy was utterly defeated, leaving Rome as the dominant power not only on the Italian peninsula, but throughout the Mediterranean.

For the next 600 years, the Romans, transitioning from a republic to an empire, ruled a united Italy and even expanded into Germania, Brittania, Gaul, and Palestine. Roman exerted its influence throughout Europe, Africa, and the Middle East, and Roman ideas of government, law, architecture, culture, and technology can still be seen today.

Eventually, however, the Roman Empire became too large to be ruled from just Rome. Vast road networks made moving goods and troops much easier throughout the Empire than in other parts of the world, but the empire was just too big to be managed easily. Emperor Diocletian established the tetrarchy, which created four administrative units. Two junior emperors ruled frontier territories, while Maximillian was given responsibility over the west, and Diocletian himself ruled the east, while at the same time retaining ultimate authority over the entire empire. In 324, Emperor Constantine built the city of Constantinople on the site of Byzantium, and Constantine ruled the empire from there. The division of the empire into these administrative units, however, made for rivalries within the Roman Empire itself. Eventually, the city of Rome was sacked by King Alaric and the Visigoths. It was the first time in 800 years that the city of Rome had been conquered by a foreign power. No longer was Rome the ruler of Italy, and the Italian peninsula was no longer unified.

In the centuries that followed, the Holy Roman Empire emerged, but the peninsula was nonetheless divided. In the north was the Kingdom of Italy. In the middle were the Papal States. And in the south was the Kingdom of the Two Sicilies. Beginning with the sack of Rome in 410 A.D. by Alaric, and the subsequent collapse of the Western Roman Empire in 476 A.D., Italy would not be unified for more than 1,400 years. In those 1,400 years, Italy saw the rise of great city-states like Venice, Milan, and Florence. Alliances, conquests, divisions, and rivalries dominated Italy for centuries.

And then came the *Risorgimento*.

. . . . .

Napoleon had designs on conquering all of Europe. His army marched across southern Europe, over the Alps, and into Italy. He had designs on Milan, and as his troops advanced, Archduke Ferdinand I of Austria, prepared to flee. The Archduke ruled Milan from the Castello

Sforzesco, the fortress in the northwestern corner of the heart of Milan. The Castello, built as a fortress by Galeazzo Visconti II, the Lord of western Milan, between 1360 and 1370, grew over the years as successors added to it. When the Duomo was built, the castello was a straight shot down Via Dante, which would become Via Cordusio, and then Via Orefici as it reached the Piazza del Duomo. In May 1796, Napoleon marched straight for the castle, and as he did, the Archduke fled, leaving only a tiny garrison behind. They were no match for Napoleon.

He conquered Italy and much of Europe. But his time eventually came to an end, and when it did, the Congress of Vienna restored the pre-Napoleonic governments, which resembled more of a patchwork of administrations rather than an organized body. Italian revolutionaries, led by Giuseppe Mazzini and Giuseppe Garibaldi, sought to create a republic instead of a kingdom. Mazzini was soon thrown in prison, and while there, he formulated the skeleton of a plan for how Italy could be unified. In 1831, he was released and he moved to France and established the *La Giovine Italia* (Young Italy), a political movement working to unify Italy. Garibaldi, meanwhile, was sentenced to death, but escaped, spending fourteen years in exile in South America before returning in 1848.

On January 5, 1848, Italian revolutionaries initiated a strike in Lombardy, and revolts began in Sicily and Naples. The Sicilian movement led to an independent kingdom of Sicily, with Ruggero Settimo as the leader. That lasted a year, when the Bourbon army reclaimed the island by force. In February 1848, citizens revolted in Tuscany, and soon afterward, three states plus Sicily all had new constitutions. In March, the people of Milan and Venice also led an uprising, and the Austrian garrison in Milan was forced to flee.

In March 1849, Mazzini arrived in Rome after Garibaldi and was appointed Chief Minister of a new Roman Republic. Papal authority was set aside – from a temporal perspective, not a spiritual one – and in April, a French force was sent to deal with the new republic. The Austrians besieged Venice, and the French did the same in Rome, and the republic capitulated, the Pope's temporal authority restored. Mazzini and Garibaldi fled and Victor Emmanuel, who had risen to monarchical power following the abdication of Charles Albert, rose to prominence.

Citizens and reformers now called for a united Italy under a monarchy, as it was clear that a republic was not strong enough to bring the disparate Italian states together. By 1860, only five states remained in Italy: the

Austrians in Venice, the Papal States, the Kingdom of Piedmont-Sardinia, the Kingdom of Sicily, and San Marino. Francis II had an army of 150,000, but a large number of them were Swiss. Suddenly the Swiss left Italy and went back to Switzerland, leaving Francis with a relatively small number of unreliable native troops. In April 1860, revolutionary movements began in both Messina and Palermo. Garibaldi brought a thousand men to the shores of Italy and marched towards Palermo. On May 14, Garibaldi declared himself to be the dictator of Italy, in the name of Victor Emmanuel. Six weeks later, Garibaldi attacked Messina. It took less than seven days for the fortress to surrender, leaving Garibaldi in control of the entire island.

He crossed the straight and began marching his swelling army up the Italian peninsula. Military resistance diminished, and smaller kingdoms surrendered, annexing themselves to the Kingdom of Italy. On February 18, 1861, Victor Emmanuel, in whose name Garibaldi was fighting, assembled the first Italian Parliament in the city of Torlino (Turin). On March 17, the assembly declared Emmanuel to be king of a unified Italy, and on Marcy 27, Rome was declared the capital.

Rome, however, was not yet in the kingdom. The Pope was not ready to surrender his temporal authority, and had even threatened excommunication to anyone who opposed him. Emmanuel and Garibaldi considered their options. They could attack, but that had risks. Emmanuel thought that he could negotiate with the French, whose army supported the Pope. Napoleon III agreed to withdraw troops by 1866, and by the end of 1866, the last of his army had left Italy.

Austria was the last to hold out. Having controlled Venice for so many years, they did not want to cede it to Emmanuel. On June 20, 1866, the Kingdom of Italy, with the support of Prussia, declared war on Austria. Prussian leader Otto von Bismarck attacked Austria from the north, and with Garibaldi and Emmanuel threatening Venice at the same time, Austria chose to sign an armistice with Prussia. Conditions of the armistice included ceding Venice to Italy.

The Roman question remained, as Napoleon III, who had been given his title by the Pope, never forgot from whence his power came, and as long as the Pope needed his armies, Napoleon would oblige. It would take many more years before Rome was firmly established as part of the Kingdom of Italy, and in July of 1871, it became the Italian capital. Italy was unified for the first time since the Roman Empire. The *Risorgimento* was complete.

. . . . .

It is said that "without seeing Sicily it is impossible to understand Italy – Sicily is the key to everything." The geography of the Mediterranean certainly puts Sicily in a strategic location with respect to the rest of the Italian peninsula. It served as a stepping stone for African migration to Europe, and over the centuries it provided a base of operations for invading Italy proper. Garibaldi, as he began his campaign to unify Italy in the name of Victor Emmanuel, understood the strategic importance of the island.

The Italian phrase *mille grazie* means "thank you very much", but it is an idiom. It literally means, "a thousand thanks". The idiom is due to Garibaldi. He landed with a mere thousand men as his unification march began. He was a cunning leader, and he waited with his fleet of two ships off the shores of Favignana, a small island just five miles west of Sicily. Two French frigates who would have put up a fight went out on reconnaissance, and Garibaldi slipped into port, docking next to two British naval vessels. When the French returned, they could not fire on Garibaldi's ships, out of fear of hitting the British warships and starting a general war between France and England.

Garibaldi marched through Salemi, declaring Italy to be united (it was not nearly that yet), and defeated a larger French garrison at Calatafimi four days later. As Garibaldi marched through Sicily, more citizens joined his army. On May 27, they arrived in Palermo and besieged the city. Fierce fighting took place in its streets. Many of the city's population joined Garibaldi against the French, and the city lay in ruin. The French fought hard, however, but the British intervened, brokering an armistice between Napoleon III's troops and Garibaldi. The French departed, leaving Palermo in Garibaldi's hands. Seven weeks later, Garibaldi took Messina.

Shortly after Garibaldi's successful liberation of Sicily from the French, Vincenzo Florio, founded the *Società in Accomandita Piroscafi Postali-Ignazio & Vicenzo Florio*, a steamship line with a fleet of nine vessels. In 1881, Florio merged with the *Rubattino* company in Genoa, and the *Navigazione Generale Italiana* was born.

Sicily was the first of Italy's kingdoms to follow Garibaldi's unification movement, but that did not mean that every citizen wanted to join. Many local lords, in fact, systematically opposed unification efforts. They fought against the government's attempts at modernizing their economy and political system. They opposed new town councils and judicial systems. In 1866, Palermo revolted against Italy, and the Italian navy had to shell the city and send troops under Raffaele Cadorna to regain control. Years of insurrections led to iron-fisted rule by the Italian government.

The unique nature of the Sicilian economy meant that adapting to unification was difficult. The rest of Italy – especially the northern segment – modernized relatively quickly, but Sicily remained agrarian, uneducated, and poor. Sicilian customs meant that men worked outside the house, while women remained at home. Because the Italian state had difficulty incorporating Sicily in its legal structures and industrialization, groups of citizens began forming to enforce their own kind of rule. These peasant "entrepreneurs" created businesses based on terror and control, profiting by "protecting" citizens by telling them that if they wanted to be kept safe, they needed to pay them. It was, quite plainly, extortion. These unruly, but slowly organizing, bands of people were called the *mafia*, which literally meant "swagger".

It was into this world that Biagio Vampatella was born, grew into adulthood, married a young woman named Angela, and started his family.

Chapter 3 – Lynching

 Antonio Randazzo and his friend, Charles Traina, walked down the dusty street in Little Palermo, an Italian section of New Orleans. In the 26 years following the end of the Civil War, the city had worked hard to get back on its feet. Unlike other Southern cities, New Orleans had the benefit of being a major port, a key location for barges along the Mississippi River and steaming in and out from the Caribbean. Randazzo had arrived just a few years before, speaking no English, but hungry for work and a new life. The Industrial Revolution had furnished northern Italy with new jobs and a growing economy, but life in Sicily was quite different. Economic conditions were poor, and Sicilians were even poorer. The Randazzos were poorer still, and so 21-year old Antonio scraped together all he could, and bought passage on a steam ship from Palermo to New Orleans.
 Upon arrival, it was clear to Antonio that opportunities for work were plentiful. As the South moved forward in the aftermath of the war, it required a new labor force to man the factories and tend to the fields. Jacob Commerce was no longer a slave in South Carolina, but the plantations still needed workers to tend to the tobacco and cotton. With black Americans moving out of slavery and out of the South, new workers

were needed; preferably, those who were willing to work for very low wages.

Enter Antonio Randazzo and the Sicilians.

Randazzo was not too proud to work low-paying, low-skill jobs. He just needed work, work that was unavailable in Sicily. And so Randazzo was hired to work a sugar cane farm on the outskirts of the city. The sugar industry in Louisiana had grown to a $25 million enterprise prior to the Civil War, and Pierre LaFell's farm on the outskirts of the city had provided a good portion of New Orleans' sugar cane. LaFell's farm had fallen on hard times during and after the war, as he lost his customer base and his labor force. But he did not go out of business, and following the war, began to see some growth again. He needed more men to work the fields, and as the blacks left, the Italians came. Dark-skinned, hard-working, with strange customs, the Sicilians provided precisely the type of labor force that LaFell needed.

Randazzo walked three miles each day to and from the farm, where he put in 12-hour days for LaFell. Randazzo had begun to learn English, enough to understand basic commands and directions for work. He had also learned enough to understand when Louisianans called him *"Dago"*, which happened to be every day. He did not care, as his life had taken a significant turn for the better since immigrating to the United States. Such was the misery of his life in Sicily that low-wage, back-breaking labor, while being subjected to ethnic slurs on a daily basis, represented a major improvement.

Italians had first immigrated to New Orleans in the early 1800s, and the population had steadily grown. As the South grew out of the Civil War, and the need for inexpensive labor grew with slavery gone, more and more Italians made their way from the southern end of the country – Sicily in particular – to New Orleans. This was the start of the "first wave" of Italian immigration to the U.S. that grew from a slow trickle to a steady stream to a rushing river across the Atlantic.

Italians were seen by the Americans in the south as dirty, low-class people of color. Many Americans considered Italians to be barely above blacks ("Negroes" was the common term of the time) in the social order. The United States, despite being a place open to different religions, was largely a Protestant nation. Consequently, there were misgivings about Roman Catholicism that gave way to suspicion. Catholics couldn't be trusted. Randazzo, like most Italians, was deeply Catholic, and faced not only ethnic persecution, but also religious persecution as well. Interestingly, the Irish – also deeply Catholic people – comprised one-third of all immigrants between 1820 and 1860, and often faced similar religious persecution. But they were at least...white. The Italians were not.

Most of the free people in America at the time were considered to be from "white" nations: England, Ireland, the Netherlands, Germany, Norway, Sweden, and Finland. Italians and Spaniards were considered to be people of color – not quite black African, but definitely not white. With the freeing of the slaves, the Italians in particular became the next lowest people group on the totem pole, at least from the largely Anglo perspective that dominated American society. In 1924 economist Robert Forester wrote, "in a country where the distinction between white man and black is intended as a distinction of value ... it is no compliment to the Italian to deny him his whiteness, but that actually happens with considerable frequency."

In the South, Italians were viewed as black, and when Jim Crow laws were put in place, Italians were grouped with blacks and subjected to the harsh restrictions of segregation placed on blacks. Northern Italians, who looked more like Germans and Swiss, did not face the same degree of racism that southern Italians – Sicilians most notably – endured. Northern Italians themselves often joke that Sicilians are really African. And there is some truth to that; after all, many immigrants into Italy from Africa would first have stopped in Sicily. Many remained, and African blood mixed with Italian blood. Genetic studies have shown that 20% of the "y" DNA lineages in Sicily can be traced back to North Africa. The further north one proceeds along the Italian peninsula, the smaller the percentage comes. Moreover, it is simply true that humans living in warmer climes tend to have darker skin on average due to the adaptations from sun exposure. The Spanish and Greek people are darker, on average, than the English and Swedish. All these factors came into play as Americans categorized European immigrants. The conclusion was: Italians are black, not white, and the treatment of Sicilians in particular reflected this view.

Randazzo, then, was treated poorly by the people of New Orleans. He was an uneducated, dark-skinned, unskilled peasant from a backwater island who did not speak much English and who possessed a spurious Roman Catholic faith. Like most Italian immigrants at this time,

Randazzo lived in what would be known as "Little Palermo", a small section of New Orleans similar to a Little Italy in New York, New Haven, or Boston. As more immigrants moved in, upper class people moved uptown, opening up sections of the French Quarter for the Sicilians. They began to establish restaurants and olive oil businesses and grocery stores and laundry services, and soon the area became so populated with Sicilians that it became known as Little Palermo. Little Palermo no longer exists, as Italians in the city are spread out and more evenly distributed, but for Randazzo, it was the one place that seemed like home.

. . . . .

Sicilians also faced another version of prejudice, but this one was not totally unfounded. In Sicily, the *Mafioso* – family-run organized crime – was pervasive. It originated as groups of peasant farmers banding together for protection against thieves, who had grown numerous in poverty-stricken Sicily. The *Mafioso* took dues from the farmers in exchange for protection, not unlike a labor union. But over time, this demand escalated, and peasants soon were required to pay dues to the *Mafioso* or else put themselves in danger from the very people they were asking to protect them. The *Mafioso* soon began extorting farmers and other peasants, and when they did not pay for "protection", violence ensued. By the end of the 19th century, Sicily had the highest homicide rate in the world. As Italians began to immigrate to the U.S., those involved in the *Mafioso* came over along with the regular farmers and tradesmen. Not only were Italian laborers and customs transported across the Atlantic from Sicily to the United States, but the *Mafioso* was as well. New Orleans was the first place where the *Mafioso* became established.

During the Civil War Raffaele Agnello, a prominent member of the small Sicilian community in New Orleans, was a leader of the "Italian Guards Battalion" of the local Confederate force. As the Union army moved in to occupy the city at the end of April, 1862, the regular army retreated. The Union forces kept the Italian Guards to keep order in the French Quarter. That left Agnello as the singular dominant person in the French Quarter, which, of course, would eventually become Little Palermo. He began to establish his own rule of law, and in effect, created the first *Mafioso* in the city, and in the entire United States. Agnello was not the only Sicilians organizing in the city, however, and when the war ended, Agnello came into conflict with the Sicilian gangs that were not part of his organization. By starting this war, Agnello actually united Italians whose roots were in Messina and Trapani. Moreover, groups from Monreale and Piana dei Greci also opposed him. The first American turf war and power struggle had taken place.

Agnello forced the Messina and Trapani groups to flee the city. Thinking he had won the war, Agnello emerged from hiding. On April 1, 1869, he took a stroll through the French Quarter and stopped at Joseph Macheca's produce shop. Creating a distraction that drew the attention of Agnello and his bodyguard, a man appeared suddenly and shot Agnello in the head, killing him instantly.

His younger brother Joseph became the leader of the Palermo mafia, and carried out the war against his rivals. He recovered from numerous injuries but in 1872 was killed by the Messina-Trapani mafia. Mateo Minafo took over but lasted just three months before dying of natural causes.

In 1879, Guiseppe Esposito, who was connected to the Sicilian mafia in Palermo, immigrated to the United States through New York, eventually making his way to New Orleans. He was immediately seen as a leader in the Palermo mafia in New Orleans and took control of organized criminal activity in the city. He supported the Provenzano family, who emerged as the leading mafia family in New Orleans.

Meanwhile, earlier in the 1870s, Charles (Carlo) and Tony (Antonio) Matranga, who were born in Sicily, had immigrated to the United States and settled in New Orleans. There they opened up a saloon and brothel and engaged in various criminal activities, including racketeering and extortion. They demanded, and received, tribute payments from Italian laborers and dock workers. Even the Provenzano family, who had almost total control over fruit shipments from South America, fell in line. In order to avoid a war, they struck a deal granting the Matrangas a piece of the waterfront racketeering action.

In 1881 Guiseppe Esposito's enemies betrayed him to police detective David Hennessey, and he was deported to Italy. The Provenzano family was, for the time, the dominant mafia in the city, but it did not last long as the Matrangas moved in on their dock and fruit operations. In the late 1880s, the two factions went to war over control of the docks. One evening, Tony and Charles Matranga were riding down Esplanade, and, approaching Claiborne, were attacked by men from the Provenzano gang. A shootout ensued, killing Tony, and nearly every man involved suffered some kind of injury. Things quickly escalated as the two factions fought for control of the docks. This war was called "the vendetta".

Their war was sufficiently large and sufficiently violent as to attract significant police attention. New Orleans chief David Hennessy – who had captured Guiseppe Esposito nearly a decade earlier who had in the ensuing years moved up the ranks – began investigating the New Orleans mafia. He held meetings with members of both mafias. They always cooperated, but witnesses never talked, and citizens feared being on juries involving mafia gangs, and so prosecuting these murders was nearly impossible. To make matters worse, more and more members of the New Orleans police force fell under the influence of the two rival gangs, and Hennessey realized that he was increasingly isolated, even on the police force. He decided to try to take down the stronger mafia – the Matrangas – and so struck a deal with the Provenzanos. They would agree to stand trial for one of the murders for which they were responsible – one out of dozens – and in exchange, Hennessey would testify on behalf of the Provenzanos.

Word of this pact got out, and the Matrangas began to issue threats unless he stopped the investigation. Several weeks later, Guiseppe Mattiani, who was working under cover for Hennessey, was slaughtered. He was found burned, his head and legs removed. Hennessey, however, was a tough character, and he did not give up. Having been appointed as police chief specifically to clean up New Orleans from mafia activity, he was undeterred.

What happened next led to one of the largest mass lynchings in U.S. history.

On August 9, 1890, a date was set for the trial of the Provenzanos, on October 17. Hennessey publicly announced his plan to testify on behalf of the Provenzanos. On the evening of October 15th, Hennessey made his way through the French Quarter, having left a meeting at the police station. He was heading for home on Girod Street, which he shared with his widowed mother. The evening fog hung in the air, the result of the day's rain in the warm, humid air. The city's new electric lamp posts glowed softly in the haze as Hennessey walked the near-empty streets.

Suddenly, at 11:30pm, mere steps from his home, Hennessey's body lurched from the bullets exploding into his body. Two men, armed with sawed-off shotguns, appeared through the fog and ambushed the police chief. He took six bullets – three in the abdomen, one in the chest, one in his right leg, and one in his left elbow – and fell back. Incredibly, he managed to pull out his pistol and fire back, to no avail. He lay on the ground, bleeding profusely.

Bill O'Connor, a friend on the police force, heard the commotion from blocks away and ran to the scene. He found Hennessey alive, but in critical condition.

"Who did this to you?" he asked.

In a weak, but determined voice, Hennessey replied with just one word: "*Dagoes.*"

He was taken to nearby Charity Hospital and surgeons attempted to save his life. That night he once again said "*Dagoes*", survived until the next morning, and finally passed away from internal hemorrhaging at 9:00am on October 16.

There were no witnesses to the murder. Hennessey did not name his assailants. All he did before dying was utter a racial slur aimed at a group of people that were seen as low-class people of color who, to be fair, had engaged in intra-tribal warfare through the various mafia gangs in the French Quarter. One mafia family, of course, had a motive to slay Hennessey, but any evidence would be purely circumstantial at best. Hennessey's murder set the city in an uproar against the Sicilian community in Little Palermo.

Mayor Joseph Shakspeare was outraged. "Scour the whole neighborhood! Arrest every Italian you come across!" he ordered his men. And that they did. In the next days police rounded up and arrested some 250 Italian immigrants – most of whom did not speak any English. Shakspeare had detectives act as moles in the prisons to try to overhear what any of the Italians were saying. Prisoner Emanuele Polizi claimed he had heard Joseph Macheca and Charles Matragna speak of having arranged Hennessey's assassination. Eventually 19 of these 250 men were charged in the murder – only six of whom had any ties whatsoever to the mafia. But the police claimed that most of them were involved with the Matragna family.

Mayor Shakspeare declared two days afterward, in front of the City Council, that Hennessey's death was due to "Sicilian vengeance" and blamed Italian "murder societies", saying, "We must teach these people a lesson they will not forget for all time." On the day of Hennessey's funeral, Thomas Duffy, overcome with grief and anger, went to the prison and shot one of the Italians in the neck. Police took him away and he called out, "If there were seventy-five men like me in New Orleans, we'd run all the Dagoes out of the city." As he was later sentenced to six months in prison for this crime, he said, "I'm willing to hang if one of those *Dagoes* dies."

Shakspeare had a terrible dislike of the Italian immigrants, not just those associated with the criminal and violent activity of the mafia. On one occasion he wrote a letter to the mayor of Athens, Ohio, and he described the Italians as "filthy in their person and in homes." He also claimed that many of the Italians were "fugitives from justice" from Sicily and who had immigrated to the United States only to escape justice in their home country. He believed Italians were unfit for citizenship and wished to see them deported. He organized a group of men called the "Committee of Fifty" – all citizens, none police – to seek out information in the case. On October 23, they published a letter in the city's newspapers demanding that Italians provide them with the names of "every bad man, every criminal, and every suspected person of your race." The letter closed by saying that they wanted to put an end to the Sicilian mafia in the city "peaceably and lawfully if we can, violently and summarily if we must." This was clearly meant to intimidate the Italian community.

The Italians arrested in the Hennessey murder were not afforded legal representation. The police treated them violently, leaving bruises and wounds of various sorts on the detainees. On January 12, 1891, the Provenzano trial began, and on January 23 and 28, the various charges against the Provenzanos were dismissed. A month later, on February 28, testimony began in the Hennessey murder case. The 19 defendants were divided into two groups, due to the sheer number of defendants and the size of the courtroom. The first group of nine were tried first. The city was enflamed in anti-Italian sentiment. On March 13 at 3:00pm, the verdict was rendered: six were judged not guilty, and three were declared "no finding". The city was stunned. They feared that the verdict was reached due to mafia bribes and threats. The city was a powder keg waiting to explode.

On March 15, William Stirling Parkerson, a resident with anti-Italian prejudices, organized a group of men he called the "Regulators" and, at the urging of a crowd of thousands of angry people shouting, "hang the *dago* murderers!", marched on the Orleans Parish Prison. They broke the gate and smashed their way into the prison with a battering ram. The guards and warden did not even try to stop them, such was the force of the angry mob. They slaughtered 11 of the men. Some were shot. Emmanuele Polizzi was the last of the men to be caught by the mob. He was dragged out of the prison and brought before the angry crowd. Men kicked him and dragged him down the street to the corner of Treme Street and St. Ann. Someone dropped a thin cord from the lamppost and wrapped it around his neck. He was hoisted in the air and struggled for life as the cord bit into his neck. But it snapped, causing Polizzi to fall to the ground, and causing the crowd to groan. Quickly someone else produced a clothesline and he was once again lifted into the air by his neck. Struggling for life, he tried to free himself but was punched numerous times while hanging by his neck. Finally, several men shot him as he hung, lifeless, from the lamppost.

Polizzi's body was left dangling from the lamppost for days as a warning to the Italian community. Thousands of citizens would come by over the next few days to see Polizzi's dead body, as well as the bodies of others slain in the lynching. One of the men killed was Charles Traina, a sugar plantation worker, who was awaiting trial despite having no connection to the mafia at all. He was dragged out of the prison and shot in the chest by the angry mob. The eleven men killed that day represented one of the largest single lynchings in U.S. history. Afterward Parkerson dismissed his Regulators by saying, "I have performed the most painful duty of my life today. Now let us go home, and God bless you and your community." Mayor Shakspeare , when asked if he was sorry to see events take place as they did, replied, "No sir. I am an American citizen and I am not afraid of the Devil. These men deserved killing and they were punished by peaceful, law abiding citizens. They [the Italians they slew] took the law in their own hands and we were forced to do the same." The New Orleans Chamber of Commerce issued congratulations to the citizens for restoring order in the city.

. . . . .

While Hennessey's murder was a national news story, the news of the lynchings quickly reached the Italian government. Furious, they recalled their ambassador and demanded that the families of the slain men be compensated. Anti-Italian sentiment was stoked across the U.S. In West Virginia, coal miners went on strike when their foreman refused to fire two Italian co-workers...simply for being Italian. In the years to come, several more lynchings of Italians occurred in Louisiana. In 1896, three others were lynched in Hahnville. In 1899, five more were lynched in Tallulah for the "crime" of treating blacks the same as whites in their shop. Three of the men were shopkeepers; two were bystanders. Louisiana would have the second highest per capita lynching rate in the U.S. by 1900. Most of those lynched were, of course, African-American, but the second most murdered group was Italians. Approximately 50 lynchings of Italians have been documented in the United States between 1890 and 1920. Sicilians comprised less than four percent of the U.S. population according to U.S. Census figures from 1890-1910, but 40% of the non-black lynchings were of Sicilians. A July 1899 report on a lynching of five Italians, said, "Five Italians were lynched here last night for the fatal wounding of Dr. J. Ford Hodge. The dead men are of a class which has been troublesome for quite some time." This, despite the fact that none of the five men were merely suspected of being involved; there was no actual evidence against them.

Teddy Roosevelt, not yet President, wrote to his sister on March 21, 1891, "Monday we dined at the Camerons; various *dago* diplomats were present, all wrought up by the lynchings of Italians in New Orleans. Personally I think it rather a good thing, and said so." John Parker, who had a hand in organizing the lynch mob, would later be elected as governor of Louisiana, in 1911. He said of Italians that they were "just a little worse than the Negro, being if anything filthier in their habits, lawless and treacherous." The *New York Times* wrote in an editorial in response to the lynchings, "These sneaking and cowardly Sicilians, the descendants of bandits and assassins, who have transported to this country the lawless passions, the cut-throat practices, and the oath-bound societies of their native country, are to us a pest without mitigation. Our own rattlesnakes are as good citizens as they... Lynch law was the only course open to the people of New Orleans to stay the issue of a new license to the Mafia to continue its bloody practices."

Later, in 1895, in response to more lynchings of Italians, the *New York Times* wrote, "The best excuse for a lynching is that the ordinary machinery of justice has broken down, and that it is a question whether the criminal shall be punished by a mob or whether he shall go free." In other words, guilt by association – simply for being Sicilian – was sufficient ground to lynch people suspected of crimes, when the justice system itself found no guilt. And it was often supported in the American press. Such was the low view of Italians held by many, or even most, Americans.

The U.S. government, in response to Italy's demand, compensated the families of the 11 slain men some $25,000 each. Secretary of State James Blaine telegraphed Louisiana Governor Francis Nicholas, "The President deeply regrets that the citizens of New Orleans should have disparaged the purity and adequacy of their own judicial tribunals as to transfer to the passionate judgment of a mob, a question that should have been adjudged dispassionately and by settled rules of the law."

. . . . .

Antonio Randazzo, like others in the Italian community in New Orleans, was stunned by the turn of events. His fellow Sicilians had been slaughtered, including his best friend, and every day he went to work on the sugar cane farm became dangerous. If the angry mob could kill Italians at will, where would he ever be safe? From that point on, Randazzo lived in fear, based only on the anti-Italian sentiment that continued to rise in New Orleans. A handful of years later, in October 1899, a ship with eight-hundred Italian immigrants arrived in New Orleans. The *Weekly Thibodaux Sentinel* expressed the still-growing animosity towards Italians, remarking, "where they will all be able to find stalls to peddle fruit is a mystery. Louisiana need not feel proud of the acquisition [of these new Italian immigrants]."

Randazzo came to America seeking only a better life from what he had in Sicily. He and his fellow Sicilians were willing to do the backbreaking work that was previously done by slaves. In exchange, he was viewed with contempt simply for his dark skin, Catholic religion, foreign customs, and national identity, being associated with the mafia simply by being a "*Dago*".

The morning after the lynchings, he put on his shoes and cap, and began his three-mile walk – alone this time – to the sugar cane farm to begin his day of work, well aware now of his place in the new world.

"Who killa de chief?" someone yelled as he trudged down the street. He would hear this taunt for the rest of his life.

Chapter 4 – Childhood

The train whistle blew as the train rumbled past the *casello*, a small two-story structure that housed the men and families who worked for the *Ferrovie dello Stato*. Sicily, like much of southern Italy, was far behind the north in terms of economics and industry. During the *Risorgimento*, the southern portions of Italy were turned over from a state-run economy to a free market economy, like that which existed in the prosperous north. It was perhaps a significant failing that this transition was forced so quickly, as the economy of places like Sicily collapsed, unable to handle free market principles in so short a time. And so Sicily was poor. But they were not without trains, and for young Philip Vampatella, this was enough.

Philip was born on September 14, 1897, and named after his grandfather, Filippo. Shortly after his birth, he was baptized in the Roman Catholic Church under the same name, Filippo. Philip was the name he would come to be known by most of his life, and the transition from Filippo to Philip was not the only name change he would experience.

Philip's father, Biagio, worked for the *Ferrovie dello Stato*, and their family lived in a *casello*, sharing it with another family that also worked for the state railroad just outside the small town of Biscari. Located in the southern portion of Sicily, Biscari sits 44 miles almost exactly due west from Siracusa, the fourth largest city on the island. In 1938, Biscari would be renamed Acate, but by then, Philip would be living in another part of the world.

Biagio made very little money working for the railroad, and he had a family to support. He and his wife Angela had two boys, Philip and Salvatore, and two girls, Giovannina and Lina. As is the case in most rural and poor areas of the world, creature comforts were hard to come by. As children, they had nothing by way of manufactured toys, and so Philip and his siblings invented games and toys of their own. Day after day was spent playing in the small space at the *casello*, and in the nearby fields. The trains were Biago's business, but they were Philip's love. Whenever the next train would come clattering down the tracks, Philip would stop what he was doing, look up, and imagine himself on the next train to…well, where did they go, anyway?

"Papa," he asked one day. "Where do the trains go?"

"They go wherever the tracks go," Biagio replied, eating a bite of bread.

"But where do they go?"

"They go all over Sicily. To Palermo. Siracusa. Catania. Marsala."

"Where is Palermo?" Philip asked.

"On the northern coast of Sicily."

"On the ocean?"

"Yes."

"Do big ships sail in and out of Palermo?"

"Yes, of course they do."

"Have you ever been on one?"

"A big ship?"

"Yes." Philip was eager in his questioning.

"No, never."

"But you've been on trains."

"Of course."

"Is a big ship just like a train, but on the water?"

"Well," Biago replied, smiling. He loved how inquisitive his son was. Always asking questions. Always learning. "The big ships are much bigger than the trains."

"Much bigger?"

"Much."

"I want to go on a ship someday."

"Maybe you will," Biagio said.

Angela smiled as she served more bread. But deep down stirrings of worry gnawed at her. She could not imagine life without Philip, but she had a sense that perhaps Philip would board a ship and never return. Life in Sicily was very hard and, like all mothers, she wanted a better life for her children. Ever since 1880 the Italian *diaspora*, as it would come to be known, had seen wave after wave of Sicilians and other Italians leave the country in search of economic opportunity. They had already seen friends emigrate across the Atlantic to the United States, and she could sense Biagio's restlessness as a father and husband, knowing they needed more money for their growing family, money that was simply not available in Sicily.

The *Ferrovie dello Stato* provided the family with a free place to live in the *casello*, but provided scant wages, and Biagio's pleas for a raise fell on deaf ears in the halls of government. His career with the railroad company was not where he had envisioned it as a boy. His first work had come thanks to his father, Filippo, and eventually the Italian Army came along and conscripted him into its service. When his time with the army was up, he returned home, married, and began to work with the railroad. Despite its low pay, Biagio made more from the railroad than he ever had before. Nonetheless, despite being better off than he had been under any other circumstance, Biagio needed more money than what the railroad was paying.

Philip, meanwhile, was growing, as the family was growing. Philip loved trains but he also loved learning. Biagio was a self-taught man who had mastered reading and basic mathematics. Philip had acquired the same passion for knowledge and began attending school at the age of seven. The Vampatellas lived in the railway *casello*, and there were no schools along the railway, but there was a school approximately five miles from the *casello*, in a medieval castle called *Donnafugata*. Owned by a duchess of Albarfiorita, the castle was nothing like anything Philip had ever seen. He grew up in rural poverty, and the castle was elegant, almost palatial. In the castle and on the grounds Philip saw gardens, hedges, large foyers, marble stairways, and perhaps most impressive of all, indoor plumbing – things he was unaccustomed to back at the *casello*.

Philip loved knowledge, and progressed in his learning, making friends, exploring the grounds, and finding new ways to get into trouble. But he did not stay long at Donnafugata, as the railway soon called Biagio to relocate. *Casellos* were interspersed along the length of the railway, and Biagio was needed elsewhere. Several times the family had to move. At some locations there were no schools but *casellos* near larger towns were close to a municipal school of some sort. The family moved to a *casello* near the town of Comiso, approximately nine miles southease of Biscari.

Comiso was large enough to have churches, schools, and a market place. When the Vampatellas arrived, Philip's education resumed from the beginning. As there were no records, and schooling was somewhat haphazard, students like Philip had to start from scratch. In Comiso, Philip grew to be a loner. He was new in town, and Philip routinely found himself in disputes with other boys, some of whom lived very different lives than he did. The harsh reality of bullying due to factors beyond one's control led Philip to dislike being around other children, and so at recess he often stood alone.

Comiso featured tradesmen of all sorts. Shoemakers, tailors, blacksmiths, carpenters all did business in the town. Biagio was determined that Philip learn a trade, and he sought out tradesmen who worked near the *casello*, so Philip could work as an apprentice during the vacation periods. Biagio first brought Philip to a shop where cotton fibers were separated from their seeds. Philip could stand that for two whole hours before deciding that this was not for him. Biagio, after administering a swift beating, then tried a shoemaker's shop. The work was hard but Philip managed to last a week before leaving. Following another beating, the next attempt was with a coppersmith. That, too, was not the place for Philip.

Biagio brought him to a stone quarry, and told the supervisor that he was free to use whatever measure he needed to keep Philip working. The work at the quarry was, as one might expect, very difficult. Workers chiseled huge blocks of stone, and Philip had to load them on carts to be pulled out of the quarry by horse or mule. But Philip was just a boy, and many of the stones were simply too large for him. At one point Philip essentially gave up trying to lift it. The supervisor took this for a lack of work ethic and, true to Biagio's instructions, proceeded to cuff Philip about the head. Philip, in a rage, threw a rock at the supervisor and even though he missed, the supervisor came at Philip ready to administer a severe beating. A worker brandishing a knife openly walked up to the supervisor.

"*Capo*," he said, "let go of Philip."

"Why should I do that?" the supervisor asked, holding Philip by the scruff of his neck.

"Because if you don't," the man said, his face betraying the seriousness with which he spoke, "the *cimitero* will soon have another client."

The supervisor let go, and that was the last day on the job for Philip.

The next stop was at a cabinetmaker's shop. Philip's job was to sweep the floor, clean out the chamber pots, and hand plane spruce boards. Philip quickly developed blisters as the work was hard on the hands. The master taught Philip how to use a saw, a hammer, and chisels, but those, too, proved difficult for Philip. He was simply not finding his niche in any trade offered to him.

. . . . .

The *Ferrovie dello Stato* moved Biagio, Angela, and the children again several more times until they landed in a *casello* overlooking the Mediterranean Sea. Philip had continued his learning on his own, developing his reading and math skills. On one occasion, as he was helping his mother Angela, he saw three dark columns rising from the water to the clouds.

"Mama," Philip asked. "What are those?"

"*Coda di drago*," she replied, and explained that the dragons in the clouds needed to drink the water from the sea, and the tails brought the water up.

Philip did not realize it, but these water spouts were dangerous, and the ensuing storm swamped the countryside. The cistern for the *casello* was filled quickly, but the overload of water posed a problem. Biagio told the family that nobody could drink the water until it had first been boiled. Naturally, he feared bacteria and parasites that often accompanied flood waters.

Shortly thereafter, Philip's younger brother Salvatore came down sick. Biagio tried to contact a doctor by telegraph, but by the time the doctor arrived three days later, Salvatore had passed away from tetanus. Angela was devastated by her son's agonizing death. She wanted out of the railway, a feeling she had had for some time, but now she blamed her son's death on the fact that the railway had placed them in harm's way in the first place. Biagio began to look for alternatives to the *Ferrovie dello Stato*.

Meanwhile, he continued to try to find Philip a trade. Philip tried a cart-building shop near Vittorio where they were stationed at the time. Philip was tasked with making a straight hole through the edge of a finished wheel – an operation that required considerable precision. If the hole was not true center, the wheel would wobble and not function properly. It took several attempts for Philip to improve this skill. Affixing a rubber tire to the wheel required heating the wheel and then being aligned by men with hammers and tongs. Philip's role was to pour water on the wheel to keep it from burning.

"Ok men, here we go," the *capo* said.

They hoisted the wheel onto the sawhorses and began to heat it up. Men hammered away to align it. Philip sprinkled water onto the wheel, but it wasn't enough. The heat intensified and smoke began to billow.

"Philip," the *capo* said, "more water!"

"I can't see," Philip cried, as the smoke rose into his eyes.

"More water NOW!"

Philip couldn't see, and was unable to pour water where it needed to be, and as a result, the tire burned. Furious, the men working on the wheel lashed out at Philip verbally.

"*Buono a nulla!*" one of the workers yelled at Philip. "You good for nothing boy!"

Philip's failure at the cart-building shop was yet another setback in his training to master a trade. He could not really even get off the ground as an apprentice, and all he seemed able to do were menial tasks, not the work of the actual tradesmen.

The next attempt was with a winery. Philip had to fill a pail with water, climb a ladder, and pour it into the large tub. Given how big the tubs were, this took immense effort and considerable time. On one such climb up the ladder, Philip slipped and toppled into the tub. He managed to cling to the side of the tub but ingested several mouthfuls of wine. Angry, the supervisor took Philip home and demanded that Biagio pay for the lost batch of wine. Angela defended her son like a lioness defends her cubs, and the supervisor left empty-handed.

. . . . .

Among the many lessons Philip learned during this time was an appreciation for other people. Sicily was a place of tribalism and distrust, and the *Mafioso* was an ever-present element in society. One's family and closest friends generally formed the full circle of trust, but Biagio had a different philosophy. He told Philip that he must sometimes make sacrifices to like other people. It was not easy to make such sacrifices, to give up something in order to like, appreciate, or love those who were different from you. Biagio put it this way to young Philip: "One travels better by trying to like people and things. By trying he will eventually like both in a genuine way and the result will eventually be reciprocal because people and things will pay back in kind."

It was a version of the Golden Rule: Do unto others as you would have them do unto you. It was a philosophy that Philip would employ the rest of his life.

Philip began to perform better in school, and became an avid reader. Books were scarce, however, and it was difficult for Philip to get his hands on reading material. On one occasion his teacher gave him a book about the adventures of Theodore Roosevelt in Africa as a reward for excelling in a homework assignment.

Philip matured over the years and turned 12 on September 14, 1909. Ever since the *Risorgimento*, the Italian armed forces utilized conscription. At 20 years of age every able-bodied male was drafted into either the army or navy. Neither Philip or Biagio knew that world was five years away from the Great War, but Italy sought to be prepared at any rate. Soldiers drilled in the town square and on one occasion Philip witnessed the harsh life of an Italian soldier. As they drilled, one of the men had difficulty following the orders from the sergeant. The sergeant proceeded to physically discipline the soldier in a way that Philip found to be exceedingly harsh. Not yet a teenager, an enraged Philip charged the sergeant and a melee ensued. Philip's two friends who were with him at the time joined in, and the sergeant suddenly found himself engaged with three aggressive and angry boys.

Eventually the fight broke up and nobody reported Philip and his friends to the police. The drilling went on as planned, but for Philip, a dislike for the Italian army – sergeants in particular – began to form. He would have to work on Biagio's life lesson to sacrifice in order to like others, although the soldier who received the physical discipline gave Philip a little smile as a way of saying thank you. What Philip did not yet understand was that military discipline was critical in order for an army to perform at the highest level necessary to keep Italy safe from her enemies. And Italy was nearing such a need.

Philip took up a new job packing crates, and he began to pick up skills in woodworking. He learned how to make furniture, and after a time made polished and veneered pieces, selling them to willing customers. It seemed that Philip finally was growing into a trade, something that had eluded him for years. Over the next few years, Philip developed this skill and Biagio recognized that his son had a real talent. Philip derived great joy from creating beautiful things, and as he learned to make marvelous pieces, Biagio began to think about what opportunities his son could have. As he assessed the situation in Sicily, his mind wandered across the world to the United States. What could Philip achieve in America? The Italian *diaspora* had been in motion for several decades, as Italians – southern Italians especially – sought opportunity for a better life in other parts of Europe and the United States. Biagio began having conversations with Angela, and Angela could see her almost prophetic vision from years before coming closer to reality.

Biagio began making plans and applied for a passport. One afternoon in July of 1912, while Biagio and Philip waited for the government to process their paperwork, Biagio decided to take the family on an outing to a piece of property in Biscari that he had been caring for. He loaded everyone up, filled baskets with bread and cheese, put his shotgun in the *carretta*, and clip-clopped down the road until they reached the spot he sought. There, Biagio noticed something disturbing, and he told his family to keep quiet. Fetching his gun, he hopped off the *carretta* and made his way across the field to a fig tree. There he saw a young man pilfering figs from Biagio's fig tree.

"Hey you, come down!" Biagio yelled. The man hopped down, knife in his hands, ready for a brawl, but the moment he saw Biagio leveling his shotgun, he lost any interest in a confrontation. He dropped his knife and stood before Biagio.

"You know, there is such a thing as asking for what you want," Biagio said firmly. But after a moment he softened and lowered his voice. "But I guess you had no way of asking, because we were not here."

The thief, trembling, merely nodded. Biagio continued.

"I'm not a vindictive man," he said. "All I want from you is that you fill your basket and be on your way. Simply remember our Sicilian way of shooting first, asking questions later. You may not be so lucky next time." He directed the young man to get after it, and he did, filling his basket with figs. Biagio picked up the young man's knife, folded it up, and helped the man fill his basket with Biagio's figs. When it was full, Biagio handed the man back his knife and sent him on his way. The grateful man hurried off, and Biagio collected his family and together they had their fill of figs, with three baskets to spare. Biagio gave Philip a live demonstration of making sacrifices to like and love others.

In February 1913, Biagio began final preparations for his and Philip's emigration. Angela and the girls would stay behind until Biagio could establish a home for them in America. Philip began to say his good-byes, and bidding *arrivederci* his best friend at school, Gaetano Alessandrello, proved particularly difficult. He would miss Gaetano, his family, and the island of Sicily that was his only home, but he would not miss the poverty, the men who owned the shops where he first worked, the beatings he received, the rigid rules of propriety in his society, nor the way that intolerant people of his country treated each other. He had visions of returning to his homeland with a fortune.

Philip had a lot to learn still.

Chapter 5 – Crossing

Saying goodbye to his mother Angela was the hardest part for Philip. Just 15 years old in the spring of 1913, all the arrangements having been made, it was time for Biagio and Philip to begin the journey across Sicily to the port of Palermo, where a steamship to the United States awaited. Biagio and Philip loaded their bags with whatever belongings they could gather (which was not much) and stood in front of Angela and the girls. Tears flowed for everyone.

"Now you be a good boy, Philip," Angela said, holding her son tightly.

"I will Mama," Philip replied, trying to show the confidence he thought a young man his age should have. His trembling voice and tears belied his fear and insecurity.

"Work hard in America. It won't be long before we see each other again," Angela lied.

"I will come back soon," Philip said, unsure if that was the truth.

"I love you so much, son."

"*Ti voglio bene mamma,*" Philip replied, wiping the tears from his eyes. One last hug from Philip to his sisters and his mother, followed by Biagio doing the same, and father and son were out the door, on the way to the train station.

The train ride to Palermo lasted six hours. Incredibly, despite working for the *Ferrovie dello Stato* much of his life, Biagio had not been on many long train trips. Nor had Philip. Certainly they had not been on many that lasted six hours without suffering some sort of break down. On the train, Biagio and Philip slept and talked about their upcoming trip. Philip asked Biagio question after question, and Biagio tried to answer them all. Even when Philip asked him a question he could not answer, he did his best to instill confidence in his son. The train chugged westward for more than an hour before turning north, stopping at every station along the way. People boarded and disembarked at various stops, but Philip and Biagio remained for the entire journey to Palermo. One such stop was at Termini Imerese, just 22 miles from Palermo. Philip needed to use the toilet and so he and Biagio found the *bagno* in the train station. Philip's eyes went wide upon entering. It was the first time in his life he had ever seen a tiled bathroom.

The train chugged onward and finally reached its destination. Palermo was the capital of Sicily, the largest city on the island, and Philip had never been there before. There Philip encountered bustling streets, crowds of people, and all the sights and sounds of an actual city. He found it fascinating but quickly his mind went back to his life in places like Biscari, which now seemed impossibly small. Philip and Biagio waited two days in Palermo for their ship to muster, and during those two days they walked the streets, window shopped in various storefronts, went to the park, and even took a trolley to visit a well-known church in Monreale. Biagio and Philip were vaccinated in Palermo, and in the evening the two of them visited a movie house, where Philip saw his first ever cowboy-and-Indian film.

. . . . .

On the day of departure, a scow took them to the *SS Napoli*, a steamship owned by *Navigazione Generale Italiana*, a shipping company formed in 1881 when two companies – *I & V Florio* of Palermo and *Raffaele Rubattino* of Genoa – merged. Florio brought to the merger some 50 ships at the time of the merger, while *Rubattino* possessed 40. In 1901 and 1906, the company acquired the assets of *La Veloce* and *Italia Società di Navigazione a Vapore*. One of the ships the *Navigazione Generale Italiana* owned was the *SS Napoli*, a passenger ship that traveled the route to the United States.

The *Napoli* was built by in 1899, originally designed as a cargo ship and named the *British Prince*. It sailed for the Phoenix Line between Antwerp and New York for *British Shipowners Ltd*. A 9,203 gross ton ship, she featured four masts, twin screws, and could reach speeds upwards of 13 knots. In 1906 *Navigazione Generale Italiana* bought the ship, refitted it with passenger quarters, and renamed it the *Sannio*. Her first Genoa-Naples-Palermo-New York voyage began on May 31, 1906. In 1913 she was renamed the *Napoli*, and her first voyage along the new route – Genoa-Palermo-Naples-New York-Philadelphia began on March 28, 1913 – the very trip that took Philip and Biagio to the United States.

A few years later, the *Napoli* would become part of a convoy during World War I, and on July 4, 1917, the *Napoli* sailed from New York to Genoa with war contraband, including munitions, destined for the Italian army. Protected from German U-boats by American, British, and Italian warships, the *Napoli* steamed for Genoa. Unfortunately, orders were confused and another convoy converged on the *Napoli's* in the Mediterranean, off Porto Maurizio, and in the darkness the *Napoli* collided with the Norwegian ship *Otto Sverdup*. There is actually some confusion on this point as some believe the *Napoli* actually collided with the British ship *Lamington*. Regardless, the *Napoli*, just a few short years after transporting Philip and Biagio to America, became a casualty of the Great War and, like so many vessels over the course of human history, currently rests at the bottom of the Mediterranean Sea.

. . . . .

Philip and Biagio boarded. It would be untrue to say that this was the largest ship Philip had ever seen, because it was anchored right next to the *Princess Irene*, a slightly larger ship. Nonetheless, the huge Napoli, smelling of fresh paint and tar, was more than Philip had ever experienced.

From 1911-1914, Sicily ranked 5th among the 16 Italian districts, with 2,270 emigrants per 100,000 leaving the island to seek their fortunes elsewhere. Every emigrant was given a trade that could be useful to the country to which they traveled. Most countries did not simply want more people; they wanted more useful people. It was imperative that you could do some sort of work that would benefit the country of your arrival. In 1913, 34% of Italian emigrants were assigned the trade of "farm laborer", the highest percentage among any other trade. Miner/forest laborer was second at 31.2%, and building/trade laborer came in a distant third at

14.4%. Philip was neither a farmer nor a miner, and his best skill was building furniture, and so he was given the designation of trade laborer.

The *Napoli* lifted anchor and sailed for Naples, another major city some 195 miles from Palermo, on the western coast of the "boot" of the Italian peninsula. Sitting approximately 115 miles from Rome, Naples was one of the leading cities in Italy for emigration. The ship sailed throughout night and in the morning, Philip found the *Napoli* anchored in the harbor of Naples. People were boarding and the ship was filling with fellow Italians pursuing their dream of a new life in America. Italians came from Sicily, Campania, Lombardi, Apulia, Calibria, and Abruzzi. In 1913, more than 300,000 men, women, and children would leave Italy for the United States; the *Napoli* carried some 2,000 of them.

The ship left port in the afternoon, heading west in the vast Mediterranean. Philip looked back east and saw his beloved Italy slowly shrink in the east, Mount Vesuvius growing more distant with each passing mile. Night came and went, and in the morning, Philip got his first glance at the Pillars of Hercules in the Straight of Gibraltar. Soon they, too, shrunk off the stern as the *Napoli* steamed out into the wide open Atlantic. Every inch forward the *Napoli* cruised was the furthest west, and the furthest away from home, Philip had ever been.

On board, Philip and Biagio engaged in all sorts of activities, as is common on a passenger vessel making a transatlantic voyage. Passengers met and talked all over the ship. They played games. They ate together in the galley. They talked about life back home and the life ahead they yearned for. The vast majority of the people on the *Napoli* were leaving for the same reasons Biagio and Philip were: to seek a better life. One thing Philip noticed was the fact that even though they were all Italians, they emphasized their differences, and those differences often led to sharp disagreements.

"*Le persone siciliane sono stupide*," said a man from Apulia.

"*Le persone della campania sono migliori delle persone della calabria*," announced a man from Campania.

"*Le persone di Napoli sono senza valore*," said a man from Genoa.

It had been 52 years since the Italian peninsula had been unified under Vittorio Emmanuel during the *Risorgimento*. But political unity had not yet led to cultural unity. The centuries of feudalism and wars between city-states like Venice, Milan, Rome, Naples, and Genoa had created a division that had yet to conquer the tribalism that was hundreds of years in the making. Philip, who had not experienced many people from other places in Italy beyond the island of Sicily, was learning quickly that to be Italian was still a messy thing.

The *Napoli* steamed ever westward. One day at around noon, the crew of the ship began closing all the portholes, up and down the length of the ship, on both the port and starboard sides. Philip, like most passengers, did not understand what was happening, but they seemed to be working with some urgency. He and Biagio were leaning over the railing watching the ship cut through the Atlantic.

"What is going on, Papa?" he asked.

"I don't know," Biagio replied, looking around. The men were hurriedly closing the portholes. "It looks like they're securing the ship for some reason."

"Securing it from what?" Philip asked.

"I'm not sure, but they're working quickly so whatever it is, it must be pretty serious."

They began to feel the ship rise and fall as it pushed through swells larger than they had experienced before. The wind picked up. The clouds darkened.

"We'd better get inside, Philip," said Biagio. The two of them hustled to their quarters, and by the time they arrived, the ship was teetering to and fro on yet larger waves. A major Atlantic storm had hit.

For most of the people on board, life at sea was something new. These were laborers, farmers, and peasants, not sailors and fishermen. The rocking of the *Napoli* in such violent winds and waves was too much. Some of the more devout remembered the gospel story of Jesus calming the storm and cried out in prayer.

"*Gesù, calma la tempesta per favore!*" they wailed over and over. Hail Marys were prayed in huddled groups all over the ship. Men, women, and children prayed to St. Nicholas, the patron saint of ships and sailors. "May Saint Nicholas hold the tiller," was the saying. He was not the only saint in people's prayers: St. Christopher (patron saint of travelers), St. Michael the Archangel (patron saint of mariners), and St. Brendan the Navigator (patron saint of navigators and sailors), among others, were called upon from bow to stern aboard the *Napoli*.

People soon got off their knees and left their rooms to rush to the railings and the *bagni* because their stomachs could not contain their freshly-eaten meals of meat and potato. People who were just talking about whether one part of Italy was better than another suddenly found themselves fully united in their misery. But not Philip. For some reason, his stomach held, and he avoided the awful *mal di mare*. He left his room when he felt queasy, went on deck despite the terrible storm, and held the railing, walking along its length, holding on for dear life. What he did not realize is that sea-sickness is a form of motion sickness, and on board a ship, when it is rocking in heavy swells, everything is moving, and one's inner ear becomes out of balance. When one is topside in a storm and looks at the horizon, the horizon is stationary, and that often helps a person return to a sense of equilibrium. Additionally, being outside brings fresh air, which helps ease the nostrils from the stench of other people's vomit. Vomiting, as most people have experienced, can be contagious, as it were.

Philip walked along the railings, gripping tightly, looking due west, and by doing so, managed to avoid becoming sick like most of the rest of the *Napoli's* passengers. The storm lasted several days, and the ship slowly crawled by the Azores, slowed by the heavy winds and waves. But eventually it passed and all was calm. That is, except for the crewmembers, who proceeded to spend a considerable amount of time and energy cleaning up the ship. Life on the *Napoli* resumed as it was before the tempest. But Philip would never forget his first storm at sea.

. . . . .

The *Napoli* continued on its journey, cutting across the warm waters of the gulfstream, drawing closer to New York with each passing hour.

Chapter 6 – Arrival

She stood proudly in the northern end of the New York harbor, some 305 feet tall, holding her torch aloft. Made by French sculptor Frederic-Auguste Bartholdi and Alexander-Gustave Eiffel – yes the man behind signature tower in Paris – the Statue of Liberty has been a beacon of hope for countless millions since Grover Cleveland dedicated her in 1886. The United States and France had developed a close and enduring relationship beginning with General Lafayette during the American Revolution. It would continue through the formation of NATO, including the two World Wars in the 20th century. As a symbol of unity and friendship between the two countries, the U.S. and France collaborated on the statue, with the United States building the base, and France building the statue. Shipped in some 200 crates across the Atlantic, it was put together over a four-month period and mounted on the pedestal.

Six years later, Ellis Island opened up as an official immigration station of the United States government. Between 1892 and 1954, Ellis Island processed some 12 million immigrants, most of whom came from Southern and Eastern Europe. On April 15, 1913, Philip and Biagio Vampatella arrived in New York harbor aboard the *Napoli*, along with approximately 2,000 others from Italy. When they pulled into the harbor, Philip and Biagio, like the rest of the passengers, stood along the railings looking out at lower Manhattan – by far the largest city either of them had ever been to – and there, welcoming them, was Lady Liberty.

Just two days earlier, one year after the sinking of the fabled *RMS Titanic*, New York City commemorated the lives lost in that tragedy with the opening of the Titanic Memorial Lighthouse and Time Ball, mounted on the top of the Seamen's Church Institute overlooking the East River. A plaque on the lighthouse read, "This lighthouse is a memorial to the passengers, officers, and crew who died as heroes when the steamship *Titanic* sank after collision with an iceberg." Biagio and Philip had no knowledge of this memorial, of course, but they **had** heard of the *Titanic*, but it was considered bad luck to mention another sinking when you yourself were at sea, and so it was never mentioned on their way across the Atlantic.

Philip's eyes widened as he saw the statue. Despite receiving a rural Italian education, he knew about the Statue of Liberty. He and Biagio had discussed it with some of the other passengers along the way and now, there she was, greeting them with open arms.

> *Give me your tired, your poor, Your huddled masses yearning to breathe free, The wretched refuse of your teeming shore, Send these, the homeless, tempest-tost to me, I lift my lamp beside the golden door!*

Philip and Biagio were indeed tired after their journey. And they were most certainly poor. They longed to be free, but it wasn't like they were political refugees like many others that had sought freedom in the United States. For them, it was simply about economic opportunity – something not afforded them in Sicily. The ship anchored in the harbor and a U.S. government inspection boat made its way towards the *Napoli*.

The inspection ship pulled alongside and government officials boarded the *Napoli*. They were not here to see Philip, Biagio, or any of the other third-class passengers – which represented the vast majority of people on board. Rather, they were here to see the relatively small number of first-class passengers, those handful of wealthy Italians who were not to be herded through the overcrowded pens on Ellis Island. The first-class passengers were given quick health and legal inspections, and only had to go through Ellis Island's immigration center if they were sick or had problems with their paperwork. Otherwise, they boarded the boat and were taken directly to the dock on the southernmost tip of lower Manhattan.

The rest of the passengers, however, were not so fortunate. Eager to get through this unknown process, they awaited orders to disembark and load the ferries that would take them to Ellis Island. The order came and Philip and Biagio boarded the ferry and they sailed a quarter mile to the immigration station's dock. Holding their only possessions they took with them – which fit in two small suitcases – they walked off the boat and stepped, for the first time in their lives, on foreign soil. American soil.

The immigration officers barked orders to the crowd of people, most of whom did not speak English and could not understand what they were saying. They handed each passenger a numbered identity tag, told them to pin them to their shirts, and ushered them inside the main building. Philip and Biagio dutifully followed the line of people inside the red brick building. Upon entering, they immediately came to the Baggage Room. Immigrations officers instructed them to put their bags down on the table for inspection. They did not understand, but they saw the people in line in front of them put their suitcases down and open them up for the officers, so Biagio and Philip did the same. The officers poked and prodded their belongings. Philip had no idea what they could possibly be looking for, but he stood in silence as the officers made quick work of their luggage inspection. They simply did not have much to inspect, and it was over in short order.

They were led down the hallway and up a winding flight of stairs to the second floor. Medical doctors observed the immigrants, looking for any sign of obvious illness – shortness of breath, difficulty walking, open sores, or anything else that might alert them to a potential health problem. Knowing that they could be denied entry if they were sick, those that were sick tried to hide it; some succeeded, but some failed. Philip and Biagio were in good health, so this was not a concern of theirs.

The stairs opened up to a huge, cavernous room called the Registry Room. It was commonly known as the "Great Hall" due to its massive size: 200 feet long and 102 feet wide – some 20,400 square feet. Hundreds of people jammed into every square inch of the Great Hall as the passengers were processed. Philip's eyes – as they often did on this entire journey – widened with awe, as he had never seen an indoor space so large before, not even at the train station in Palermo.

Men, women, and children stood in long, winding lines, with metal railings dividing them and keeping the flow orderly. Wooden benches – added to the room in 1903 – enabled exhausted passengers a few moments of rest before moving on again. The noise, to Philip's young ears anyway, was deafening. People talked excitedly about America, and answered dozens of questions from immigrations officers. Finally, after an hour and a half of waiting, Philip took his turn for inspection.

The immigration officer looked at his passport, and then up at him.

"Filippo Vamp—a—tell—a?" he stumbled. Having worked at this immigration station for three years, it never ceased to prove to this officer how difficult so many of these Italian and Eastern European names were to pronounce. Not everybody was a Smith or an O'Leary.

Philip did not know what he was saying, but he understood his name, so he nodded. The officer scribbled notes in his file. The doctor came over to look Philip over. He used a stethoscope and listened to Philip's heart and lungs.

"Breathe deeply," he said, but Philip did not understand, so the doctor demonstrated. Philip nodded and took several deep breaths. The lungs were clear. He looked in his ears and nose and mouth, and did a quick bodily inspection for any obvious issues. Philip showed no sign of pain or discomfort anywhere the doctor prodded. Everything seemed to be in order.

The doctor then took out what was called a buttonhook. This device was, as its name suggested, originally meant for fastening buttons to clothing, but on Ellis Island, doctors put it to a different use. Each immigrant had to be inspected for trachoma, a dangerous eye infection that if left untreated, could blind a person. Rumors had spread on the *Napoli* about this device and this part of the inspection process, and not a single passenger looked forward to it. Some dreaded it. For Philip, everything was so new that it was all both fearful and a wonder. He stood patiently as the doctor probed with the buttonhook, lifting his eyelids, looking for any swelling or other obvious signs of trachoma, such as a roughening of the inner eyelids. The disease was spread through contact, and though most people did not touch other people with their eyes, all it took was a quick wipe of the eyes and now the bacteria was on the fingers, which could then be passed on. It was often even transmitted by peoples' handkerchiefs. Trachoma was one of the leading medical reasons for people to be denied entry into the United States.

· · · · ·

The United States at the time held to an immigration policy that could be best described as *qualitatively restrictive*. During the first century of America's history, the United States had open borders, and immigration was highly encouraged. There were no barriers to immigration at all. In fact, one of the chief complaints the colonists levied against King George III was his restrictive approach to immigration. In the Declaration of Independence, Thomas Jefferson charged the British king thusly: "He has endeavored to prevent the population of these states; for that purpose obstructing the laws for naturalization of foreigners; refusing to pass others to encourage their migration hither...." The colonists wanted more immigrants, not fewer, but King George understood that the more people populating the colonies, the more perilous his hold on them would become.

For a century after gaining independence the U.S. government adopted the same philosophy, advocating for open borders. There were some in the Federalist Party that were concerned that too many immigrants – especially from particular countries – would change the uniquely American culture. In 1790, though, the Naturalization Act sought to legalize this policy of unabashed immigration. But only to a point. Section 1 of the Act declared, "Be it enacted by the Senate and House of Representatives of the United States of America, in Congress assembled, That any alien, being a free white person, may be admitted to become a citizen of the United States, or any of them, on the following conditions, and not otherwise—". Slavery still being very much legal in the United States in 1790, the government restricted immigration to free whites, which naturally excluded Mexicans, slaves, or even free blacks.

The Naturalization Act required immigrants to swear allegiance to the United States, renounce all foreign citizenship, and renounce any and all titles that he or she may have possessed in their home country. In other words, if an immigrant was a Duke somewhere in England, he was no longer a Duke when he swore his allegiance to the United States, and no rights and benefits of being a British Duke came with this immigrant to the United States.

Over the years, more and more people began to seek restrictions on immigration. The "Know-Nothing" movement, which gained considerable support and won 70 House of Representative seats in 1854 as the American Party, argued for restrictions on immigrants from non-Anglo-Saxon nations. Italy, of course, would fall under those restrictions, and if they had ultimately won the day, Philip and Biagio may never have made it to the United States.

Things changed in 1875 following the Civil War. From 1875-1920, the United States adopted a policy of qualitative restrictions. That is, people had to be of a certain "quality" in order to immigrate to the U.S. In 1901, future President Woodrow Wilson stated, "Immigrants poured in as before, but...now there come multitudes of men of lowest class from the south of Italy and men of the meanest sort out of Hungary and Poland, men out of the ranks where there was neither skill nor energy nor any initiative of quick intelligence; and they came in numbers which increased from year to year, as if the countries of the south of Europe were disburdening themselves of the more sordid and hapless elements of their population."

Wilson, of course, was not alone in his distaste for certain immigrants, especially those from Southern and Eastern Europe. Prior to Wilson, attitudes in the U.S. had changed so that instead of open borders, the government wanted only healthy, fit people of good character immigrating. In 1875 the US declared that convicts, prostitutes, and polygamists need not come to America. And in the Immigration Act of 1882 barred paupers and people who were "mental defectives." And the Chinese Exclusionary Act, passed that same year, denied Chinese immigrants – the first time that people from specific nations had immigrations restrictions placed upon them. Congress three times would pass literacy tests in 1896, 1913, and 1915, but each time those bills were vetoed by the sitting President.

When Biagio and Philip had arrived, the U.S. required all immigrants to be healthy and possess a useful trade. On the *Napoli*'s manifest, Philip was designated a "laborer", and the U.S. certainly could use more of those as it expanded and grew. Italians had been immigrating to the U.S. for several decades by the time Philip and Biagio pulled into New York harbor, and that was long enough for a saying to develop amongst Italians coming to America expecting riches: "The streets weren't paved with gold; they weren't paved at all; and I was expected to pave them."

. . . . .

Philip and Biagio passed their health inspections easily. Those that didn't were herded to the Hearing Room, where their case was heard. Most likely, these unfortunate souls were then kept in quarantine in the island's hospital, sometimes for weeks or even months. After that time, they would sit before the Board of Special Inquiry and a decision would be made whether they were well enough to then immigrate, or if they were sent back to their home country. For these people, the "Island of Hope", as Ellis Island was commonly called, became the "Island of Tears".

After the health inspection came the paperwork. It was time to make sure it all lined up correctly. In an age when records were kept by hand, without the aid of multilingual translators, it was very easy for paperwork to be filed improperly, for names to get changed inadvertently, or for documents to go missing. But Philip's information checked out – his passport and the ship's manifest matched, and so on April 15, 1913, Philip Vampatella, along with his father Biagio, were given permission to enter the United States of America.

Chapter 7 – Beginnings

The population of New York City in 1913 was a little under 5 million inhabitants. Of those five million, more than 300,000 were of Italian descent. Starting in 1870, when the first waves of Italian immigrants began to make their way to New York, a community of Italians had settled in the Bowery section of the city. Located just west of the Bowery section, on the lower east side, large Italian families lived in tight quarters on Canal Street, Centre Street, Mulberry Street, Hester Street, Mott Street, Baxter Street, and Hester Street. Immigrants have always had the tendency to find people most like themselves – it is a common human trait to seek those who share one's language and culture. In many cases, Italians coming over had relatives who had made the journey across the Atlantic in the preceding years, and it was natural, of course, to seek those relatives out in order to live with them.

By the time Philip and Biagio had arrived at Ellis Island, some 3.5 million Italian immigrants had settled in the United States, all over the country. Many of these had chosen to live in these tightly packed Italian communities. Many of the first wave of Italian immigrants were from Northern Italy, and were merchants and artisans. But by the time Philip and Biagio had arrived, the majority were like them – common farm and trade laborers, people just looking for any kind of work they could find. Like Biagio and Philip, most planned on amassing what to them would have been considerable wealth, and then sailing back to the mother country to be reunited with their families. These Italians who had gone back to their homes in Sicily, Naples, and other regions were called *ritornati* ("returned"). That was the plan Biagio and Philip had been operating under. Time would tell if it would come to fruition.

Biagio and Philip left the Great Hall and made their way to a large staircase leading down. There were three aisles on the staircase: if you were detained, you had to walk down the center aisle. If you were traveling west or south, you walked down the right side, and if you were heading to New York or north of the city, you walked down the left. Biagio and Philip were heading into the city and so they followed the mass of people walking down the left aisle. At the bottom of the stairs, Biagio and Philip were greeted by a railway ticket office, a currency exchange office – though Biagio and Philip did not have much money, they did exchange what little they had from Italian *lira* to U.S. dollars, being guided by the blackboard where the day's currency exchange rates were posted. There were also government social workers available to provide help to anyone who needed it. Philip and Biagio eschewed their help and, after retrieving their cases from the Baggage Room, came to what became known as the "kissing post". Many immigrants already had family or friends in New York waiting for their arrival. The two travelers saw many people hugging and kissing loved ones as they had finally been reunited after what was for some a considerable number of years.

Biagio and Philip did not have any family or friends in the U.S. They represented the totality of the Vampatella family on this side of the Atlantic. They boarded the ferry for Manhattan and in no time, they set foot in Battery Park. They had made some arrangements for their arrival, but without any easy way of making contact, and given the difficulty and unreliability of cross-Atlantic communication at the time, such plans were likely to go awry. And so they did.

An acquaintance in Palermo had recommended a man in New York who could help them with their transition. Biagio had no personal knowledge of this man and so did not even know what he looked like. This contact would help them find a place to stay for the princely sum of $25. All Biagio knew was that they were to meet in Brooklyn, on Union Street. They consulted the subway map and looked around for the subway terminal. Neither Philip nor Biagio had ever experienced anything like this before. Biagio eventually found a fellow Italian and asked for help.

"*Dov'è la metropolitana?*" Biagio asked. The man smiled and pointed to Whitehall Street and the sign for the South Ferry Station.

"*C'e la stazione dei traghetti sud,*" he said.

"*Grazie,*" Biagio replied, and he and Philip made the short walk to the subway.

Biagio was not a city man but he was intelligent, despite having little formal education. He was also familiar with trains, having worked for the *Ferrovie dello Stato* most of his adult life. The New York subway system, having been first built nine years earlier in 1904, and, being relatively new still was somewhat simple compared to what it would become, but it was nonetheless far more complex than the rail lines of Sicily. But Biagio read the map he had picked up and the two of them clattered over to Brooklyn, where they got off at Union Street.

Miraculously, they met up with their contact. They made their introductions but it seemed evident right from the start that this man had no idea what he was actually supposed to do to help them. He did not seem to be aware of the agreement made in Palermo. He was an insurance agent, and instead of talking about a place to live, he began to work his pitch on Biagio.

"You are new to America," he said. "You need what I am selling."

"What's that?" Biagio asked.

"Life insurance."

"Life insurance? What's that?"

"If something happens to you, the insurance company will give money to your son here in order to take care of him."

"So I pay money to buy insurance, and if I die, they give Philip money?"

"Yes," the man replied, sensing interest.

"How much does this insurance cost?"

"I will sell you a policy for….how much do you have?"

Biagio dug into his pockets and counted. Fifteen U.S. dollars. He knew he needed money for a place to stay. "*Dieci,*" he said.

"Ten will work," the man said, and reached into his case and pulled out a paper insurance policy. He told Biagio to hold onto that and keep it safe, and he took ten of Biagio's fifteen dollars.

The man went on his way and Biagio and Philip turned southeast and walked down Union Street, crossing Third and Fourth Avenues. People were everywhere. More people than either of them had ever seen in one city. They saw a nickelodeon – a five-cent movie theater – across the street, a spaghetti factory next to a saloon, and public baths on Fourth Avenue. A drug store sat on one corner while a bank sat on the opposite corner. There were more businesses, never mind people, than they'd ever seen people in a city before. Horses drew carriages, and their droppings littered the streets.

They also saw motorcars – an extreme rarity in Sicily. But this rarity was not because Italy did not produce cars; rather, it was a simple matter of the poverty on the island. Italy, as it were, was one of the world's leading manufacturers of automobiles. In the late 1880s, Stefanni-Martina became the first auto company, and in 1888, Giovanni Battista Ceirano started building Welleyes bicycles, before turning to motorcars in 1898. In July 1899 they contacted a consortium of businessmen and together their conglomeration produced the Fiat 4 HP, capable of achieving speeds upwards of 22 miles per hour. In the century following, of course, Italy would produce some of the finest luxury and sports cars the world has ever seen. But on the poor, rural island of Sicily, these Italian cars were hard to come by.

New York City was not like Sicily in any meaningful way. Their *casello* was in rural country, a place for two families, and they were spaced out along the miles of railroad track. In New York, homes were lined along every city street, either in brownstone row houses in residential neighborhoods or above ground-level shops, restaurants, and businesses of every imaginable kinds. In 1913 the tallest building in New York was the Woolworth building in Manhattan, rising into the sky some 792 feet. On Madison Avenue the Metropolitan Life Insurance Company Tower, built in 1909, stood 700 feet in the air. No city in Italy – or anywhere else in the world at that time – could one find buildings of such soaring height.

They managed to find a place to stay on Union Street for the night. It was small, hot, and smelly. The beds were infested with cockroaches and bed bugs. But it was a room with a roof and beds and they fell asleep contented. They had made it to America.

. . . . .

It took just two days for Biagio to find work. He was hired at two dollars a day by a company working on a subway station on Fourth Avenue. He worked for ten grueling hours a day, working hard labor, came back to the tiny apartment, ate a plate of spaghetti, and quickly dropped off to sleep. It was about as difficult a way to start life in America, but they had a place to live and money coming in.

15-year old Philip also needed to work. He lacked motivation, but necessity – and Biagio – drove him. The challenge for Philip was the barrier of the English language. He was not in Sicily, nor was he even in Little Italy in Manhattan. He was in a section of the city where English was the dominant language, and it proved to be nearly insurmountable for Philip. Nonetheless, he got his first American job at a clock factory south of Union Street. His task was to sort little brass gears that subsequent workers would assemble. He could not easily understand his instructions, but his foreman, believing he could himself speak Italian, served as a sort of interpreter. Somehow they managed to get the message across to Philip and he did his job to the best of his ability. However, when pay day came, the foreman took Philip's pay envelope and took a portion of Philip's pay for himself, leaving Philip with a mere three dollars – far below what he was supposed to make. Philip left the job and sought different work.

In May he found work at a rope factory. He left that and in June he picked up work at a bowling alley, setting up pins, making a dollar a night. His father left every day for his exhausting job, and the two hardly ever saw each other. Philip was lonely, homesick, depressed, and in a bad state. The apartment was far worse than his home in any of the *casellos* in which he lived back in Sicily, and the food was far worse. Neither he nor his father could cook on a level anything close to his mother Angela. Most nights at the bottom of his spaghetti he found cockroaches. The best food was found in the small restaurants and street vendors scattered throughout the Union Street area of Brooklyn. He experienced hot dogs and sauerkraut and thick American beer. But those cost money, and they didn't have money to spare on eating "out", as it were. They were once-in-a-while treats, while the bland, homemade, roach-infested spaghetti was the main fare each day.

This continued into July and August. The same routine. Nothing fun or glamorous about their life in America so far. But it was a start. At the end of August they found a new place to live – slightly better, with a much better landlord – landlady in this particular case. September and October featured the same, day after day. Biagio had never felt so isolated, having made no friends, and never getting much time with the only family he had on the continent. Biagio at work during the day. Philip to the bowling alley at night. Their paths hardly ever crossing. Loneliness like he had never known consumed Philip. Something needed to change.

The change came unexpectedly as both Biagio and Philip lost their jobs at the end of October. One thing about Biagio – he was a very hard worker. He found an ad about an employment agency in Manhattan. He walked across the Brooklyn Bridge to Mulberry Street and there they let him know about a project building a water reservoir in Connecticut that seemed like a good opportunity. But....what was Connecticut? Philip had never heard of it before, but Biagio explained to him that it was the next state over to the east of New York. And so Biagio and Philip packed their meager belongings and spent $1.50 a person for train tickets to Connecticut. This train was the first "regular" American train for either of them. It was very different from the subway cars they had ridden on, and likewise, very different from the trains in Sicily. This was big and comfortable. They took the train from Grand Central Station. As they watched the miles of track go by, the conductor made his rounds.

"Stamford," he said. "Tickets please."

Chapter 8 – Rapuanos

Roughly 32 miles north of Naples, Italy, lies the small town of Puglianello. In the 1990s, between 1,200-1,300 people lived in this small community. Looking in the public records, of the 130 last names registered in the phone book, seven of them fell under the name Rapuano. That made the Rapuano family the eighth largest listing in the Puglianello public records in the 1990s.

Sebastiano Rapuano was born and raised in Puglianello, and in his early teens immigrated to America, ultimately ending up in New Haven, Connecticut. He found work with the Connecticut Company, a railroad outfit that traced its origins back before 1895. A long series of mergers and acquisitions had led to the formation of Consolidated Railway, and in 1907, they acquired the Waterbury and Pomperaug Valley Street Railway in April, and the Thomastan Tramway in May. This new joint venture was renamed the Connecticut Company, and they operated all of New Haven's electric railways formerly owned by Consolidated.

Rapuano started out in a standard entry-level labor job with the Connecticut Company, laying paving blocks on track repairs, earning less than a dollar a day, but after some time, he had moved up in the company, earning some $18 a week, a considerable sum. Along the way, Rapuano had married, and by late 1913, he and his wife Mariella had six children:

fourteen-year old Tony, twelve-year old John, ten-year old Antoinette, nine-year old Alfonso, six-year old Louise, and Edward, still just a baby. The Rapuanos lived in a third story, three bedroom flat on Myrtle Street. Not far from the Rapuanos lived Mariella's sister, Jennie Bruno, and her husband Nicola, on Wallace Street, near Wooster Square. The Brunos lived with Nicola's parents, John and Teresa, and his two brothers, Armando and Steve.

Philip and Biagio had disembarked from the train from New York and found themselves in New Haven. They knew nobody in New Haven, but that was where the work apparently was, so that is where they went. Standing at the train station, having no idea where to go or what to do, Biagio tried to make sense of the confusing situation. Fortunately, a man noticed the blank looks on their faces.

"Can I help you?" he asked.

"Yes, my son and I just came from New York," Biagio replied. "We are looking for work and a place to live."

"What kind of work?"

"I heard there was a big project at a reservoir."

"Oh yes, at the end of the trolley line. Well I'm sorry," the man said, "but there is no way that you can get there today, given how late it is. You're going to have to find a place to stay for the night and go tomorrow."

"That's fine," Biagio replied. "Do you know where we could find a room for the night?"

The man pointed off in the distance. "There's a hotel that way. There are always rooms available."

"Thank you," Biagio replied, reaching out his hand. The man shook it.

"You're welcome, and good luck."

Biagio and Philip headed for the hotel and on the way, found a grocery store. There they bought bread and salami and checked into the hotel. It was a very low rent, low quality establishment, and they spent a dollar apiece for the privilege of staying the night. In the morning they headed to the job site. It was a long hike in the cold, damp morning. By the time they got there, they were told that there was no work to be had. Discouraged, they retraced their steps and walked back down to the trolley line from whence they came, wondering what to do next, when an elderly man and woman overtook them in a wagon.

"Hello there," they asked in Italian.

Biagio and Philip looked up. *"Buongiorno,"* Biagio replied, happy to hear his native tongue.

"Dove stai andando?" the man asked.

"Non lo so," Biagio replied, shrugging. "We are looking for work."

"Hop in," the man urged. "We are heading into the city."

So Biagio and Philip tossed their valises in the wagon, climbed in, and the horses clopped down the muddy street. The four people chatted the whole way into town, until they arrived on East Street. On the next block they came to a bakery with wagons meant to deliver bread. The man and woman offered Biagio and Philip a place to stay for the night.

"Unfortunately, I don't have a room to offer you," the man said. "But you can stay the night in the hay loft. It should be comfortable enough for a night."

"I'm grateful," Biagio said, smiling. "I am Biagio Vampatella, and this is my son Philip." Once again he offered his hand.

"John Bruno," the man said. "This is my wife Teresa." They all shook hands. "And this is our bakery, and our home. Please won't you stay for supper?"

"We would be very grateful for that," Biagio replied. *"Mille grazie."*

"Prego," John replied, opening the door and letting them in.

Once inside, John and Teresa introduced Philip and Biagio to their sons, Armando, Steve, and Nicola, along with Nicola's wife Jennie. The dinner was excellent, and the Brunos took to Biagio and Philip right away. They again apologized for not having a room available, and promised to help them find a better place to stay.

The next morning, Armando led Philip and Biagio to Myrtle Street and introduced them to Jennie's sister, Mariella Rapuano, who was pregnant at the time, and her children. Mariella was readying the kids for school, but they all stopped to look at the strangers with Armando. Their reaction was not warm and inviting. Tony turned and left. John frowned and went back to combing his hair. Alfonso glanced over, said nothing, and waited for his turn to use the comb. Neither of them knew it at the time, but Alfonso would become one of Philip's best lifelong friends.

Ten-year old Antoinette looked at Philip with disdain. She was well-dressed for school and, carrying her books under her right arm, spun around and walked out. Philip was stung at this brazen act of snobbery, and instantly Philip took a disliking to her. Antoinette's younger sister

Louise simply laughed at Philip and hurried off to kindergarten, which was just a two-minute walk away.

The children all left for school, leaving Armando, Biagio, Philip, and Mariella alone, along with baby Edward. More formal introductions were made, and they began to share about themselves. Biagio told his story quickly, but sufficiently and pleasantly enough to engender a sense of trust in Mariella. Mariella then opened up about her life. She had married Sebastiano Rapuano when she was just fifteen, in opposition to her parents' wishes. He was a handsome 19-year old and she was star struck by his appearance. She did not know much about love but she knew enough that if you said, "I do," that meant you were committed for better or worse. Unfortunately for Mariella, worse was all too often the word of the day, though she never stopped hoping for better.

Steve – as Sebastiano would be known to Philip – was a hard worker, having risen up in the ranks of the Connecticut Company. But for years now he had made it a daily habit of stopping at nearly every bar on the way home from work for a beer, which meant that every night he came home, he was drunk. Nothing good came of that once he arrived at the house, and Mariella was dutifully expected to tend to his every need at that point, even after spending all day taking care of the children and the home.

Armando returned to Wallace Street, leaving Philip and Biagio at the Rapuanos. That evening, to Mariella's pleasant surprise, Steve came home sober, met Biagio and Philip, and quickly cleaned up from his long day of work. Mariella set out supper, put on a plate for Biagio and Philip, and a lovely dinner was enjoyed by all. Biagio and Steve hit it off right away, perhaps sensing an affinity given their similar upbringings in Italy. Like Steve, Mariella had immigrated from Italy but unlike her siblings – including her sister Jennie Bruno – she struggled with English. She worked when she arrived in the United States but soon met Steve, fell in love, and married. They agreed to let Biagio and Philip stay with them.

Philip and Alfonso became friends quickly, despite the sizeable difference in age. They immediately learned to enjoy one another's company, laughed at each other's jokes, and went to the nickelodeon on Grand Avenue, having maneuvered their parents into giving them nickels for the show.

"Alfonso," Philip said as they sat in their seats, "*sei un buon ragazzo.*"

"Don't say that!" Alfonso replied sharply, but almost in hushed tones.

"Why not?" Philip asked.
"That's a bad word!"
"No it isn't."
"Yes it is, and you shouldn't say it."
"*Buon ragazzo* just means 'good boy'. I'm saying you're a good boy."

Alfonso frowned, his eyebrows tilting downward. "Ok," he said. But Philip got the message that in the Rapuano home, *ragazzo* was not a word to be used, and so he never did.

. . . . .

Biagio managed to find work in bits and pieces, but nothing permanent or steady. They had come to love the Rapuanos and were grateful for their help, but they also realized that there were limits. Philip landed a job at an electric plating shop on Grand Avenue for $3.50 per week. Given the struggles Biagio was having in his efforts to work, Philip's pay became their main source of income for that winter, with most of that money being paid to the Rapuanos for room and board. Almost every penny Biagio earned was sent back to Angela and the children back in Vittoria.

At the end of November, something strange happened to Philip. It was a cold 31 degrees and clouds darkened the sky. Temperatures in Sicily, even in the winter, almost never got below 40 degrees farenheit, and this was without question the coldest weather Philip had ever experienced. Suddenly, out of the sky, soft white flakes fell to the ground. Philip looked on in wonder. It was the first snow he had ever seen.

. . . . .

The Rapuanos' home on Myrtle Street – a small connector road linking East Street and Hamilton Street, crossing over Wallace Street (where the Brunos lived) in-between – bordered the railroad tracks that led to Cedar Hill to the northeast. Every day Philip and Biagio encountered the sounds of the locomotive chugging its way up the slope. The noise took some getting used to, but then again, they had both spent many years at the various *casellos*, and were quite familiar with train noise.

Snow piled up that winter, and Biagio got work for the city shoveling snow. But he did not yet have anything steady, and Philip's small earnings kept the two of them afloat financially that winter. Meanwhile, Philip and Alfonso's friendship grew, and Philip soon discovered that Alfonso shared a similar hunger for knowledge. They taught each other new words and struggled to pronounce them correctly. Alfonso learned Italian, while Philip learned English.

One day Alfonso shared the idea with Philip that they should get some books to read.

"*Dove?*" Philip asked.

"At the library," Alfonso replied.

"That's *biblioteca*," Philip said slowly.

"Biblio…what?" Alfonso asked, trying to pronounce the word.

"Tek-a. *Biblioteca.*"

"Ok," Alfonso replied. "We can get books at the *biblioteca*."

"How much do they cost?" Philip inquired.

"Cost?"

"Yes, they must cost something."

"No, we just borrow them."

To Philip, this was not something he had ever heard of before. To be able to access books without buying them was…new. The New Haven public library lent books in almost any language, opening up a storehouse of learning and knowledge for Philip that he had never imagined possible. He and Alfonso would stay up late at night reading, learning, and talking together. This displeased Steve, who wanted peace and quiet in the house, but even more, did not like paying the extra money for the gas to light the lamps that were left on in order for the boys to read into the wee hours.

. . . . .

Most Americans today associate the Italian term *Don* with the mafia, specifically the fictional character Don Corleone of Mario Puzo's *Godfather* fame. It literally means "Lord", as the word was first used to speak of Italian royalty, nobility, and people in power. It was not to be used as a substitute for someone's name, or to be used on its own (one would never simply say, "*Don*"), but rather as one might use the term "Mister". Hence, "*Don* Corleone", not merely "*Don*". It stems from the Latin "*dominus*", which means "gentleman, lord", and is a shortened version "*donno*", the Italian modification of the Latin. Over time it became more used as a term of great respect, and of course, mafia family leaders were called *Don* this or *Don* that. Sometimes a man was called *Don* because of his position or power, whether he was personally loved or not. But in many cases, *Don* was used for a person who was respected and loved.

As Biagio and Philip went through the winter lodging with the Rapuanos, Biagio began to get to know many people in the Myrtle Beach community. Biagio was always a gentlemen – kind, polite, deferential, hard-working, and helpful. He truly practiced his version of the Golden Rule he had taught Philip as a young boy. To the people of Myrtle Street, New Haven, he was worldly wise, properly religious, and modest. When he helped someone, he refused payment for his services. "A good word is easier to say than a bad one, and the best reward for a man saying the good word is friendship," he would tell Philip. Biagio had the proper sense of the value of good relationships, and he always extended his hand to others. As a result, people in the community began calling him *Don* Vampatella, or *Don* Biagio.

Giuseppe Lacana was one such man, and one day he came to *Don* Biagio for help. He had a brother who had been locked up in the state prison in Wethersfield, some 35 miles north of New Haven. Giuseppe's brother worked for the railroad, and an issue had come up, creating a significant disagreement between Giuseppe's brother and his job foreman. The conflict became so terse that the two men could not resolve it, and the foreman fired Giuseppe's brother. In reprisal, he derailed a train, causing considerable damage. For this action, he was sentenced to prison.

Giuseppe, meanwhile, had a wife and a young daughter named Nancy, and it was Giuseppe's dream to make his fortune in America and move back to Girgenti, a Sicilian town approximately 60 miles northwest of Vittoria. There he hoped to buy a farm and get Nancy married off to a rich Sicilian. Nancy was ten, and in light of Giuseppe's dream, she was instructed to learn Italian. Giuseppe, having gotten to know and respect Biagio, asked for help.

"*Don* Biagio," he said. "I know you are from Sicily and you speak fluent Italian."

"Yes, of course."

"I want my daughter Nancy to learn Italian, and I cannot teach her. Will you help?"

"Of course I will help. I cannot teach her, Giuseppe, but my son Philip would be glad to." Biagio, of course, had no idea whether Philip would be *glad* to help, and in fact he suspected quite the opposite, but that did not matter. And so Biagio made arrangements to have Philip teach Nancy all the Italian he knew. Payment would come in the form of a few beers on the weekends.

"*Grazie, Don* Biagio," Giuseppe said, shaking his hand energetically.

Nancy took a liking to Philip and became a good student. Philip, however, grew bored with the arrangement and soon lost interest. One Sunday, he tried to teach Nancy his favorite poem. One stanza said:

Nell 'orto alcuna volta
Scinta, il bel ppiede sale
Su giovin pero al quale
I pomi fura.

(Sometimes in the orchard
Naked, the fair foot climbs
On a young pear tree from where
The fruits are stolen.)

Nancy understood the words *pero* (pear tree) and *pomi* (apple), but could not understand how the poem could speak of apples growing on pear trees. Philip explained the nuances of the words and said, "*Pomi* are the unripened fruit of several trees." Nancy disagreed, sticking to the literal terminology, and an argument ensued. Neither gave an inch. Eventually the argument got so heated and loud that Giuseppe and his wife intervened and Philip was ejected from the house without his usual payment of beer.

. . . . .

Biagio's job prospects in New Haven did not improve in the spring of 1914, and he eventually got a tip about a job in Ansonia, a town 10 miles or so to the west. Biagio walked the considerable distance to Ansonia to meet the man in charge of the job, and the two of them talked it over. Biagio would start the following Monday, earning $1.50 per day on a long road paving job.

He and Philip had to say goodbye to the Rapuanos, who by then had become another family to them. It cut both ways, of course. For the Vampatellas, the Rapuanos were the family they needed to find in America. For the Rapuanos, Biagio and Philip were a breath of fresh air and a source of great joy. Mariella wept at their departure. Philip had the hardest time saying goodbye to Alfonso, who clung to him and did not want him to leave. Even Antionette by now had grown to at least appreciate Philip and hated to see him go.

But off they went, having secured a ride in a truck heading to Ansonia. They arrived and the two of them went to live on Main Street with Santo, the Floridian in charge of the project. Santo was gregarious, and Philip and Biagio liked him instantly. His wife, Carmela, was a beautiful woman, and the two of them had a pair of young daughters. Biagio worked with great energy, and Santo promised him a raise when he could come up with the money. Philip, meanwhile, was jobless, but he came up with a creative idea. Ansonia did not have much industry, save for two foundries, who would take scrap metal and turn them into slid ingots to be refined elsewhere. Philip saw an opportunity, and scoured the town dumps for discarded brass and copper. From his previous job experience, he knew how to clean them up, and he was able to sell them to a middle man who turned around and sold them to the foundries for a tidy profit. Philip usually spent the money on entertainment, watching Charlie Chaplin movies at the theater.

Philip visited the Ansonia public library but found that it lacked books in Italian, still the language through which he wanted to learn about the world. His English, while improving, simply was not improving rapidly enough to read whole books. Having become accustomed to borrowing books in his native tongue, he would occasionally walk the ten miles, skirting the hill town of Derby by the Housatonic River, to the New Haven library.

Biagio's job lasted throughout the summer and began to wrap up as August arrived. He began the process of looking for more work and soon he and Philip found themselves pushing wheelbarrows full of muck from the town's main sewer. Not glorious work, but it was work, and it paid the bills.

Then came the news from Europe, and it was not good.

Chapter 9 – The Great War

Philip and Biagio's journey to America can be traced directly to the Italian purchase of Assab Bay. And that's largely because Giuseppe Sapeto was a man of vision. The Suez Canal was nearing completion in 1869, and he imagined what it would be like for Italy to have a coaling station and port of call for Italian ships in the Red Sea. Understanding the economic advantages inherent in such a station, he made his pitch before King Victor Emmanuel, who was sold. He commissioned Sapeto, along with Admiral Alfredo Acton, to go to the Red Sea and investigate the possibilities. They found Assab Bay, off the eastern coast of Africa near the mouth of the Red Sea, appealing, and began negotiations with the Danakil chiefs for its purchase. They paid a small deposit in exchange for promises to sell the territory upon their return.

The Emmanuel government, meanwhile, knew that entrepreneur Raffaele Rubattino was planning to establish a commercial sea route through the Suez Canal, and the government arranged a deal with Rubattino for him to buy the Assab Bay territory, but to use it to advance Italian national interest. Sapeto sailed back to Assab Bay, completed the deal, adding more territory just to the south, and by 1870, Italy had its first port in the Red Sea since the Roman Empire. Rubattino's personal merchant fleet would grow considerably thanks to this deal, and in 1881, after merging with *I & V Florio* of Palermo, founded the *Navigazione Generale Italiana*, the company that would eventually purchase the *British Prince* from *British Shipowners Ltd.* in 1906, rename it the *Sannio*, and then in 1913 refit it as a passenger ship and rename it the *Napoli*.

In 1882, the Italian government took over ownership of the territory, establishing its first overseas colony for the new united Italian kingdom. Other countries began to see the value in similar actions, and the scramble for Africa, as it became known, was on. By 1914, Italy succeeded in acquiring Assab Bay in Etitrea along the coast of the Red Sea, a protectorate in Somalia, and influence in Libya. Italy pursued colonization elsewhere in the world as well, as it continued to expand its territory and influence.

Naturally, this push by European nations for colonies brought tension between European powers, as quite often, their interests and efforts came into conflict. In 1870, France and Germany went to war as France sought to deter Germany from bringing southern states Baden, Wurttemberg, Bavaria, and Hesse-Darmstadt into the national fold. France worried that the balance of power in Europe would shift should German expansion continue unabated. In what could only have been considered an upset of historic proportions, Germany wasted very little time in dispatching the French, and just six months later, on January 28, 1871, German troops occupied Paris. In victory, Germany claimed Alsace-Lorraine, a long-disputed territory that bordered both France and Germany. In the halls of Versailles, the French domination of the European continent that had existed since 1648 ended as Kaiser Wilhelm began to rule over the united nation state of Germany. France never forgot this defeat, and set about to rectify this loss.

Tensions mounted as the nations pursued colonization. Germany rightly understood that France would not take defeat kindly, and as a way to secure its position in Europe, began the process of establishing alliances with other European powers. France, of course, was not the only threat to Germany, and in 1879, Germany entered into the Dual Alliance with Austria-Hungary primarily as a hedge against Russia, ever looming over European affairs. Meanwhile, France had begun to establish greater influence in North Africa, causing Italy to seek protection. Mutual concern over France brought Germany and Italy to the table together, and in 1882, Italy joined Germany and Austria-Hungary in what became known as the Triple Alliance. This pact guaranteed that if France attacked any of the three, the other two would come to its aid. They would seek to add Britain – longtime rival of France – into the fold, but they were unsuccessful. However, Russia was under the impression that England had an agreement in place with the Triple Alliance.

Italy and Austria-Hungary, despite being in the Triple Alliance, were not comfortable partners, as they had numerous conflicts of interest, particularly in the Balkans. Germany tried to iron these out between their partners, but Italy entered into a secret agreement with France in 1902 to remain neutral should either be attacked. Europe was tying itself in a Gordian knot, and they were not yet finished.

In 1887, Russia and Germany entered into the Reinsurance Treaty, with Germany promising to support Russia in case Austria-Hungary – longtime enemies of Russia – attacked their eastern neighbors, and Russia supporting Germany in case France attacked from the west. Over the next two decades, however Russia drifted away from this agreement. Meanwhile, France, looking itself for support, courted Russia and in 1894 the two nations signed the Russo-French military-political alliance. Ten years later, Britain aligned with France and finally, in 1907, Russia joined the two European powers to form the Triple Entente, which acted as a massive political, economic, and military counterweight to the Triple Alliance.

Each nation believed that having the support of each other would ensure its protection. Why would any nation attack another when it would immediately invite the wrath of two more great powers? What they did not understand was that if, for some reason, one nation **did** attack another, it would trigger war on a massive, continental scale. Which, of course, is exactly what happened.

Tensions rose in Europe. Nations prepared for war. Philip watched Sicilian units of the Italian army drill, not realizing what was happening around the world. It is likely that the soldiers on drill had no idea either, but it would not be long before Italy found itself embroiled in an all-encompassing war.

The flashpoint, of course, came in the assassination of Archduke Ferdinand on June 28, 1914. The Hapsburg royal was on a visit to Sarajevo, capital of the Austro-Hungarian province of Bosnia-Herzegovina. The Black Hand, a terror group from Serbia, was responsible. The Austria-Hungarian government weighed its options. It did not want to precipitate a war with Russia or France, but it believed that neither country would come to the aid of little Serbia, not after they had responsibility for an assassination of one of its royal family. On July 23, they issued an ultimatum. But they did so only having received assurances from its alliance partner Germany that it would help Austria-Hungary in the case of Russian or French attack.

Russia, meanwhile, saw clearly what was happening and sought French support should Russia get involved. On July 27, France began mobilization. Tensions were thick throughout Europe. Now, those same alliances designed for the purpose of keeping Europe **out** of war, were about to engage all of it **in** war.

Austria declared war on Serbia on July 28, and on July 30, Russia began a general military mobilization. Two days later, Germany declared war on Russia, and two days later still, on France. On August 4, Germany entered Belgium, according to their war plans. Great Britain promptly declared war on Germany in support of Belgium, and the Great War was on.

War raged for eight months. Italy, which was obligated by the Triple Alliance to join in the effort with Germany and Austria, sat idly by, watching and waiting. The German-Austrian-Italian alliance had formed a solid wall through the heart of Europe, and Britain knew it needed to chip away at that and put pressure on the mighty German machine. It began negotiations with Italy in secret, and offered Italy the territories of Tyrol, Dalmatia, and Istria in the Adriatic Sea region. Italy, flush with colonial aspirations, found that offer too tempting to refuse, and on April 26, 1915, Italy spurned the Triple Alliance and entered the war on the side of the Triple Entente. War had come to the homeland.

. . . . .

When the war began in 1914, Italy needed men, and so immediately began a massive recruiting effort. Biagio and Philip's sewer job ended, and they looked for the next work they could find. They made contact with a Sicilian from Vittoria living in Paterson, New Jersey, who turned out to be an old friend from Biagio's past. Biagio and Philip soon found themselves in the industrial city of Paterson but no job was to be found. They survived on the meager savings they had, and when 1915 rolled around, Philip finally found work in a piano factory sawing wood with a circular saw. He cut off the end of his left thumb, and was sent home by the foreman. He went back to work and wheeled material from one department to another, earning him $4.50 a week.

The Sicilian community in Paterson was well aware of events in Europe. Their home country was on the brink of war. Angela sent a letter telling Biagio that there was urgent business at home, and Biagio made the decision to return. He borrowed enough money for a ticket to Sicily, told Philip he would be back soon, and boarded the first ship back to Italy. Philip was now alone in America, and homesickness ate at him day after day.

As the days passed by, Philip's homesickness turned to depression. He got little joy from the people around him. Even going to the theater to watch Pearl White's "Perils of Pauline" did little to lift his spirits. Biagio sent him letters from home, but the news was not good. Biagio told Philip that he could not return to the United States right away, but assured Philip that he would as soon as he was able. He exhorted Philip to work hard and behave well. These letters helped some, but in the end only reinforced the idea that he was separated from his family, whom he missed dearly. On numerous occasions, Philip felt the urge to take his own life, such was the hopelessness and isolation he felt, but he never followed through and continued to slog along, day after lonely day.

More bad news came when the piano factory let him go. Now without a job, Philip thought of the Rapuanos again, and after packing his few belongings, left Paterson, and took the train back to New Haven. He found Myrtle Street more easily than he thought he might, and without any warning, knocked on the door. Alfonso opened it up and saw his friend standing outside.

"Philip!" Alfonso cried and embraced a teary, but smiling, Philip, who hugged him back.

Alfonso's cry rustled the home, and the Rapuanos rushed to the door. Mariella, who had already had another baby named Rose, was pregnant again, and she kissed Philip and brought him inside. Steve grinned widely and clapped Philip on the back, saying it was great to see him. Even Antionette smiled at Philip's return. It wasn't even a question that they would let him stay as long as he wanted. A forever grateful Philip brought his things up to Alfonso's room where he stayed previously. It was like old times, except that his father was in Sicily, and Alfonso was no longer Alfonso – he was called Jimmy.

Naturally, Philip asked for an explanation. It turned out that Alfonso had found a job at the dry cleaners on Grand Avenue, and for some odd reason the people at the cleaners started calling him Jimmy. It stuck, and before long, everyone but his father Steve was calling him Jimmy. It was difficult for Philip to adjust at first, but it did not take long before he, too, was using that moniker on his old friend.

. . . . .

It was April, and Philip had now been in the U.S. for two full years. The war in Europe accelerated, and with it came the need for more men and, of course, more materiel. The Winchester Repeating Arms Company of New Haven had been in existence since the middle of the 19th century, and as the Great War in Europe intensified, Winchester found their rifles in high demand. The British government contracted with Winchester for the .303 Pattern 1914 Enfield rifle, and later in the war, the United States bought Winchester's .30-06 M1917 Enfield rifle for its soldiers.

As demand for Winchester rifles increased, the need for labor increased as well. Philip applied for a job at the Winchester plant and was hired at $0.32 per hour, plus overtime. Philip's work contributed to the war effort for Britain, who suddenly found themselves allied with Philip's native Italy. Philip and Steve had come to some disagreements, and Philip decided to move in with a friend on nearby East Street. Philip had to learn how to cook, and he was wildly unsuccessful. Not knowing a thing about nutrition or having any skills in the kitchen, Philip became ill, and for the first time in his life, had to see the doctor. He recovered, continued working, and chose to eat as much food as possible that required no preparation.

The spring of 1915 represented the start of the Presidential political season, as candidates began to traverse the country, hoping to win the White House in 1916. Democrat Woodrow Wilson won in 1912, having defeated Republican incumbent William Howard Taft and third party candidate, former President Theodore Roosevelt. As the war erupted in Europe, Wilson campaigned on the theme of "He Kept Us Out of War", and argued that a Republican victory would inevitably lead the U.S. into war with both Germany and southern neighbor Mexico. In 1915, they were still well before the primaries, but that didn't stop the candidates from traveling around the states to give their stump speeches.

One day during his lunch hour, Philip, like other workers, left the building and ate his lunch on the crowded street. An open car stopped in the center of the street. A huge man with a moustache and reddish hair, dressed in a black suit, stood up in the back of the car and began to deliver a speech. A crowd of nearly 2,000 people surrounded the car as he spoke. For five minutes his voice thundered as he criticized President Wilson. Philip watched on in great amusement at the scene in front of him.

Finally, a man from the crowd yelled out, "And what did you do while in office?" The man, face flushed with anger, shouted back something that Philip could not understand, and began waving his arms violently. The car, yielding under the immense weight of the man, began bouncing up and down almost comically. The exchange lasted several more minutes before the man sat back down and the car drove off.

The man was former President, and future Chief Justice of the U.S. Supreme Court, William Howard Taft.

. . . . .

At the Winchester plant Philip grew close to a middle-aged co-worker named Bob, whose last name Philip never got to know. Bob was kind to Philip, and he taught him much about the work Philip was being asked to do. Philip came to respect and love Bob as if he was an older brother. Bob also taught Philip more English, as the two of them often sat down and read books together, including some of the great English writers like Chaucer, Shakespeare, and Keats. Bob's philosophy was straightforward: Every man is every man's brother. In other words, it was imperative to live a life where you cared for others and looked after them. Philip never knew much about Bob's past, except that it was a troubled one, but he quickly realized that Bob was educating him in more ways than in just English.

Italy and England were now allies, at war with Germany, and Biagio wrote Philip from time to time. He told Philip that he needed to return to Sicily to do his duty in the army, a suggestion that Philip had no interest in pursuing. He did worry about his family, however, and he occasionally sent what money he could spare to his mother and father back home.

At work he was moved to a different part of the plant and no longer saw Bob, who had by then become a dear friend. The New Haven railway had a track that split the Winchester operation into two halves, with a very busy intersection at one of the crossings. One day Philip joined other workers in crossing this intersection on their way to lunch when he heard the screech of brakes as the train tried to stop suddenly. People screamed in horror. Philip ran over to see what had happened, and he saw a man, lifeless, against the rail, struck by the train with violent force. Philip instantly felt nauseous as he recognized the face. It was his friend Bob.

Over the next few weeks Philip spent considerable time in his grief thinking about Bob, their friendship, and the life lessons Bob had taught him. Bob had encouraged Philip to pursue the virtues that God had put in him, to seek knowledge and wisdom, to walk in modesty and grace and always be thankful for good fortune and the many blessings that came his way. Bob instilled in Philip a deep sense of personal responsibility. He did not know Bob that long and never knew his last name or his background, but in that short time Bob taught Philip more about life than anyone else had in his whole two years in America.

Philip took Bob's death hard, but what Philip didn't realize was that much more death was on the horizon.

Chapter 10 – Enlistment

Italians, like other Europeans with family members in the United States, sought to stay in touch with them as much as possible. The only practical way to achieve this was through the sending and receiving of hand-written letters. Biagio and Angela occasionally wrote to Philip, sending him word of tidings back home, and often the news was bad. Philip returned the favor with letters telling them about his latest job, how the Rapuanos were doing, and any other news they might find interesting. He also sent small amounts of money – such as he could spare – back to his family, knowing that they were in tough financial shape. Immigrants in the U.S. often had no fixed addresses, and the post office had no way of contacting them, so a system developed over time whereby the post office would publish in the newspaper a list of people who had received a letter from Italy. The immigrants would check the paper's *Lettere Degli Italiani* listing and if their names were on it, they would go down to the local post office to retrieve them. Philip would keep Biagio informed as to where he was staying, but always Biagio could send letters to the Rapuanos at 35 Myrtle Street in New Haven.

August and September had rolled around, and the war in Europe raged on. Germany had begun using U-boats against British and French vessels, as well as merchant ships carrying supplies from the U.S. At the end of

April France and Germany clashed again in the Second Battle of Ypres, during which time Germany first began using poison gas on the battlefield. Italy had entered the war on April 26 on the side of France and Britain, and a week later revoked its commitment to their defensive alliance with Germany and Austria-Hungary. On May 23 Italy declared war against Austria-Hungary and between June 23 and July 7 they fought their first of eleven battles of the Isonzo, failing to achieve victory. The Italian war cry of "*Sacro egoismo!*" (sacred egoism) seemed odd and proved to be of little use as the Austrians piled Italian bodies high on the slopes of the Alps.

Shortly thereafter, they fought again in the same spot, as General Luigi Cardona attempted to smash the Austrian lines. For the second time, he failed, as he did not appreciate the value of barbed wire, which created killing fields for the Austrian infantry. That was a lesson every nation was learning the hard way in the early stages of the war.

On August 21, Italy declared war on the Ottoman Empire, increasing the strain on its resources, and in September, a letter arrived from home.

The war effort in Italy, like in every other European nation involved, put a tremendous strain on the economy and on its resources. Industry was switched from peacetime to wartime efforts, and rationing began to take place to support the army and navy. Farm produce was sent to the front lines. Metal was used not for household items but for shells and guns and barbed wire. Families at home suffered. The work on farms normally done by men had to be done by women, as the men were now serving in the armed forces. That meant that women had to pull double duty, doing their work plus their husbands'. As was the case for most families, rationing meant less food at the dinner table for Biagio, Angela, and the rest of the children. Hunger gnawed at them.

Philip was not exactly living in the lap of luxury enjoying five-star dining either, of course. He could feel his own stomach tighten as he read Biagio's description of things back home. It was Italian custom to write letters in a more formal tone, even between family members. Even so, Philip could clearly feel their pain.

Biagio had more to tell. Cousin Rosario had been shot by an Austrian during one of the battles of Isonzo. Cousin Giovanni waited to enter the army. Cousin Biagio was too young but was eager to sign up anyway. Sister Giovannina had a boyfriend in the army. Sister Lina helped Angela care for newborn twins in the home. Philip had new brothers that he had never met! Sadly, they passed away in infancy and Philip never knew them.

Biagio sent letter after letter, with more frequency and urgency, calling on Philip to return home and join the Italian army. Philip did not think he had enough money for a ticket back, not realizing that Italy would happily have covered his cost if it meant another man on the front. He pushed away his father's suggestions, however urgent and demanding they were, more and more firmly resolved not to fight in the Italian army. Something was nagging at him to stay. But Biagio was relentless, and in one letter he warned Philip that he would contact "people in high places" to compel Philip to return and do his duty serving Italy.

Philip was frightened by this prospect, and not a little bit angry. He had come to like America, and feared that Biagio, who stayed true to his word as a matter of habit, would follow through on this threat. All Philip could picture was a young, scared Italian soldier standing on the front lines, obeying orders from sergeants that he only remembered from his youth as being vicious bullies with no regard for the well-being of the men. The last thing in the world Philip wanted was to enter that life. He realized that he had to do something drastic, and so that's precisely what he did, deciding that two significant changes had to be made. First, he needed to move out of New Haven, since Biagio knew that's where he was living, and second, he needed a new identity. And so, in order to free himself from a worsening and increasingly desperate situation at home, Filippo Vampatella became Philip Vamptell.

In 1916, Philip moved from job to job and from town to town. He worked for P&F Corbin in New Britain polishing hardware. He took a job in Milford putting salvaged tire rubber into steel rollers, but quickly left it after hearing about a worker being crushed to death after having been caught in the rollers. He worked as a maintenance man in a carpentry shop in Branford. There Philip learned a lesson in window repair and roofing – something he would take with him in the years to come. He found himself working short stints at jobs in Hartford and East Hartford, but never holding a job down long enough to actually launch a career. But it was enough – barely so – to survive.

He did manage to visit the Rapuanos as often as he could, always being welcome in their home. Steve's drinking and disposition was getting worse, but he loved Philip nonetheless. Jimmy was doing well. Mariella had had another baby and the Rapuano family continued to grow.

They handed Philip a letter from home, as 35 Myrtle Street was the only place Biagio was sending letters. Philip had stopped writing back, but Biagio kept sending them nonetheless. This particular envelope had a black border, and that was not a good sign. Philip, hands trembling, opened the letter.

His mother Angela had died.

Philip reeled. He never imagined, boarding the train to Palermo, that he would never see her again. Biagio wrote, "*L'ultime parole sulle sue labbra erano una preghiera per il suo figliolo cosi lontano.*" (The last words on her lips were a prayer for her son so far away.) Devastated, Philip was filled with grief at the loss. He felt overwhelming guilt for not writing, an act that seemed at the time to be of self-preservation, but now felt like it was pure self-centeredness. He was consumed with depression and grew sick with peritonitis, eventually losing his job in the process. He wrote back home that he loved everyone, and that as much as he loved his home country, he did not want to go back, explaining that the doctors in Italy couldn't care for what ailed him.

. . . . .

By 1917, Europe was weary of war, but because all nations had so much invested by this point, none of them wanted to give up. It was the most bloodshed the continent had ever seen, and men were dying by the millions. The famous Battle of Verdun was fought between France and Germany throughout almost all of 1916, a battle that would claim some 750,000 casualties on both sides, 120,000 of them deaths, absolutely staggering figures. To put that number into perspective, it has been estimated that in the entire six-year American Revolutionary War, the total number of American, British, and German deaths were estimated at roughly 52,000, most of them dying of diseases like scurvy or smallpox, not from battlefield wounds.

The United States had thus far managed to stay out of the war. An immigrant nation, the U.S. had citizens from every European nation, including large contingents from each of the primary powers. It was not at all clear which side the U.S. should be on, should it be drawn into the conflict. Woodrow Wilson had been re-elected in 1916 on a neutral/isolationist platform, but events in Europe were growing increasingly difficult to ignore. The Wilson government had arranged with London to start sending war supplies to Britain and her allies, but in order to not provoke the Germans into war, did so secretly, bringing them over on passenger vessels. Germany, naturally, got wind of this, and could no longer allow supplies to continue to flow unimpeded from America. In 1915 they sunk the British passenger ship *Lusitania*, which was secretly transporting material to Britain from the U.S. for the war effort. 1,128 people died, including 128 Americans. By 1917, the U.S. was not using passenger ships, but more conventional merchant vessels. Germany resumed a policy of unrestricted submarine warfare, which meant that they would now attempt to sink any and every ship in a declared war zone around Britain, France, and in the Mediterranean. Attacks would come without warning.

Wilson was stunned, as he himself had negotiated Germany away from this very policy following the *Lusitania* attack. But the German situation was growing desperate. Wilson withdrew the U.S. ambassador to Germany, James Gerard, and sent German ambassador Johan von Bernstoff home. This official break in diplomatic relations beginning on February 3, 1917, did not mean war necessarily, but it was a strong signal to Berlin. The Germans did not back off, however, and in the eight weeks that followed, German U-boats sank nine American merchant ships.

On April 6, the United States declared war on Germany. The *New York Times* blared, "President Calls for War Declaration, Stronger Navy, New Army of 500,000 Men, Full Co-operation With Germany's Foes". The *Buffalo Evening News* headline cried, "U.S. Now at War With Germany; Interned Ships Seized by U.S. More American Nations to Join". The *Daily Missourian* headline read, "U.S. Officially at War". And the *Portsmouth Herald* announced, "State of War is Declared".

This news, of course, quickly reached the ears of Americans and immigrants alike, from Maine to Florida to California. The U.S. began the process of enlistment drive through the Selective Service. Philip continued to work in Hartford and East Hartford, all the way through 1917. January 1918 came, and while in Hartford he came across a poster of Uncle Sam, famously pointing the finger and declaring, "I want you." Philip began to be pulled in by the war effort – the American one, not the Italian one, from which he still had every desire to avoid. But Uncle Sam was calling, and by this time, despite its challenges, he had come to love America.

By this time, the Russians had pulled out of the war, dealing with their own internal problems. The Bolsheviks had revolted against the government of Czar Nicholas II, and Vladmir Lenin would ultimately seize power for the communist rebels. Philip continued to work every day with the world around him in chaos. Every day to and from work he passed Uncle Sam pointing his finger at him. Every day Philip felt greater compulsion to respond.

Finally, one day, Philip found himself at the U.S. Army recruiting station, standing before an army officer.

"What is your name?" the officer asked.

"Philip Vamptell," came the reply. By now, he was so used to using it that it even rolled off his tongue somewhat naturally.

"What branch do you want?"

"Infantry."

"Sign here," the officer said, pushing a form across his desk. Philip signed it and the next thing he knew, he was on a train to New Rochelle, New York, landing at Fort Slocum. There, he took the oath of allegiance, got his uniforms and shots, and began life in the U.S. Army. Shortly thereafter, he was sent to Fort Jay on Governor's Island in New York as part of Company B, 22nd Infantry Regiment. The 22nd was the largest organized combat-ready army presence in New York, tasked with homeland protection duties: securing tunnels, bridges, rail lines, and other important forms of transportation. Back in April the regiment had boarded U.S. Coast Guard cutters and seized German-owned freighters and passenger ships all along the Hudson River. This represented the very first U.S. military action in the war.

As was the case with every new man arriving at Fort Jay, Philip's records were screened. Officers were looking for any history of crime, specific skills the men might have, aptitudes, and education. Two of the new recruits were found to have been born in Italy: Philip Vamptell and Anthony Bressi. Officers figured that Philip was uneducated and couldn't spell his own name, so a sergeant named Francois pulled Philip aside to ask him some questions.

"You seem to know your ABCs pretty well," he said. "I know most Italian names end in an a, e, i, or o. Why not yours?"

"Simple, Sarge. I like to Americanize my spelling. That should be reason enough. But I don't mind telling you the real reason: I don't like to be in the Italian army."

"That's a reason? Pretty slim, isn't it?" Francois asked.

"I'm not ashamed of the Italian army. I'm not ashamed of the misspelling of my name. I'm simply afraid," Philip admitted.

"Afraid of what? Do you think the American army is going to pamper you?"

"No. My father is still in Italy," Philip replied. "For the last two years he has begged me to enlist in the Italian army. Since I have turned a deaf ear to his please he has finally threatened to have some responsible people in Italy contact some responsible people here to force me back to the old country."

"That's a lot of bunk. They couldn't do that in the first place." The sergeant paused. "Or could they?"

"I don't know," Philip shrugged. "I just want to play it safe."

"Yes? But what have you against the Italian army?"

"Nothing but a fight," Philip said.

"A fight with the army?"

"No, with an army sergeant."

"What happened?" Francois asked, curious.

"I spit on him, called him names, kicked him in the shins."

"Wow, you must have been pretty mad. What did he do to you?"

"He slapped me, kicked me in the rear, threw me to the ground, and stepped on me."

"Son," Francois said with a chuckle, "that was enough for both of you to get court-martialed."

"Yes?" asked Philip. "I didn't know that. All I knew was that he was beating up one of his men because he couldn't march right."

"When did that happen?"

"Over eight years ago. I wasn't in the army."

"What?" Francois was incredulous that Philip, while still a boy, would enter into a fight with an army sergeant. Philip shared the story as it had happened when he was just a boy. He explained to Francois that this is how Italian sergeants were, and he wanted no part of that.

"That was only one sergeant," replied Francois. "I don't think all Italian army sergeants act that way."

"I don't know. I didn't want to take chances. So here I am."

Francois began to explain that armies all over the world, throughout the history of the world, had done horrible things.

"That's the way it is; that's the way it has always been. With time refinements have come about in the art of killing. From the very beginning discipline has taken a very large part in all armed organizations. The top man had always made his generals; the generals have made their subordinate officers and these their non-commissioned officers down to the rank of corporal. The rank and file take orders without question. All this has always been done, is done, and always will be done, not on the basis of 'if you please', but by direct and unswerving orders of 'do it or else.' Where the orders come from no one questions. The ones in command shout them, many times, much as they hate to." He paused. "I don't like to see my men hurt, son, but my job is to carry out orders as it was for the Italian sergeant with whom you fought."

Philip still had a lot to learn, but he was getting there. Meanwhile, it didn't take long for his story to make the rounds in the 22nd.

One day new arrivals showed up at Governor's Island. They were a group of prisoners, wearing American uniforms, but definitely not Americans. They did not speak English, and the unattached women living on Governor's Island quickly developed an affinity for them. These men, as it turned out, were Italians, and they, like so many others, were conscripted into the Italian army. They were captured by German troops and sent to work camps in eastern Germany. Before the Bolsheviks revolted, the Russians had managed to capture the portion of German territory the camps were in, and these men were taken by Russian troops and brought back to Russian POW camps. When Russia pulled out of the war to concentrate on dealing with their own serious internal issues, American diplomats learned of the existence of these prisoners. They negotiated to have them put on a train to Vladivostok, and from there were shipped to the United States. Eventually, they were assigned to stay on Governor's Island, with the men of the 22nd Regiment.

For most of these men, this was a breath of fresh air, and they mingled freely with the citizens on the island. One man, however, mostly kept to himself. He was older than the rest, and Philip couldn't shake the suspicion that he recognized the man from somewhere, but he couldn't figure out the connection. It took a while, but then it dawned on him. This man was from Vittoria. He was the very same sergeant that he had spit upon and from whom he had received the beating eight years prior. Now he was living in the same army camp as Philip, all the way across the Atlantic.

Philip asked questions.

"Was that man ever a non-commissioned officer?"

"Yes," one of the others answered. "Some time ago he was a sergeant."

"What happened?" Philip asked.

"He was demoted and put in prison."

"Why?"

"Brutality," they answered.

Philip felt anger towards this man but knew that starting any trouble would have terrible results. He was not worried about a fistfight. Philip was bigger, stronger, and younger and had no doubt that this time, he could deliver a serious punishment to the sergeant. But he also knew that, as Francois had explained, he could get put in military prison for such an act. Philip decided that discretion was the better part of valor, and kept his fists to himself.

. . . . .

In 1790, The U.S. Congress passed the first naturalization law, laying out a two-step process that took a minimum of five years to complete. The first step was for an "alien" living at least two years in the U.S. to file a *declaration of intent* to become a citizen. The second step, which required three more years of residency in the U.S., was for the applicant to *formally petition for naturalization*. This rule became the norm for all immigrants looking to become citizens of the United States.

Three major exceptions exist to this general rule. First, wives and children of naturalized men could be granted so-called "derivative citizenship." Between the years of 1790 and 1922, wives of naturalized men automatically became citizens, and immigrant women who married U.S. citizens also automatically became citizens. Thus began the storied tradition of marrying for the purpose of citizenship. Between 1790 and 1940, children under 21 automatically became citizens when their father was naturalized.

A second exception existed from 1824-1906, minor aliens could file their declaration of intent and their formal petition at the same time.

A third exception came into play during the Great War. In 1862 a law allowed honorably discharged veterans of any war to file a formal petition for citizenship after just one year, without the need for a declaration of intent, and this after needing just one year of residence in the U.S. On May 9, 1918, a law enabled aliens serving in the U.S. military during "the present war" to file their formal petition without needing either a declaration of intent or 5 years' residency. Between May 9, 1918, and June 30, 1919, more than 192,000 aliens became citizens thanks to this exception to the general rules of naturalization.

In June, Philip and three other soldiers were given orders to report to Sergeant Bogel, who led them to the ferry, crossing the harbor, and then a walk to City Hall. The four soldiers had no idea what was going on, so they asked the sergeant questions, but he kept quiet. A short time later, they found themselves standing in a courtroom and a judge in a black robe stood before them, told them to raise their right hands, and led them in taking an oath of allegiance to the United States and a pledge to defend the Constitution.

On June 19, 1918, Philip Vamptell became an American citizen.

Chapter 11 – Reunions

The United States entering the war, it is argued, tipped the balance in favor of Britian and her allies. In the course of a year and a half, the U.S. sent more than a million men to Europe to fight, and in many cases, die, for its European friends. The Italian-American community, having a deep love for its home country, as well as a fervent sense of American patriotism, wholeheartedly supported the war effort, and rushed to sign up in huge numbers. Despite a population far smaller than its war contribution would suggest, some 12% of the total American armed force in the Great War were either American-born citizens of Italian descent, or Italian-born immigrants. The U.S. military featured a significantly disproportionate representation of Italians.

The "War to end all wars" concluded on November 11, 1918, when an armistice was signed with Germany in a railroad carriage at Compiègne. The eleventh hour of the eleventh day of the eleventh month brought about a general cease-fire all across the lines. While still technically in a state of war, the armies all over Europe disengaged, leaving the rest of the work for the diplomats. On June 28, 1919, the warring nations signed the Treaty of Versailles.

For Italy, the war was an unmitigated disaster. In just three years of fighting, Italy suffered 600,000 dead and 950,000 wounded – some

250,000 of those crippled for life – all while wrecking the economy. The war alone cost more than the entire nation had spent in the previous 50 years combined, and by 1918, inflation and unemployment were at unfathomably high levels. For Biagio, life at home was incredibly difficult. Now a widower, he found it difficult to find work. He wrote to Philip often to get any news.

When Philip wrote back telling him he had become an American citizen – *"Pater, civic Americanus sum"*, he wrote – Biagio at first felt a sense of resignation. But soon he felt a sense of joy and pride at what his son had accomplished. More than half a million sons of Italy had perished in the Great War, but his own son, staying true to his convictions and serving in the military himself, somehow managed to survive. Biagio longed to see Philip again, and wrote that he would soon return to America with the rest of the family to once again be reunited.

At the beginning of June, before the Treaty of Versailles was formally signed, the United States began the process of demobilization. By mid-June, every eligible man was given an honorable discharge and $60 separation pay. Of course, some chose to remain in the service, but that life was not for Philip. He received his discharge and soon found himself standing on the subway platform on 4th Avenue in Brooklyn, where his father had labored to help build six years earlier. Philip boarded the first available train to New Haven.

When he knocked on the door at 35 Myrtle Street, he found himself staring at a familiar face. Jimmy, his dear friend, had answered, and his face burst into a wide grin.

"Philip!" he cried, gripping his friend in a big bear hug. He and Philip had continued to exchange letters all while Philip was stationed at Fort Jay, and through these letters, their friendship had continued to grow.

The rest of the family rushed to the door to greet Philip. Mariella looked tired, having added another child to the Rapuano brood, but she was not pregnant, a state in which he often found her. Steve was sober, to Philip's grateful surprise. Antoinette, now 16 years of age, smiled at him through eyeglasses she had begun to wear a couple of years before. Her smile this time was different, almost shy, but Philip wondered if he noticed a little sparkle in her eyes. She looked…pretty, Philip thought, and somehow that thought must have been communicated in the way he glanced at her, because after a moment, her face flushed with redness, and she excused herself to her room.

Shortly thereafter, dinner was served. Oh how Philip had missed Mariella's cooking! Huge mounds of pasta – made far better than either Philip or the Fort Jay mess hall could make – covered in a rich, garlic-flavored sauce was almost too good to be true. As Philip gulped down helping after helping, the Rapuanos peppered him with questions.

"How many times were you shot?"

"Where did you go?"

"How many generals did you meet?"

"Was there any beer in the army?" Steve wanted to know, as a push was being made for a Constitutional amendment prohibiting alcohol. It would pass on January 16, 1919, and despite claims to the contrary, had significantly positive effects on society. Alcohol consumption declined dramatically, cirrhosis deaths rates for men fell, admissions to state mental hospitals for alcoholic psychoses declined, and arrests for public drunkenness and disorderly conduct decreased as well. Moreover, people reported to work more often, as absenteeism declined considerably during Prohibition. But in the process, billions of tax dollars were lost, and organized crime grew out of liquor bootlegging. Prohibition, which had enjoyed considerable popular support initially, was repealed in 1933 with the passage of the 21st amendment.

"Did your father write?" asked Mariella, the only one who seemed interested in how things were back in Sicily.

It felt so good to be back with the Rapuanos. He loved them all. Steve and Mariella were like a second set of parents – especially important because of Angela's death and Biagio being back in Italy. Tony and John were like brothers. Jimmy, of course, had become his best friend in the world. The little ones were easy to love. And then there was Antoinette. There was now something different about her. He was very glad to see her.

Philip could not stay long, because the search for work in New Haven proved fruitless. He had spent some time in Jersey City while on leave from Fort Jay, and there he had visited a factory that he now hoped was hiring. He took the train and found an opening with the Mengel Box Company. Philip was assigned the task of feeding rough boards into a double-headed planer, which smoothed both sides at once. It was laborious work, but Philip, energized by Biagio's promise to come back to America, wanted to save money to help them with the passage, and so he stuck with it. In the process, he learned more valuable woodworking skills.

Things were going well for Philip. He boarded with Vitale and Antonia Gualtieri on Broadway, and their son Pasquale, who would become a good friend of Philips, had also served in the army. Not long after boarding – three others did the same at the Gualtieri home – he was treated like family. Philip worked and saved as much money as he could, and after a year, had enough to pay for passage for his father and sister. He sent that money to Biagio, and proceeded to rent a three-room flat, some furniture, and cooking supplies. He even had enough money left over to buy a new suit and a bicycle.

. . . . .

At the beginning of the summer of 1920, a ship arrived to New York from Palermo. Biagio and his three sisters disembarked, went through Ellis Island (for Biagio, a second experience), and were reunited with Philip after a long separation. As glad as he was to see them, and vice-versa, he could see the strain that the years of war had upon them. Biagio looked considerably older and more worn out. Giovannina was not the vivacious girl he knew seven years before. Lina was a late teenager and grown tall and beautiful. Maria was nearly 16, slender and frail. All of them looked exhausted, and Philip knew it wasn't just from the journey. It was from years of privation thanks to the burden put on families by the war.

Biagio, Giovannina, and Lina all quickly found work. Maria stayed home, taking care of the flat, doing all the housework, and preparing meals for the family over the hot coal range Philip had purchased before their arrival.

The Vampatella ladies quickly made an impression on the men in the neighborhood, and it was not long before there were frequent requests for their company. Pasquale found favor with Giovannina and soon after, they were married. They lived at the Gualtieri home on 128 Broadway. Jim Prestia, a man Philip met and befriended at the Mengel works, made a valiant effort to win Lina over, finally succeeding, and the two were married, living with his mother on Sip Avenue.

Biagio, Philip, and Maria continued to live in the flat Philip had originally rented. Philip, now 23 years of age, had begun to spend any extra money he had earned on train tickets to New Haven to visit the

Rapuanos. Of course he wanted to visit Jimmy, but his attention – and purpose – turned to 17-year old Antoinette. He made it clear that he had intentions for her hand in marriage, but the family felt she was too young for that. Moreover, her income - $16 per week from the L. Candee Rubber Company – was crucial to help the ever-increasing Rapuano family's financial budget. Steve had gone back to drinking and was in rough shape, so her income helped pick up the slack. Philip would have to wait.

The Rapuanos moved to a new place on Wallace Street, behind the Hamilton Street School, south of Grand Avenue. As the months went by, Philip appeared at their door more frequently on weekends, and even occasionally during the week. He would travel for a very short overnight visit, take the train back, and be home just in time to start work the next day, using the hours on the train as his only rest. By this time, Philip had left the factory to pursue carpentry work, getting a job with Hanson Coleman in downtown Jersey City. He earned a dollar per hour, a handsome salary of $44 per week – far more than he had ever made in his life. But money disappeared as fast as it came in, spent on rent, food, tools for his trade, train tickets to New Haven, and small loans to Antoinette's mother, Mariella.

Weeknight visits were always interesting occasions. He would arrive around midnight, when everyone else was in bed. Jimmy would let him in, asking what time he had arrived.

"Just now," was how Philip usually answered.

"When are you going back?"

"Pretty soon."

"Why don'tcha say?"

"Gotta work," Philip would reply, the same routine over and over. Mariella would wake Antoinette, make everyone coffee, and enjoy a visit with Philip, who made such trips two to three times a week.

. . . . .

Antoinette was actually Philip's second serious romantic pursuit. The first began shortly after his discharge, with a young lady named Catherine Kalkieviecz, from Hamden, Connectiut. Her brother Mike was a private in Company B at Fort Jay, and he had taught Philip how to play checkers while serving together on Governor's Island. At first, Mike won handily, but Philip improved to the point of winning from time to time. The two

92

began to bet on the games, and on one occasion Mike bet his sister's name and address against a pack of Philip's cigarettes. Mike lost, and Philip began sending letters to Mary Kalkieviecz.

But Mary never wrote back, and Philip was puzzled. Eventually, he received a letter from her sister Catherine, explaining that Mary had run away with a sailor and had ended up in a home for wayward minors. Catherine included a photo of herself, and the words, "Please write to me and think of me as your sweetheart. I love to read your letters and I know I can love you." Philip wrote back, but was wary, as he did not want to lead this girl along.

Their correspondence continued, and a month after Philip was discharged, he took a ride to visit her at her family's farm in Hamden. He was taken in by her long, flowing blond hair and natural beauty. Immobilized by the vision in front of her, he struggled with words. It was one thing to write letters or see pictures; it was another thing to see her in person, and what he saw in person was far more beautiful than anything he had imagined.

"Hello," he managed to say. "I'm Philip."

Catherine smiled, stepped towards him, took his head in her hands, and softly kissed him on the lips.

"Hi. I'm Catherine."

They stared into each other's eyes for a lingering moment, before the spell was broken. Catherine excused herself to get herself more presentable, as she had greeted him at the door wearing plain, everyday clothing, not something meant to impress. But Philip couldn't have been more impressed by her than she already was. He was fully smitten. Nonetheless, she scooted to her room, leaving Philip with Mrs. Kalkieviecz in the kitchen.

"Have a piece of *bapka*," she said, putting a slice of cake on a plate and pushing it in front of him. Philip said thank you and took a bite. It was delicious.

"You like Katy?" she asked in accented, but passable, English.

"Very much," he replied.

"You think me pretty like Katy?" she asked. Philip did not know what to say, given the oddity of the question. Philip knew enough to answer kindly.

"Any mother with a daughter as beautiful as Catherine must be beautiful inside," he said diplomatically. She laughed.

"Me more pretty once. You see me now: ugly."

Philip frowned, unsure what to say. Mrs. Kalkieviecz continued, "Katy someday look more ugly than mother. Soon she get married. Soon she look ugly."

Philip's face betrayed the fact that he did not believe anyone as beautiful as Catherine could ever not be beautiful. Nor could he believe that she was soon to be married. She noticed his doubt.

"You no believe? Come next year, you see. She marry Andrew Dollar next month."

"Marry? Next month?" Philip was stunned.

"Andrew give me three hunnert dollars. He buy Katy forty dollar ring."

By now Catherine had returned and interjected herself into the conversation, reminding her mother that she had no interest in marrying Andrew. He was thirty years old, twice her age.

"He give me money to marry you," Mrs. Kalkieviecz said to her younger daughter.

"You can't make me marry him, mama! I'll run away like Mary!"

Mrs. Kalkieviecz pointed a plump finger at Philip. "You run away with this boy? He got no money, maybe he no got job. Andrew got money, got job, got automobile. You look like important lady with Andrew. You run away with this boy, you walk. Maybe you get hungry too."

Philip suddenly realized what he was up against, not just with Catherine, but in life. He had worked hard and had made something of his life in America, but make no mistake: he had very little to offer a young woman like Catherine, and he knew it. His heart sunk. But he knew he couldn't give up.

"Mama," he said, mustering as much confidence as he was able. "I have a job. It may take some time before I can save enough money to marry and buy a car, but I am a good worker."

"How long?" she asked, skeptically. "Five, six years? Too long. Katy old lady before you get ready. Maybe you change mind, marry another girl more young. No, no can be. And how me pay back Andrew three hunnert dollars?"

Philip had no response, and no solution to the problem suddenly placed before him. She was right, of course. He was unprepared for marriage, and it would take a while before he would get there. In the meanwhile, anything could happen. Catherine was not old enough to decide for herself whether to marry or not. Philip knew he could run away with her, but the law nor her mother nor his father would be pleased. He knew he had to honor his family, and realized in that moment what he must do.

He reluctantly kissed Mrs. Kalkieviecz and her beautiful daughter, and left.

Six weeks later he returned to Hamden to pay the Kalkieviecz' a visit, hoping the situation had changed. It had, but was worse than Philip had imagined, for two weeks prior, she had indeed married Andrew. He was at work and Mrs. Kalkieviecz left Catherine alone with Philip, a move that puzzled Philip as it seemed to court danger. Catherine brought him up to her room and Philip followed, afraid at what was about to take place.

They sat on her bed and Philip waited nervously. She reached under her pillow and pulled out a revolver.

"I keep it with me all the time," she said, "to keep Andrew away from me."

"Why?" Philip asked, astonished.

"I don't want him near me," she continued. "Mama made me marry him because she needed the money. Now you have come back. What do you think I should do?"

Philip thought of several options, but only one course seemed correct.

"First, you get rid of that gun. Then you get a legal annulment of marriage. Then you let me know when you are free. We will get married then."

She wept, and as tears poured down her face, she nodded. "If you say so."

Philip kissed her tenderly and left. For a long time he waited for word from her, but it never came.

. . . . .

In March of 1921 Philip began working for a local contractor, building houses. Philip learned much about framing, roofing, and finishing – skills he would later employ when the time came for him to build his own home.

The spring and summer led to fall, and in September Biagio saw an advertisement in the newspaper for land that was selling on Long Island for just $250. They traveled to Great River, on Long Island, and saw that the description of the land was accurate. It was beautiful land with plenty of timber and space and nobody around for miles. They surveyed the land and agreed to buy one acre. They paid a deposit, and once they had finished paying off the rest, Biagio and Philip, for the first time in their lives, would be landowners.

In December Biagio, Philip, and Maria moved from Jersey City to Long Island, to a drafty house on Connetquot Avenue in Great River. Back in Jersey City, Philip became an uncle and Biagio became a grandfather, as a baby boy Philip was born to Giovannina and Pasquale Gualtieri. Lina soon gave birth to a girl, Jennie, and the next generation was well on its way.

The Spring of 1922 brought about a resumption of Philip's visits to New Haven to visit the Rapuanos. He informed the family that he had bought a lot on Long Island. Antoinette looked beautiful and spent the night giggling with Philip as Steve grumbled, "When the hell are you going to bed?"

Chapter 12 – Restrictions

Italians passing through New York City's Castle Garden immigration station on a chilly February day in 1873 were greeted by men offering them work. What luck! Broken Italian combined with a smattering of English, and before they knew it, these Italian immigrants were on a train to Coalburg, Ohio. They arrived the next day, along with 300 black men from Richmond, and found themselves in a tempest. Hundreds upon hundreds of men were walking around with signs, picketing. The Italians had no idea what the signs meant, but because Italy was no stranger to labor disputes, they quickly understood what was happening. These men were on strike. So why were the Italians and blacks being brought in?

They pulled up to the work area and were immediately showered with insults and threats from the striking coal miners. The mine produced bituminous coal, soft and tarlike, a mid-grade quality better than lignite but worse than anthracite. It was common in these parts of Ohio and Pennsylvania, and the workers in the Mahoning Valley were laboring day after day under dangerous conditions – some 250 miners died each year – to extract the precious natural resource. They were getting paid $1.10 per ton that they mined, and in 1872 they decided that they needed a raise, and demanded a fifteen cent per ton pay increase. Naturally, the company thought differently, and actually began to lower their pay by twenty cents per ton. On January 1, 1873, more than 6,000 men stopped working and went on strike.

The mine operators had a problem. Business was completely shut down while their labor force was not working. Sure, they were holding fast to not acceding to the workers' demands, but every day they did not mine coal was another day of lost business. They developed a plan and sent men to the South and East to recruit. Recruiters found 300 black men in Richmond willing to work the mines, and hundreds more Italians getting off ships in New York who were desperate for work, and they brought them in by train. Now these men were getting off the train, ready to work, but clashing with those on strike. The company had brought these men in to break the strike, and unbeknownst to the new recruits, their employment was contingent upon being replacement workers. That is to say, if the original crew remained on strike, the black and Italian men would be hired to replace them. However, if their presence brought an end to the strike, the original mining crew would go back to work, and these black and Italian men would be out of a job.

Before they could even enter the mines, they faced harassment from the striking workers. Rocks were thrown. Insults were hurled. Threats were made, and on occasion, those threats were carried out. Fistfights became a daily occurrence. Eventually the strike ended, but the Italians and blacks were linked together as strikebreakers. Thus, in the American mindset – the strikes were covered by national newspapers – Italians were seen as uneducated, unskilled peasants coming to take the jobs of everyday Americans.

Between 1880 and 1924, some four million Italians immigrated to the United States, most from Sicily and the southern portion of the peninsula. Half of them arrived between 1900-1910, and reached a high of 283,738 in 1914, the year the Great War started. But once the war began, immigration tailed off dramatically, shrinking to 49,688 immigrants in 1915, 33,665 in 1916, 34,596 in 1917, 5,250 in 1918, and just 1,884 in 1919, a low number not seen since 1869. Why did Italian immigration decline so much and so rapidly? The answer is clear: the war effort demanded every able man and woman; men were conscripted into the military, and women stayed to tend the farms and the home front.

In the United States, Italians contributed to society in innumerable ways. They joined the U.S. military effort in disproportionately high rates. They built bridges and subways and railroads. They opened shops and restaurants. They also worked jobs that many other Americans did not want to take, replacing former slaves in the fields on cotton, sugar, and tobacco plantations in the South.

But Italians – especially southern Italians – were not viewed positively in the United States, despite these significant contributions. There were three primary reasons for this negative disposition towards Italians. First, white Americans associated Italians with uneducated peasantry, good for very little more than to work the most basic and unskilled labor. Second, Italians were believed to be of a criminal class, engaged in more crime and believed to be capable of worse behavior than other ethnic groups. And third was the unique brand of Roman Catholicism they brought to America, characterized by superstition, devotion to the saints, and long-held rituals.

When Italians first started immigrating in larger numbers in the 1870s, they took the kinds of jobs normally reserved for slaves and peasants. The work needed to be done, slavery was no more, and Italians were willing to do it, seeing as how it represented an improvement over life in southern Italy. They were not viewed with respect or admiration for this, but rather as a group of some of the worst classes of people, and those jobs appeared all they were fit to do.

This stereotype was emphasized by the newspapers, which spoke openly and with shocking sentimentality. One paper wrote in the 1890s, "The floodgates are open. The bars are down. The sally-ports are unguarded. The dam is washed away. The sewer is unchoked. Europe is vomiting! In other words, the scum of immigration is viscerating [sic] upon our shores." The *Fort Worth Weekly Gazette* accused Italian immigrants of being "fruit dealers of the very lowest type, men who just arrived to this country and scarcely speak a word of English."

The prevailing sentiment in the United States was one of unease over the influx of Italian immigrants – especially those from southern Italy. A book written in 1907 said, "immigrants from eastern and southern Europe are storming the Nordic ramparts of the United States and mongrelizing the good old American stock." Regarding the religious concern, Episcopal Bishop Charles Henry Brent said, "the United States is in far greater danger from the quality of immigration that comes from Southern Europe than from any peril that could come by Japanese ownership of lands in California, or from Asiatic immigration."

Of all immigrant classes, Sicilians were held in the lowest regard. The most favored were English, German, French, and Scandinavian. Southern and eastern Europeans were held in lesser regard, and among southern Europeans, Sicilians were held in the most contempt of all. After the New Orleans lynchings, the *Lewiston Teller* in Idaho called Sicilians "a baser kind of Greek." The *Arkansas Gazette* tried to link Sicilians with their Arabic and northern African ancestors, saying that their violence was "a direct and reasonable result of their Bedoin descent."

It wasn't just because Italians were poor and uneducated peasants that Americans held them in such low regard. It was the common perception that Italians were criminals, at least moreso than the rest of the population and other immigrant groups. The New Orleans lynching brought about a widespread criticism not of those who did the lynching, but of the Italians who were lynched. Reporting on the massacre, one newspaper said, "The little jail was crowded with Sicilians, whose low, receding foreheads, dark skin, repulsive countenances and slovenly attire proclaimed their brutal nature." The *Thibodeaux Sentinel* warned that "If the Italian Government does not want her assassins and murderers killed in the United States let her keep them at home." The *Opelousas Courier* took it one step further, calling Italian immigrants "a gang of desperate foreigners ready to do any bloody work for hire." And the *The Watauga Democrat* from Boone, North Carolina, claimed that the "Italians who were killed were not worth the protection of any decent government".

It wasn't just the sense that Italian immigrants were criminals; it was that they were considered to be linked to organized crime. To be fair, there were some Italians who were connected to organized crime, as was the case in New Orleans. Of course, it was a small percentage of Italians that were involved in the mafia, but that didn't stop people from associating Sicilians with the mafia – a view that persists in many respects to this day.

Following the New Orleans lynchings, the December 1890 issue of *Popular Science Monthly* printed a scathing, racially-charged article titled, "What Shall We Do With the *Dago*?" The author, Appleton Morgan, wrote: "What shall we do with the '*dago*'? This '*dago*,' it seems, not only herds, but fights. The knife with which he cuts his bread he also uses to lop off another '*dago*'s 'finger or ear, or to slash another's cheek. He quarrels over his meals; and his game, whatever it is, which he plays with pennies after his meal is over, is carried on knife at hand. More even than this, he sleeps in herds; and if a '*dago*' in his sleep rolls up against another '*dago*,' the two whip out their knives and settle it there and then; and, except a grunt at being disturbed, perhaps, no notice is taken by the twenty or fifty other '*dagoes*' in the apartment. He is quite as familiar with the sight of human blood as with the sight of the food he eats. His women follow him like dogs, expect no better treatment than dogs, and would not have the slightest idea how to conduct themselves without a succession of blows and kicks. Blows and kicks, indeed, are too common an experience with them for notice among '*dagoes.*' When a woman is seriously hurt, she simply keeps out of sight somewhere till she is well enough for the kicking and striking to begin over again, and no notice whatever is taken of her absence meanwhile. The disappearance is perfectly well understood, and no questions are asked. The male '*dago,*' when sober, instinctively retreats before his employer or boss, or any other man, and has no idea of assaulting him, or indeed of addressing him, or having any relations with him except to draw his pay. But, when infuriated with liquor, he will upon any fancied occasion use the only argument which he possesses—his knife. I say the only argument, for it is inevitable experience that he will not talk; however little or however much he may understand of what is said to him, he will pretend not to understand. He has a pretty clear idea of how much money is coming to him, and manages to convey that information to his paymaster. But it is rather dangerous for the paymaster to give him much less than the amount which, in his idea, is coming to him. He will refuse to accept it, withdraw, jabber and gesticulate, and it will be well for that paymaster to be on his guard until something representing that month's wages is accepted."

The slander, the generalization, the accusations, the outright racist remarks in this article can hardly be believed to have been put to print. But that was the prevailing view among many, possibly most, Americans. It certainly was enough to cause the United States government to reconsider its position on immigration, and so in 1907, the U.S. Congress formed a special committee on immigration. It undertook the task of examining the origins and consequences of immigration in the U.S., with members of both the House and the Senate taking part. It would be known as the Dillingham Commission, named after its chairman, Senator William Dillingham of Vermont, and in 1911 it issued a wide-ranging report.

The commission described the ethnicity of Sicilians this way: "All of Italy south of the Apennines and all of the adjacent islands are occupied by a long-headed, dark, 'Mediterranean' race of short stature. This is the South Italian, supposed to be descended from the ancient Ligurians of Italy and closely related to the Iberians of Spain and the Berbers of Northern Africa. Indeed, the foremost Italian ethnologist, Sergi, traces their origin to the Hamitic stock of North Africa. It must be remembered that the Hamites are not Negrotic or true African, although there may be some traces of an infusion of African blood in this stock in certain communities of Sicily and Sardinia, as well as in northern Africa."

Addressing the issue of crime amongst Italians, the report said, "Italy still holds first place for the number of crimes committed against the person, although these have greatly diminished since the betterment of educational facilities and large outflow of emigrants....The secret organization of the Mafia and Comorra, institutions of great influence among the people, which take the law into their own hands and which are responsible for much of the crime, flourish throughout southern Italy. The chief difficulty in dealing with the crimes of Italians seems to be their determination not to testify in court against an enemy, but to insist on settling their wrongs after the manner of the vendetta."

The report concluded, "Certain kinds of criminality are inherent in the Italian race. In the popular mind, crimes of personal violence, robbery, blackmail and extortion are peculiar to the people of Italy."

The Commission made several recommendations. First, it called for a literacy test for future immigrants. Given the low literacy rate among southern Italians, this seemed particularly aimed at them. Second, it suggested, "limitation of the number of each race arriving each year to a certain percentage of that race arriving during a given period of years."

In 1917, Congress passed the Immigration Act, the first law imposing a general restriction on immigration via a literacy test. Woodrow Wilson vetoed it twice, but Congress eventually overrode his veto, and it became law. It had a significant impact on Italians as well as a large percentage of Asians. The United States was putting the squeeze on Italian immigration.

. . . . .

The man in the brown shirt pulled the wagon down Wall Street. The forecast had called for rain on September 16, 1920, but the weather had held off. Nonetheless, it was damp and threatening. People milled about dressed in suits and ties, doing the work of bankers and investors and stock traders. The man stopped in front of the Assay Office and pulled the wagon to the side. Nobody paid him any mind as he got out, patted his gray mare on the neck, walked behind his wagon, lifted the canvas tarp, and fidgeted with something in the back. It only took a few moments, after which time he recovered the wagon and stepped away. Checking the time, he glanced up at the high-rise, looked both ways, and crossed the street. Nobody noticed the man leaving his wagon alone, and nobody had any reason to care.

Andrew Dunn worked at J.P. Morgan on Wall Street. Dunn was just leaving his desk for his noon lunch, ready to walk into the busy intersection of Wall and Broad Streets in the heart of New York's financial district, right next to the New York Stock Exchange. Dunn had taken his lunch in his hand, pushed his chair in, and turned towards the door.

The concussion of a massive explosion ripped through the air, knocking Dunn back a step. A hundred pounds of dynamite, carried in the nondescript horse-drawn carriage detonated in front of the Assay Office, derailing a streetcar and blew the horse drawing the carriage to pieces. Fragments from the blast reached the 34th floor of the nearby Equiable building. Dozens of people were killed instantly by shrapnel, and hundreds were injured.

Two thousand New York City police converged on the scene, which looked like the front lines from the Great War after an enemy shelling. Bodies were strewn about the street, riddled with holes. Blood filled the gutters. Limbs were missing. The cries of shock and agony rose like a cacophony on the street. Trading at the U.S. Stock Exchange stopped as Red Cross workers came to deal with the carnage. The 1920 Wall Street bombing was the largest act of terrorism the U.S. had ever experienced, and it would hold that distinction until the 1995 Oklahoma City bombing.

Police immediately began to investigate. Anti-capitalist anarchists led by recently deported Luigi Galleani were suspected. The evidence was exceedingly thin, but the Italians believed to be affiliated with Galleani drew the ire of the public. Thousands of people – mostly Italians – were arrested, and roughly 500 were deported. Italians were once again seen as a criminal class, this time with monumental consequences.

. . . . .

By this point in time, Italian immigration had slowed to barely a trickle. Sicilians were suspected of being mobsters and mass murderers.

Newspapers all over the country had cast dispersions on southern Italians. Despite serving heroically in the Great War, Italians were believed to be among the worst possible people on earth, and the United States appeared desperate to prevent more from arriving.

In 1924, Congress passed another Immigration Act, called the Johnson-Reed Act, continuing the theme of creating further restrictions on immigration, particularly from "undesirable" parts of the world. The law developed a strict quota system, set at three percent of the total population of the foreign-born of each nationality in the United States. That was bad enough, but it was made worse by the fact that the date from which these population figures would be counted was 1910, not 1920. As such, it severely limited the number of Italians that could legally immigrate.

None of this, of course, impacted Philip or Biagio, who by then were safely living in the United States, with Philip having become a naturalized citizen. But for many of their native countrymen, the U.S. quest for white homogeneity ended their chance at the American Dream.

Chapter 13 – Antoinette

Philip neared the age of 26 in the summer of 1923. He had managed to find consistent work as a carpenter for a man named James Thurber in Bay Shore, a town just a few miles from Great River. Lina and Jim Prestia needed more space, and they moved their family – two children now – from New Jersey to a house near a railroad station on Connetquot Avenue in Great River. Lina assumed ownership of the property on Cedarhurst Street and took over the payments. Meanwhile, Philip, Biagio, and Maria moved to a house in Islip, just a few miles from Lina and Jim, at the cost of $18 per month. At 26, Philip had now spent ten years in the United States, and had endured hardship, suffering, job loss, family loss, a broken heart, service in the U.S. Army in wartime, and several moves. But he had settled in nicely and turned his attention to his future.

He began to think of marriage. And Antoinette. She was now twenty, and still single, and Philip thought that perhaps the time was right to revisit the question of their possible union. He traveled to visit the Rapuanos and sat with Steve and Mariella.

"Mr. and Mrs. Rapuano," Philip said nervously, trying to muster as much confidence as he could. "I would very much like to marry your daughter." He did not need to say which one, of course.

"Philip," Steve replied. "I've known you for ten years now. In that time you've worked hard to become successful. You've survived some difficult things, and you've managed to keep your head above water. You know our family loves you. You've been patient, waiting for Antoinette to grow old enough to marry."

"Yes sir," Philip replied.

"You've done well," Steve said. Mariella wiped her eyes with gladness.

"Thank you."

"Well," Steve said, looking at Mariella, then back to Philip. "You have my permission to marry Antoinette."

Philip broke into a huge grin. He stood up and shook Steve's hand. Mariella would take nothing less than a giant hug.

"Thank you," Philip said. "Now I must go talk to Antoinette."

The "Yes" answer came with no hesitation, and Philip took a moment to think back on their first interaction, when Antoinette viewed him with contempt. Well, perhaps not contempt, but there was a strong sense of dislike right from the start. How times had changed. The date was set for September 10, four days before Philip's 26th birthday. In the meanwhile, Philip continued to work for Thurber for $1.25 an hour, bought some furniture, and continued to save money as best he was able.

In August Philip visited the Rapuanos and handed Mariella two envelopes. Each contained one hundred one-dollar bills. Mariella opened them and could not believe her eyes. She had never seen so much money before in her life. Choking away tears, she kissed and hugged her future son-in-law, grateful for how he was willing to help pay for the wedding, an expense typically reserved for the bride's family.

Protocol at St. Michael's Church required that Philip go before the priest for confession prior to the wedding. Dutifully, Philip sat in the confession booth rattling off his sins, one after another. Philip was skeptical about confession, the reason being that the Bible mentions confessing sins to one another, and he had never experienced a priest confessing his sins in return for the penitent's. The priest, growing grumpier by the moment, told Philip that he did not wish to hear Philip's good points, told him to go home and repent of his immodesty. On the way home, Philip stopped at Terry's jewelers and spent $10 on a wedding band with his and her initials inscribed in the inner edge. Philip would forever be proud of that ring.

The morning of September 10 was bright and sunny and as beautiful a day anyone getting married could hope for. Philip stayed the night with family friends on Blatchley Avenue in New Haven, and the couple helped get him suited up in his tuxedo, also figuring that a shot of rum would help calm Philip's nerves. He paced nervously, waiting for the car to arrive to take him to the church. At this point, he wondered why the wedding couldn't be done in front of a justice of the peace, but there was nothing to be done about that now. He thought of Mariella, and how she would have wanted her daughter to be married properly, despite the expense that the Rapuanos really could not afford.

Philip waited at the door of St. Michael's, while Antoinette waited in the back, ready for the ceremony to begin. But they would have to wait longer. The church, as it turned out, was occupied. The hall was filled with mourners, and a funeral mass was underway. Philip grumbled under his breath – someone had picked a bad time to die. Making matters worse, the priest had overslept and so everything was running late. Not liking to be rushed, the priest displayed a grumpy attitude for the funeral, his words almost certainly not putting the grieving family at ease. Finally, the mass ended, the coffin was rolled out of the church, and the sanctuary emptied. Philip and Antoinette could finally marry.

The ceremony went off smoothly, and Philip couldn't help but wonder how deft the priest was, moving from a funeral mass to a wedding mass – from one end of the happiness spectrum to the other. Before he knew it, Philip and Antoinette had said "I do" and the two of them were married. Philip thought that the next step would be to take his long-waited-for bride away, but, of course, he was sadly mistaken. They first had to go to get pictures, to be taken by a photographer on Grand Avenue. Then there were the festivities at the Rapuano's home. More people than Philip thought possible had been invited, as the Rapuanos were a popular family in the community. The house simply could not fit everyone. Everyone ate and danced and drank and sang. Everyone fully enjoyed themselves except for the groom, who had a splitting headache. Mariella was in her element, overwhelmed with joy that her daughter was married.

Antoinette fainted three times during the day as the time drew near for she and Philip to leave. She did not want to leave her family. Mariella encouraged her to go and embrace this new stage of life. Antoinette resisted. Philip's headache worsened, and he very nearly decided to go on his honeymoon alone. Their friends accompanied them to the train station to see them off.

. . . . .

Philip and Antoinette lived in Islip with Biagio and Maria. They loved Antoinette very much, and did everything they could to please her and make her feel welcome. But she missed her mother, and was often in tears. Maria tried to comfort her, and Philip tried to make her happy, but he understood – Mariella was a special woman and she should be missed. He made a decision to take Antoinette twice a month to New Haven. That lasted until his job with Thurber ended.

Unemployed again, Philip tried to kill two birds with one stone. He spoke with the his old friends the Brunos on Main Street in New Haven, and agreed to rent some attic rooms from them. They lived about their grocery store, and Nick gave Philip some temporary cabinetry work that needed to be done, seeing as how they were remodeling the store. In this arrangement, he had found work and had brought his bride closer to her mother, and indeed Antoinette was much happier. She had grown up with very little, and so did not ask for much. Still, Philip wanted to provide for her needs and her desires. He worried that if he had moved in with the Rapuanos, and couldn't find steady work, the Rapuanos would be stuck with two more mouths to feed.

In the spring of 1924, Philip got a job building a house for a Mr. DeArchangelis on Dixwell Avenue in New Haven. The owner planned poorly, however, and, though he was able to pay for the material, could not pay Philip for his labor. Philip left the job having been owed several hundred dollars. Leaving Antoinette in New Haven, Philip went back to work with James Thurber on Long Island, working for several weeks.

On Friday, June 13, Philip entered the home where he, Biagio, and Maria were staying, and he found a telegram waiting for him. It was from Antoinette. She had just delivered their first child, a beautiful baby girl. Excited and frightened by the prospect of being a father, Philip sped to New Haven to meet his new daughter, Angelina, named for his sister, Lina.

Mariella was thrilled beyond belief. Not to be outdone, however, she gave birth to yet another child, a girl, and named her Dorothy. And so in two weeks Mariella became a grandmother and a mother again, and Antoinette became a mother and a sister again. Aunt Dorothy would always be in the odd situation of being two months younger than her niece Angelina.

·····

During that spring and summer, Biagio had bought and cleared an acre of land at the northeast corner of Greenlawn Avenue and Seacliff Street, in North Great River. He dug the hole for the foundation, all by hand, all by himself. He mixed and poured the concrete, all by hand, all by himself. He proceeded to erect the foundation and outer walls, using clay blocks, all set by hand, all by himself. One thing could be said about Biagio: the man could work. Philip helped him from time to time from that point on, and together they built Biagio a home.

When the house was completed, Philip took a job building a new home for Nino Cottone, a wealthy man from Palermo. The house took a month to complete, and when it was finished, Nino paid Philip the astounding sum of $2,000, plus a bonus of $200. Philip could not believe his good fortune. He gave his father some money, bought his first car – a used Chevy that lasted several weeks before dying, and saved the rest.

·····

Time passed and on January 10, 1925, Philip and Antoinette received horrible news. Mariella, beloved mother and mother-in-law, valued wife, and dear friend to so many, passed away. Her life was not an easy one. Steve had his strengths, but too often his neglect of her caused her great pain, which she bore admirably, but bore nonetheless. She had loved her family well, living sacrificially for the benefit of those she cared about. She had a deep duty to her family, her husband, and to God. She lived without many things that could have made life so much easier for her, but she never complained. She gave of herself right to the end, bringing another beautiful life into the world just six months before. Antoinette was, of course, devastated, and for the second time in his life, Philip lost a mother. These wounds would never fully heal, for any of the Rapuanos.

·····

Antoinette still lived in New Haven, while Philip continued to work on Long Island. Now that Mariella was gone, Antoinette's longing for New Haven lessened, despite the fact that there were younger Rapuanos that needed care. Her sister Louise filled in admirably, though there would never be another Mariella. Philip wanted to be together as a family – he, Antoinette, and Angelina – but he knew the timing wasn't right. He wanted to wait until he had a home ready for them all, and he wasn't there yet. So he continued to work and travel back and forth between Long Island and New Haven every other week to see his wife and daughter.

On July 4, 1925, just over a year after Angelina was born, Philip was given word that his second child had been born, this time a boy. Biagio, he was called, after the Italian tradition of naming the first-born son after the child's paternal grandfather. The second son, if one were to come about, would be named after the father. And so Philip, who had been named after his paternal grandfather Felippo, became father to Biagio, named after *his* paternal grandfather Biagio. Young Biagio had healthy lungs and, after screaming loudly to demonstrate how well they worked, proceeded to urinate all over the room. Philip could not have been more proud.

Philip picked up work again on Long Island and moved his growing family to his father Biagio's house for the time being. He continued to rent the flat in New Haven, though it was rarely, if ever, used. He dedicated himself to providing for his family and to making Antoinette happy. He had been in the United States for more than twelve years, and by this point, he knew that he could take care of a family. Philip had come into his own as a man. He continued to master his trade as a carpenter, honing building skills and developing as a craftsman, looking for the right place and time to build a home of his own.

Chapter 14 – Great River

The Algonquin tribe's oral history says that their people migrated into Canada – of course it wasn't called that at the time – from the Atlantic coast of North America, via the St. Lawrence River. From there, they settled in what would become Quebec, Ontario, and for centuries would live as hunters, fishermen, and trappers in the frigid north. They first met Europeans in 1603 when Samuel de Champlain made contact with Algonquin Kitcisipirini Chief Tessouat at Tadoussac, a small village at the delta where the Riviere Saguenay deposits into the St. Lawrence. Champlain quickly and wisely formed an alliance, an arrangement that benefitted both sides greatly. The Algonquin tribe came into conflict with the Iroquois, who, with the help of the Dutch, drove them from their lands, forcing them to settle west.

The various tribes of the Algonquin people ended up being spread across Canada and the northern parts of the United States, reaching as far south as Virginia. Being made up of various sub-groups, it is difficult to trace the exact history and heritage of the larger Algonquin family, but what is known is that for centuries, Algonquins lived in both western and eastern Long Island.

The town of Great River is almost exactly at the midpoint of the island, on the southern shore. The Secatogue sub-group of Algonquins occupied the territory of what is now Islip, a larger municipality comprised of numerous hamlets, including Bay Shore, Oakdale, Great River, and North Great River. Presently, Islip Terrace and North Great River – technically two distinct municipalities – share the same zip code within the larger city of Islip. This came about as a result of the U.S. Postal Service, choosing to make life easier by merging the two hamlets into one mailing district.

Great River takes its name from the Algonquin word *Connetquot*, which means "Great River". Before the 1900s, Great River was home to primarily wealthy mansion-owners. Its location was ideal, being close to the southern shore of Long Island. Originally, it was called Youngstown, named for Erastus Youngs, who built and repaired boats, which he would then launch into the Connetquot River. In 1870, the hamlet was renamed Great River. Slowly, starting in the early part of the 20th century, more common folk began to move in.

. . . . .

Biagio had built his home in North Great River in a neighborhood that could hardly be called that, so few were the people that lived there at the time. Two blocks south, at the northeast corner of Cedarhurst Street and Greenlawn Avenue, Jim Sutton and his wife Susan owned two acres of land. On that plot of land sat a shack covered in tar paper, a model T Ford, a Fordson tractor, numerous children, numerous dogs, and a herd of cats. Jim was an Irishman who had over the years developed numerous skills, having worked at several different trades to make ends meet. He had also spent his childhood in an Italian neighborhood in Brooklyn, and had learned to speak Italian more fluently than many from Naples itself. After spending his early adulthood traveling all over the country, he returned to Brooklyn and married Susan, who herself came from an Italian family.

Jim's in-laws moved in with him and tried their hand at raising chickens. It did not work out, so soon afterward, they left their coops in Jim's back yard and left town. Jim and Susan continued to produce more children, without the requisite increase of income needed to provide for the larger crew. He used his tractor to help break ground for new families moving into the area looking to build homes. It helped, but not enough. Susan began to grumble. Jim gave a go at working as a teamster for a lumber dealer, and that went well enough for a while, until horses were replaced by trucks. Jim was once again out of work. As their situation worsened, so did Jim and Susan's marriage.

Philip had known the Suttons for some time, given how close they lived to each other. Philip came into possession of a large stash of lumber, and he asked the Suttons for permission to build a small house on their property. The arrangement was that after seven years, Philip would move out and leave the house as payment. The Suttons could then sell the home and make a profit. The Suttons agreed. It took three weeks, but Philip had managed to build a small 10x20 foot structure, finished with one bedroom, a kitchen with one sink complete with a hand water pump, and an outhouse in the back. Philip, Antoinette, Angelina, and little Biagio – called Ben – moved in.

Things were good until Susan Sutton began meddling. She stopped over regularly and inserted herself in conversations and situations unasked-for. She offered advice aplenty, and rarely took it in return. She proved to be helpful to Antoinette, but at times became too helpful.

In January of 1928, the third Vampatella child was born, another girl, this one named Marie. At the tender age of six months, Marie demonstrated a flair for the dramatic. In her crib, she tried to suck the paint off a doll's head instead of playing with it. She fell into convulsions. Antoinette, unsure what to do and frightened for her child, ran to Susan. Susan, upon seeing the girl, immediately diagnosed her with a case of the "*il Malocchio*", the "evil eye", an old Italian superstition of bad luck. She offered a prayer or spell – Antoinette couldn't tell which – along with a few hand gestures meant to ward off the bad spirits, and left. Marie continued to writhe, unaffected by Susan's incantations. Philip, once he returned home, summoned a doctor, who prescribed an antidote for paint poison, and Marie recovered.

. . . . .

In the fall of 1927, Philip put a $200 deposit down for two acres of ground 600 feet east of the Sutton's, on Cedarhurst Street. Two hundred more dollars and several weeks later, Philip had constructed a 20x26 foot garage, with windows, doors, and imitation brick on the outside. He used it for a garage and storage, not having any idea of using it for a home. That would come later.

Antoinette had begun to tire of Susan, and the "evil eye" incident had not helped. She was sick of Susan's meddling, kerosene lamps, hand pumps, wood burning stoves, outhouses, and other signs that they were not living a civilized life. She wanted to go back to electricity, indoor plumbing, and at least a couple of creature comforts, such as the Rapuanos could afford.

The best Philip could come up with was a flat on Fifth Avenue in nearby Bay Shore. Philip did not like it, but as a concession to his bride, he put his head down and continued to work at making the best of it. He had hoped the arrangement would not last long, but his timetable was sped up when he received his first electric bill: $30 for one month for two electric bulbs! Quickly, Philip thought through his alternatives, and one promptly came to mind – the garage he had built. He took the next week to turn the garage into a bedroom, kitchen, and garage, finished the ceiling and walls, laid a wooden floor, covered it with linoleum, and even bought an old range for the kitchen.

Proudly, he brought Antoinette to their new home, and she wept with gladness. She saw the value of not having to pay rent to anyone, and being far enough away from Susan was a bonus. She loved it. Philip had pleased her, and in turn was pleased himself, and for the time being, the Vampatella family was as happy as it had ever been.

. . . . .

Things were not so rosy with Philip's sister Lina and her husband Jim. They had sold their place on Cedarhurst Street and had bought a new home on the west end of Seacliff Street. They had a rapidly growing family that threatened to overrun the neighborhood, and Jim found it increasingly difficult to support such a large group of hungry mouths. The struggle was real, and arguments grew more frequent. To make matters more difficult, Lina experienced a change in religious affiliation, much to Jim's consternation. Lina had fallen in with a group of devout Christians unaffiliated with the Catholic Church, or any other major Christian denomination. This group, Jim felt, was a collection of "holy rollers", named so because of their loud forms of prayer and worship. They lived modestly in accordance with their understanding of Scripture, and Lina soon found a comfort and sense of peace with them that she lacked at home with Jim. More and more, they would become family to her, to the point where she would eventually become a missionary with their church.

In the meanwhile, Lina kept getting pregnant, and Jim, who loved the baby-making part of marriage but did not want to actually have more children, grew desperate to stem the tide of offspring. Abortion, of course, was unthinkable, for both religious reasons and for legal ones, as it was outlawed in the United States at the time. Birth control was forbidden by the Catholic Church. Abstinence was more than allowed, but Jim would have none of that. So he resorted to a barbaric solution. When he found out that Lina was pregnant again, he kicked her abdomen with all his might. Lina doubled over from the blow, and would recover from the injury, but he had achieved his purpose. She miscarried.

The next time she got pregnant, Jim was even more cruel. He took a carpenter's hammer and pummeled her belly violently. Enraged by her pregnancy, he even resorted to punching her in the face, as if somehow Lina was responsible. Lina, a bloody and beaten mess, prayed for forgiveness from God and struck back at Jim with all her force, landing a tremendous blow to his face that knocked Jim unconscious. Nevertheless, once again, the damage was done, but not as Jim envisioned. The baby survived and was born, but with significant intellectual and physical disabilities.

It would be 35 years later before anyone else knew what Jim had done to Lina and the baby.

. . . . .

In Girgenti (later changed to Agrigento), a sulfur mining region on the southwest edge of Sicily, a legend persisted for centuries. Young women thought it *sfortuna* (bad luck) to marry men who did not have at least one murder on their record. Mike Scilabro was from Girgenti, and had successfully immigrated to the United States. Given the immigration laws in place at the time, assuming officials did not miss anything – always a possibility one supposes – Mike had not murdered anyone.

Mike had children from two marriages: Helen, Paula, and Frank were children from his first marriage, and Nick, Joe, and Sam from his second. He had moved, along with his second wife and the children, to North Great River in 1921, hoping to make a life for himself there. An honest and hard-working man, Mike looked for a steady job. He met Philip, and asked him to build a six-room house. Philip agreed, and Mike gave him a first payment of $50, with more promised upon completion of the house.

Mike had calculated everything shrewdly, but Philip saw the figures and shook his head.

"I'm sorry," Philip said. "You don't have nearly enough money to pay for this job."

"No?" Mike asked quizzically. "How close am I?"

"Not close. It will take many times as much as you list here just to even get started."

Mike's eyebrow furrowed. "Hmmmmm…" he muttered, thinking. Philip had taken a liking to Mike and came up with a solution.

"I'll tell you what. If you pay for the materials, I will build the house for you. That way you can save money on materials you'd prefer instead of what I'd prefer. You probably can do it cheaper that way."

"That's a great idea," replied Mike. "Give me a list and I'll get it." Philip drew up a list and handed it back to Mike, and after a couple of days shopping, Mike returned, not with the materials, but with a request for a new list.

"Can you make a new list, but this time based on a four-room house instead of one with six?" he asked. Philip agreed. Mike managed to secure lumber from a contractor, enough to build a 20x20 foot building. Philip went to work, and in short order built a small home for Nick and his family.

Mike's older son Frank was trouble, and that had been true from the very beginning. It proved a difficult task for Mike to reign Frank in, and in fact, never truly succeeded. If trouble was there to be found, Frank was sure to be in the thick of it.

On one occasion, Biagio's son-in-law Pasquale came by for a visit. The two of them talked for hours and Pasquale helped Biagio with a task around the house. Pasquale owned an expensive watch, and in order to not damage it, he left it on the kitchen counter by the sink. The two men worked outside. Frank, sensing an opportunity for mischief, snuck into the house and began rummaging around. It didn't take long before he spotted Pasquale's watch, and quietly slipped it into his pocket. When the men returned, the watch was gone, and there was no sign of a thief. Pasquale was distraught. He did not own many expensive things, and this had cost him a substantial sum. After searching the house – a task that did not take long given the small size of the structure – Pasquale left, despondent. Biagio relayed the story to Philip later that evening.

Many years later, Philip was talking with a neighbor, and the time was drawing near for the neighbor to go home. He pulled out a fancy watch and glanced at it.

"I'm sorry Philip," the man said, "but I have to go."

Philip had to take a second glance but then realized that he recognized the watch.

"Where did you get that nice watch?" he asked.

"I bought it."

"Where?"

"From Frank."

"Scilabro?"

"Yes."

"How much did you pay for it?" Philip asked.

"Ten dollars."

Philip paused in thought as to his next move. His neighbor did not seem to do anything wrong, and all signs pointed to Frank being the culprit.

"Did you know where Frank got it?" he asked.

"No, I never really asked."

"Well I'll tell you," he said, and promptly relayed the story of Pasquale "losing" his fine new watch that just happened to look exactly like that. The neighbor apologized profusely, realizing that Philip's story was almost certainly true. Frank by this point had amassed a low reputation in the neighborhood and thus it came as no surprise to the neighbor to hear how he may have come into possession of such a fine item. He offered to return the watch to Pasquale, but Philip waved him off.

"No, don't worry," Philip said. "You didn't know, and you paid ten dollars for it. We will deal with Frank."

Three years later, Frank, by this point a 16-year old troublemaker, engaged in much more serious behavior, with far worse consequences. The DiCapua family lived at the west end of Babylon Street, next to the state hospital grounds. Joe and Teresa DiCapua had one child, Concetta, who was six years old at the time. Teresa's brother, Feliciano Tartaglia, would occasionally stop by for a visit, but mostly, with Joe at work, Teresa and Concetta were alone.

One day Concetta was playing alone in her room when she heard a gunshot. Startled, she looked up and heard a loud thud, and then some heavy, hurried steps, and then…nothing. She rushed to the front room to see Frank rushing down the street, removing a bandana from his face. Frank had no idea he had been seen, a fortunate thing for Concetta. Frank had snuck into the DiCapua home to rob them, but Teresa had caught him in the act. In desperation, he had shot her in the neck. She did not die instantly, and was rushed off to the hospital. The bullet was lodged in her neck, rendering her speechless, and the doctors feared attempting to remove it.

Frank was arrested, tried, and sentenced. Unfortunately, because he was still just sixteen, his sentence was light and after a short term, was released. Meanwhile, Teresa's brother Feliciano and his wife Julie had tended to Teresa while she was incapacitated. Upon her death, Feliciano swore that if he ever saw Frank, he would kill him, but Frank evaded Feliciano for years. Feliciano spoke of Frank and all Sicilians with vile contempt. Philip took considerable time persuading him that not all Sicilians were like Frank, and that there were good and bad people in every ethnic group. Feliciano grew to appreciate Philip and his wisdom, and the two became friends, even though they viewed the world differently. Philip sought to settle scores with discussion; Feliciano with his fists.

Feliciano was born an American citizen in the Bronx, had been raised in Italy, and had returned to the United States, and over the years had become a wonderful cook. His Danish wife Julie was a wonder, and they and Fannie, their daughter, had relocated to Great River following Teresa's death. When the depression came, they moved into Philip's two-room garage after Philip had moved into his four-room house, and Philip let them live there rent-free until they found a more permanent situation.

As years went by, Philip helped Feliciano open a restaurant. Feliciano changed his name to Fritz, attached the same name to his restaurant, and served good food for years. His business grew and he was able to buy several houses in Bay Shore. Following the Second World War, he retired in the 1950s and moved to Florida, collecting rents on his properties back on Long Island.

Fritz remained forever a good and faithful friend to Philip the Sicilian.

Chapter 15 – The Klan and the Mafia

The crowd filed into the Orpheum Theater in Ogden, Utah. March 26, 1916 was a cool spring day and the exclusively white audience took their seats in anticipation of what was promised to be the greatest motion picture they had ever seen. For three hours people watched, wept, cheered, gasped, cried out with fear, and celebrated as the scenes unfolded before them. It was a silent picture, but the 25-member orchestra performed a brilliant musical score that helped set the mood for each defining moment on screen.

D.W. Griffith's *The Birth of a Nation*, an adaptation of Thomas Dixon Jr.'s book *The Clansmen*, roared to life in theaters across the United States, following its release on February 8, 1915. Following the showing in the Orpheum Theater, the Ogden Standard newspaper wrote, "'The Birth of a Nation' motion picture reincarnation of the period of the reconstruction in American history, too vivid for pen to describe, made its long-looked-for appearance at the Orpheum theater last night and held a large audience in its spell for three hours. And, there is little doubt, it will be held in memory for days to come. The play…has a deeper purpose than the justification of the organization of the 'Ku Klux Klan' or 'Night Riders'. This, it seems, is to deepen the inborn love of Americans for their country. That this purpose has been achieved in many parts of the land, was evidenced last night in the reception of the picture by the representative Ogden audience, the applause being as enthusiastic at the victory of the Ku Klux Klan over the negro militia, excited to deeds of frenzy by 'carpet baggers' from the north after the war, as it was at the surrender of General Lee to General Grant, marking the close of the war."

The scene was similar at the Oregon theater in Pendleton, Oregon, a month later. In the April 28, 1916 edition of the *East Oregonian* newspaper, the story read, "So much had this great picture been advertised and so widely heralded that a crowded house saw the first matinee yesterday afternoon and there was standing room only last night. The best tribute to the picture is to say that those who went there all eagerness and expectancy came away with nerves still quivering with the excitement of the two hour photo drama. The photography of 'The Birth of a Nation' is wonderful, but wonderful as it is, it is still only half of the picture as presented by the company yesterday. No silent picture could stir an audience again and again into cheering and wild applause."

These were just two of many examples of theaters outside Dixie that reported immensely favorable reactions to the film. In the South, of course, the reception to *The Birth of a Nation* was even more exuberant. Katharine DuPre Lumpkin wrote of her experience watching the film in her autobiography "The Making of a Southerner". She wrote, "Here was the black figure—and the fear of the white girl—though the scene blanked out just in time. Here were the sinister men the South scorned and the noble men the South revered. And through it all the Klan rode. All around me people sighed and shivered, and now and then shouted or wept, in their intensity." The *Los Angeles Times* called it "the greatest picture ever made and the greatest drama ever filmed."

Civil War defeat, of course, never sat well with the white South. Following the war, on December 24, 1865, the Ku Klux Klan was born. It began as essentially a terrorist organization, committing atrocities like flogging and lynching blacks, and burning the homes and shops of black men and women. Its main purpose was to frighten ex-slaves into not exercising their newfound freedom, especially the right to vote. Civil War general Nathan Bedford Forrest, the first "Grand Wizard" of the KKK, had led a group of Confederate veterans in organizing to reverse the government's Reconstructionist policies, and the Klan had for a half a decade rampaged throughout the South intimidating black Americans.

In 1871, Congress passed the Ku Klux Klan Act, outlawing the organization, and it led to nine South Carolina counties to be placed under martial law. Law enforcement arrested thousands of Klansmen, and support for the organization began to slip. The law was challenged in court and in 1882, the U.S. Supreme Court ruled that the KKK Act was unconstitutional. But by that time, Reconstruction had ended and the Klan had nearly disappeared. It had, however, achieved much of its purpose.

Following the emancipation of slaves and the end of the Civil War, a new wave of immigration began. Millions of immigrants – many from eastern and southern Europe – poured into the United States. Sicilians took the place of blacks on southern plantations, and were promptly placed on the lowest rung of the social ladder, being seen as uneducated, uncouth people of color fit for only the lowliest of tasks in a civilized, white society.

But they kept coming into America. Italians were lynched in numbers second only to blacks. Sicilians were relegated to the ghettos of American cities and were held in contempt for their religion, customs, and skin color. Good white southerners led the charge in resisting the integration of *"dagoes"* in American society.

As immigration grew, resistance to these immigrants grew as well. A new movement rose from the ashes and the revitalized KKK was born. The Klan portrayed itself in this iteration as a Christian, white, patriotic organization that opposed various vices and sins, such as the use of alcohol. Many saloons and bars were owned by immigrants, and so were seen as the people most responsible for proliferating liquor. The Women's Temperance League and the men's Anti-Saloon League blamed Catholic immigrants – mainly from Italy – for this plague, and began to push for a Constitutional amendment outlawing alcohol.

As this push happened, D. W. Griffith released *The Birth of a Nation*. Southern whites rejoiced in what they believed was vindication of their anti-black and anti-immigration worldview. Seeing blacks as barbarians who would just as soon invade a wedding to rape the bride, their views were confirmed over the course of the three hour blockbuster film. Northerners were more split, but a sufficient number of northern whites sympathized with what they saw on screen, and anti-black sentiment rose even outside the former Confederacy. In Boston, for example, there were widespread protests by blacks even as thousands of whites attended the show. On February 18, 1915, the film was given a special screening before a Presidential audience. Though this quote is disputed, Woodrow Wilson allegedly said in response to the movie, "It is like writing history with lightning. And my only regret is that it is all so terribly true." For Griffith, the White House viewing was taken as an honor, and he considered it an endorsement of his work. The next day, Griffith took the film to New York City to present it before the National Board of Censorship. They referred to Wilson's "endorsement" and the board approved the film by a vote of 15 to 8.

Wilson may or may not have said that, but he certainly did little to dampen the rising enthusiasm for the project. He and Dixon were friends from Johns Hopkins University, and he undoubtedly knew the content and character of the film before seeing it, seeing as though it was an adaptation of his college friend's play. In the film Wilson himself is quoted three times, each one from Wilson's book "History of the American People". Wilson is quoted as saying, "Adventurers swarmed out of the North, as much the enemies of one race as of the other, to cozen, beguile and use the negroes.... [Ellipsis in the original.] In the villages the negroes were the office holders, men who knew none of the uses of authority, except its insolences."

"....The policy of the congressional leaders wrought...a veritable overthrow of civilization in the South.....in their determination to 'put the white South under the heel of the black South.'" [Ellipses and underscore in the original.]

"The white men were roused by a mere instinct of self-preservation.....until at last there had sprung into existence a great Ku Klux Klan, a veritable empire of the South, to protect the southern country." [Ellipsis in the original.]

Wilson's words gave weight to the argument Griffith put forth on screen. The South was the victim of northern aggression. Good white Christians were seeing their world invaded by people of color who were largely criminals. If the Klan had not come to the rescue, the entire South would be overrun. This argument struck a chord with southern whites and even a large number of northern whites. The ranks of the KKK immediately began to swell.

Meanwhile, some 350,000 blacks had served in the Great War – in segregated units only, as Wilson had made sure of that – and upon their return from the war began looking for new economic opportunity. That was not to be found in the south, and so by the tens of thousands they migrated to the industrious north. The northern economy began to boom, while the southern economy stagnated, giving rise to old hatreds. After watching the film, William J. Simmons held a rally and on the top of Stone Mountain, Georgia, burned a cross as a symbol of the KKK's rise, and declared himself to be the "Imperial Wizard" of the KKK.

The new Klan was not, however, just against blacks. The new targets included immigrants and Catholics – essentially, anyone who was not a white conservative Protestant. Its efforts during this time were less violent than the first iteration in the 1860s, but rather focused on politics and policy and social action. The Klan became a force in mainstream politics. Many people in national politics – allegedly including Harry Truman, who paid the $10 membership fee to the KKK on the advice of supporters, but who later appears to have had significant disagreements with them – joined the Klan. 40,000 Klansmen marched openly in Washington, DC. The Klan used its prodigious influence to push through laws restricting the flow of immigrants from eastern and, especially, southern Europe. The Immigration Act of 1924 was a direct result of, among other things, the Ku Klux Klan's political power being exercised on a national level.

The Klan also used its influence to help get the 18th amendment passed, and just like that, the Prohibition Era was born. While the Women's Temperance League and the Anti-Saloon League were interested in ending the vice of alcohol consumption, the Klan had another agenda. As immigrants were largely the owners of bars and other establishments that served alcohol, this represented a perfect opportunity for the Klan to deal a crushing economic blow to the dark-skinned Italian Catholic population that had become an infestation on white protestant America.

. . . . .

Woodrow Wilson did not run for the Presidency on a platform of racism. He ran for office in 1912 on a platform titled "New Freedom", and it included such ideas as supporting a federal income tax, the rights of labor, tariff reform, business reform, and banking reform. Wilson was a progressive that wished to keep the United States out of European conflict and he championed states' rights. By the time 1916 rolled around, Wilson, whose party platform ironically called for presidents to serve only a single term, campaigned on the theme of keeping the U.S. out of the war in Europe. These ideas won the hearts and minds of enough voters in the right states and Wilson served two terms as President. But though he did not campaign on racist ideas, Wilson's actions revealed a heart that was, if not outright racist, at least turned against people of color.

Wilson said during his campaign in 1912, "Should I become President of the United States, [Negroes] [*sic*] may count on me for absolute fair dealing and for everything by which I could assist in advancing the interests of their race in the United States." A little over a month after his inauguration, on April 11, 1913, President Wilson sat in on a cabinet meeting and listened to Postmaster General Albert Burleson make the argument for why the Railway Mail Service should be segregated. Burleson was personally disturbed by the presence of black workers working in the same train cars with whites, where they were sharing glasses, towels, and washrooms. He argued that the Railway Mail Service was best served if the workers were segregated, claiming his goal was not necessarily to make the Service "lily white", but rather to segregate all government departments.

Wilson listened to Burleson, and then replied, "I have made no promises in particular to Negroes [*sic*], except to do them justice." He then said that he "wished the matter adjusted in a way to make the least friction." Burleson took this comment to be, if not tacit approval of segregation, at least a green light to implement his plan. Soon after that meeting, Burleson and Treasury Secretary William McAdoo segregated all employees in their departments. Wilson, who was fully aware of this development, and obviously had the power to stop it with a single command, let it happen, further emboldening those who wished for greater segregation.

The Washington, DC, post office headquarters was quickly segregated, and numerous black employees were either demoted or outright fired for no reason other than that they were black. Those who were demoted were transferred to the "dead letter office", being placed in positions where they could not interact with the public. Both the Treasury Department and the Post Office Department segregated workspaces, lunch rooms, and washrooms. In a letter written to Wilson in 1913, W.E.B. DuBois wrote of "one colored [*sic*] clerk who could not actually be segregated on account of the nature of his work consequently had a cage built around him to separate him from his white companions of many years."

Wilson, in personal correspondence to NAACP board chairman Oswald Garrison Villard, defended these forms of segregation. He told Villard that segregation in these federal departments was not "a movement against the Negroes [*sic*]. We are rendering them more safe in their possession of the office and less likely to be discriminated against." This, while actively removing blacks from their roles and separating them from their white colleagues.

Wilson, whose father – a Presbyterian minister – defended slavery from the pulpit, himself fired 15 out of 17 black supervisors in the federal service, replacing each of them with white people. The director of the Internal Revenue division in Georgia fired all his black employees. He said upon the dismissals, "There are no government positions for Negroes in the South. A Negro's place is in the corn field." When friend and Harvard alumnus Monroe Trotter and other black business leaders confronted Wilson on the issue of federal segregation in 1914, Wilson simply said, "Segregation is not humiliating, but a benefit, and ought to be regarded by you gentlemen."

Trotter could not believe his ears and passionately pleaded for Wilson to reconsider. Wilson rebuked him, saying, "If this organization is ever to have another hearing before me it must have another spokesman. Your manner offends me….Your tone, with its background of passion."

Trotter was incredulous and told Wilson that segregation, "must be a humiliation. It creates in the minds of others that there is something the matter with us—that we are not their equals, that we are not their brothers, that we are so different that we cannot work at a desk beside them, that we cannot eat at a table beside them, that we cannot go into the dressing room where they go, that we cannot use a locker beside them." The meeting ended unsatisfactorily for Trotter and his colleagues.

Wilson's book "A History of the American People" was thrice quoted by D.W. Griffith in the film *The Birth of a Nation*, but one of Wilson's most horrifyingly racist quotes was left out. He had written, "The white men of the South were aroused by the mere instinct of self-preservation to rid themselves, by fair means or foul, of the intolerable burden of governments sustained by the votes of ignorant negroes [*sic*]…." He wrote that at the end of Reconstruction, "Negro [sic] rule under unscrupulous adventurers had been finally put an end to in the South, and the natural, inevitable ascendancy of the whites, the responsible class, established."

Wilson spoke in front of Congress in his State of the Union address on December 7, 1915, and, speaking firmly against immigrants, said, "Such creatures of passion, disloyalty, and anarchy must be crushed out." He would add, "There are citizens of the United States, I blush to admit, born under other flags but welcomed under our generous naturalization laws to the full freedom and opportunity of America, who have poured the poison of disloyalty into the very arteries of our national life; who have sought to bring the authority and good name of our Government into contempt, to destroy our industries wherever they thought it effective for their vindictive purposes to strike at them, and to debase our politics to the uses of foreign intrigue. Their number is not great as compared with the whole number of those sturdy hosts by which our nation has been enriched in recent generations out of virile foreign stock; but it is great enough to have brought deep disgrace upon us and to have made it necessary that we should promptly make use of processes of law by which we may be purged of their corrupt distempers. America never witnessed anything like this before."

For people of color, the Wilson Administration, which was elected with great promise, served as one of the great barriers for advancement and equality. Blacks and immigrants – especially those from southern Europe – suffered immensely from Wilson's words and actions. Wilson's unspoken support for *The Birth of a Nation* helped launch it to blockbuster status. His policies brought the nation down the path of segregation. He supported immigration reform that would end up restricting immigration against darker-skinned southern Europeans. And he helped grow the second incarnation of the Ku Klux Klan. Together, though they were not formally working in concert, the President and the KKK pushed for policies that would set back people of color – from American descendants of slaves to immigrants from Sicily – culturally and economically, for a generation.

What neither Wilson or the Ku Klux Klan realized, however, was that their efforts to suppress people of color – blacks and immigrants – would contribute to the rise of something that would impact how Americans viewed Italians: the mafia.

Chapter 16 – Prohibition

Al Capone rubbed his face, running his finger along the edge of one of three scars that bothered him so much. He traced the line from his ear down across his jaw and frowned. He had received these scars thanks to a nasty brawl he engaged in while working for mob boss Frankie Yale at the Harvard Inn on Coney Island in New York. The Harvard Inn was a speakeasy that Yale had begun in response to the growing tide of prohibition, as the push to make alcohol sales illegal increased. Speakeasies had their origin in Britain in the early 1800s, the term meaning "smuggler's house", in reference to an establishment that bought and sold illegal liquor. In the United States, it is said that the first speakeasy was run by Kate Hester in McKeesport, Pennsylvania in the 1880s, as she would often tell her loud customers to "speak easy" to avoid unwanted attention from law enforcement.

Capone worked at the Harvard Inn as a bouncer and waiter, and on that fateful night in 1917, Frank Galluccio entered with his sister Lena and his date Maria Tanzio. Tanzio was strikingly beautiful, and she had caught Capone's eye, and his gaze was unrelenting. She noticed him staring, and that made her uncomfortable. She mentioned Capone's incessant gawking to Galluccio, but before the hoodlum could say anything, Capone leaned over to Tanzio.

"Honey, you got a nice ass and I mean that as a compliment, believe me."

Galluccio was enraged.

"Hey asshole, I don't need to hear that from anyone," Galluccio said through gritted teeth. "Apologize to her right now."

"Or what?" Capone replied, unafraid. He did, of course, work for a powerful mob boss, and he was on his home turf.

"Or I'm gonna make you wish you had," Galluccio replied, standing.

Capone smiled a toothy grin. "Come on buddy," he said. "I'm only joking."

Galluccio responded with some choice words and Capone's smile left his face. He was not used to people talking to him like that. He lunged at Galluccio, who quickly pulled out a knife. Attempting to stab Capone in the neck, he missed, his blade slashing through Capone's face three times. Blood poured from Capone's face as the fight was quickly broken up. Capone received 30 stitches at a nearby hospital, and considered his revenge.

Meanwhile, Galluccio met with New York mob bosses, who called Capone in for a sitdown. There they ordered Capone to stand down, and not retaliate, as they had agreed with Galluccio that Capone was at fault for insulting Galluccio's date. Capone, in a rare moment of humility, agreed, and apologized to Galluccio. The two men shook hands and all was forgiven.

But not all was forgotten. Every time Capone touched his face, he felt the scars. And years later, when he gained notoriety and became the most famous mobster in America, the media would give him the nickname "Scarface", a moniker he detested. He routinely turned his face so that photographers would only capture the right side of his face, and over time editors would touch up pictures of Capone's left side, making the scars more apparent. Capone may have forgiven Galluccio, but he never forgot that night, as he was reminded of it every single day.

. . . . .

He fidgeted with the scar as he contemplated his options. His old friend, Johnny Torrio, had presented him with an offer. Torrio had spent time with Capone in the Five Points gang in New York. Five Points represented a new generation of young Italian-American criminals, with Capone, Torrio, and Charlie "Lucky" Luciano being three of the most prominent members. In 1909, Torrio had moved to Chicago to work for "Big Jim" Colosimo. Colosimo ran hundreds of brothels and gambling rackets, and engaged in racketeering, and his organization would come to be known as the "Chicago Outfit".

Colosimo, who had immigrated to the United States from Calabria, Italy, in 1895, started his life of law-breaking in typical fashion, through a variety of petty crimes. As his wealth and influence grew, he organized prostitution rings and gambling rings. Dressed in his white suit and wearing diamond pins and rings, and his marriage to Victoria Moresco, an established Chicago madam, launched his career in the brothel business.

As his power grew, threats from the outside grew proportionally. So-called "Black Hand" extortion threatened Colosimo, and to combat this, he called upon Johnny Torrio to serve as his enforcer and second in command. In 1919, Colosimo and Torrio opened a brothel at 2222 South Wabash in Chicago, and named it the "Four Deuces". Torrio was given authority to run the establishment, and he needed help. Thinking back on his personal network, he had one man in mind: his old friend Al Capone.

The offer was extended. Torrio invited Capone to move to Chicago to join him and work at the Four Deuces. Capone read the cable thoughtfully, stroked his scar, and thought deeply for several moments. But it did not take long. Capone folded up the telegram, and sent his reply. He would be in Chicago by the end of the week.

Capone arrived and Torrio put him to work in the Four Deuces in a familiar role: bouncer and waiter. Capone had learned his lesson from the Harvard Inn incident, and he ran a tight ship. Outgoing and social, he made an excellent waiter. But mean-looking and street tough, he was also an imposing bouncer. Capone took to his duties and the Four Deuces quickly became prosperous.

. . . . .

On January 29, 1919, the 18th amendment to the United States Constitution was ratified. It had broad national support, and powerful political groups such as the Women's Temperance League, the Anti-Saloon League, and even the Ku Klux Klan had pushed for Prohibition. Opponents cited the economic impact – particular the loss of tax revenue – but that opposition was silenced when the federal income tax became firmly – and permanently – established in 1913. The government could now afford to do the "moral" thing, without fear of losing needed tax revenue.

The amendment read, "After one year from the ratification of this article the manufacture, sale, or transportation of intoxicating liquors within, the importation therefor into, or the exportation thereof from the United States and all territory subject to the jurisdiction thereof for beverage purposes is hereby prohibited." It went on to say that Congress and the states had the power to enforce this by appropriate legislation, and they promptly passed such legislation. Federally, the Volstead Act – named for Representative Andrew Volstead – set guidelines for federal enforcement of the 18th Amendment.

. . . . .

Capone, Torrio, and Colosimo sat at a table, sipping their drinks – for Capone, that meant his favorite, Templeton Rye whiskey. They surveyed the political and legal landscape. Colosimo's brothels were bringing in huge money, and his gambling rings were productive as well. But Capone and Torrio saw other opportunities.

"We need to move into liquor," Torrio said.

"Why do you say that?" Colosimo replied.

"It's going to be huge. The government has outlawed it. But if they think that people's appetite for drinking is going to go away, they're crazy," Torrino said, setting his own glass down on the table.

"I know Johnny, but we're doing fine selling alcohol in our establishments. We don't need to expand."

"But the money–" Torrio was cut short by a wave of Colosimo's hand.

"I know. The money is big. But we're making millions of dollars each year, and this new law is going to be heavily enforced. I've got the Chicago cops in line here, as far as everything goes, but if we expand into bootlegging, we're going to attract way too much attention from the feds."

"Maybe," Johnny admitted. "But maybe you're just too afraid to take the next step." That earned Torrio a glare. Capone just sat and listened. He was involved, but not involved enough to step between Colosimo and Torrio.

"You sound like your aunt Victoria," Colosimo said, referring to his wife, who happened to be Torrio's aunt. "She says the same thing. Says I'm scared."

"Maybe she's right," Johnny said slowly and quietly, being careful. "I just think this is the path we need to take."

"I'll think about it," Colosimo replied. "For now, we stay put, but I'll think on it."

"Ok," Torrio said. "Just know that every day we wait, someone else is stepping into that business."

"I get it, I get it," Colosimo said. And with another wave, Torrio and Capone were out the door, walking and talking about the opportunity that they feared Colosimo was wasting.

A year later, Colosimo had divorced Victoria Moresco, and had stubbornly refused to enter the business of bootlegging. The divorce was the final straw for a frustrated Johnny "The Fox" Torrio. He contacted leaders in the New York mafia, soliciting their support for a hit on "Diamond Jim" Colosimo, and he asked them to name him head of the Outfit once Jim was dead. They agreed, and Frankie Yale joined Torrio and Capone in Chicago. They informed Colosimo, who had just returned with his new wife, Dale Winter, that a shipment of booze had arrived at one of his establishments. Colosimo drove over and waited. The shipment did not arrive and Colosimo grew impatient and irritated, and, turning to leave, suddenly found himself face to face with a gunman who had been hiding in the coatroom. Moments later, on May 11, 1920, Jim Colosimo was dead, and Johnny Torrio became the new head of the Chicago Outfit.

It was long rumored that Al Capone was the man that pulled the trigger.

. . . . .

For five years, Torrio ran the Outfit, expanding business in prostitution, racketeering, gambling, and now, bootlegging. It was incredibly profitable, but naturally, such an expansion of business attracted competition, and Torrio found himself in a struggle with the North Side Gang, led by Dean O'Banion. Tensions mounted as each moved into one another's territory, but neither side wanted a full-scale war. But it was too much for Torrio, who ordered O'Banion to be taken out. On November 10, 1924, Frankie Yale and two other men murdered O'Banion in his flower shop, and a large, city-wide war erupted.

In 1925, North Siders attempted to murder Torrio, in retaliation for the O'Banion death. On January 24, Torrio was returning to his apartment and men riddled his car with bullets, the shattered glass and bullets lodging in Torrio's jaw, legs, and torso. Additionally, Torrio was kicked in the stomach and smashed with a billy club. Incredibly, Torrio survived the attempt on his life, but realized at that point that it was time to get out of the business.

He recovered from emergency surgery and called Capone in to talk.

"Al," he said, "I'm done here."

"What do you mean, you're done?"

"That's it. I'm out of the business."

"What? Why?" an incredulous Capone asked.

"I don't need this. I've made plenty of money. I'm out."

"You're kidding," Capone said, still in disbelief. Torrio had been his friend and mentor for years and could not believe he was just...leaving.

"It's all yours, Al. Me? I'm quitting. It's Europe for me."

Torrio left organized crime – and the United States – and moved to Italy. He passed leadership of the Chicago Outfit to Capone, an organization that brought in an unfathomable sum of $70 million annually.

Al Capone had become the undisputed leader of the biggest criminal organization in Chicago, and he had Prohibition to thank. Ironically, Torrio would return to the United States several years later, and head up an organization of mob leaders, called the National Crime Syndicate. Its purpose was to establish a national body of *Mafioso* that could prevent full-scale war. The respect that mafia leaders all over the United States – particularly New York, Chicago, and Kansas City – had for Torrio led to the idea being accepted.

. . . . .

The Ku Klux Klan had played a major part in getting the 18th amendment enacted. In turn, the 18th amendment had created conditions that led to the rise of illegal bootlegging of alcohol, which directly led to the rise of the notorious Al Capone.

. . . . .

Philip was not much of a drinker himself, and so Prohibition had little to no effect on him personally. But he saw firsthand the impact the 18th amendment had on people around him.

In North Great River, a town with few people but plenty of open space and oak and pine forest, small shanties sprung up in the early 1920s. Some were made out of tin and others out of pine logs. Some were used as homes by people with very little money, and others were used for more nefarious purposes. Various buildings that dotted the landscape were turned into small enterprises for the production and sale of now illegal liquor. Many of the people engaged in this activity got caught and spent time in prison, but whenever one was incarcerated, more took his place. North Great River – a town where normal citizens were in short supply – had more than its share of bootleggers.

Philip saw that Prohibition had created a sort of struggle between law enforcement, finding their job exceedingly difficult most of the time, and those flaunting the law, making money on illegal liquor. He read the story of a sick woman in the Midwest who had a prescription and a bottle of wine on the table. An overeager police officer shot the woman for possession of the wine, and the woman's sons retaliated by shooting the police officer. As Philip recalled, it was a case of two lives wasted for nothing.

Philip saw in his small town the scene playing out across the nation. Men who struggled to find honest work suddenly found there was lots of money to be made in the illegal manufacture and sale of liquor. Petty thieves turned into murderers as other petty thieves and would-be murderers moved in on their bootlegging territory. Men organized and the criminal element grew before Philip's eyes in North Great River, as it was elsewhere, in response to Prohibition. Philip understood then, as he would the rest of his life, that Prohibition was a mistake. Not that it was a mistake to seek temperance. No, rather, that the law should have been based on abuse of alcohol, not simply the sale and use of it. He never saw the point in Prohibition, but regularly saw the rise of the criminal element that accompanied it.

. . . . .

The speakeasy culture grew in the 1920s as federal and local authorities tried to enforce Prohibition. These speakeasies featured quiet conversation – and undoubtedly tens of millions of dollars of business deals brokered – and a new kind of music: jazz. Jazz originated in New Orleans as a form of black ethnic music, evolved through the experience of African-Americans in the U.S. It found a home in the 1920s in these speakeasies, and there, a unique culture began to form. By the end of the 1920s, there were some 32,000 speakeasies in New York City alone. Louis Armstrong's first paid gig was put on by a Sicilian mobster, and for much of his early career, another gangster, Joe Glaser, managed him.

People of different ethnicities visited these speakeasies, to enjoy company, incredible jazz music, and of course, illegal alcoholic beverages. These establishments were usually run by organized crime, and that brought about a partnership between blacks and whites, jazz musicians and bootleggers, and all the while, the Ku Klux Klan fumed. This represented everything they were against: the integration of the races, the promotion of black music and entertainers, and the financial success of Sicilians. And so they fought back. Hard.

The KKK served as the paramilitary wing of vigilante "justice", enforcing prohibition, but limiting their activities to the south, where they had great support. Generally speaking, they wanted no part of speakeasies in the north, where the mafia was strong. In the south, the Klan tarred and feathered bootleggers, burned speakeasies, and murdered tavern owners. But the mafia, whose business was being hurt by the Klan's actions, used their muscle to combat the KKK, and for the first time, Sicilians had almost an organized army helping them in the fight against white supremacists. Over the course of Prohibition, Italians and blacks joined forces in terms of culture and business interests against the Klan and those who despised people of color. By the time Prohibition ended, jazz culture had grown, the mafia had become more powerful than ever, and the second incarnation of the Ku Klux Klan had shrunk back in power and influence.

By then, something worse had come along: the Depression.

Chapter 17 – The Great Depression

In the summer of 1929, Philip was once again looking for work, and for the second time in his life crossed paths with Arnold Elliott, for whom he had once worked. The Elliotts lived in Bay Shore and Arnold had secured work at the newly formed Belmont Lake State Park in Babylon. The park was named for August Belmont, who had been a banker of great renown, and upon his death had donated a 463-acre parcel of land to the state. Originally, Belmont used the grounds – a beautiful stretch of green bisected by Carl's Creek and aptly named Belmont Lake – for equestrian activities, and by the time Philip began work there, the park had been open to the public for three years.

Elliott was a man of great skill, but equally great character, and Philip came to love and respect him immensely. Elliott understood people, worked quietly, deflected praise, and was dedicated to helping others. He had a penchant for complimenting the fine work of others, while never complaining about his own problems. Philip considered the Elliotts to be uncommon people, as good a representative of what Christians ought to be as anyone he had ever met.

When he ran into Arnold Elliott in the summer of 1929, he stared at the work being done on the park. Belmont's old stables were being torn down, and work was beginning on new quarters for the assistant chief engineer. The two of them looked at the piles of lumber, and hordes of people milling about, performing various tasks as appropriate to their expertise. Arnold was working on concrete forms when he saw Philip approach.

"Well hey there Philip!" he said, grinning from ear to ear.

"Arnold!" Philip replied. "What are you doing here?"

"What does it look like I'm doing?" he said, extending a worn hand. Philip happily shook it.

"Looks like you're working hard," Philip said.

"Looks like you're here to work too," said Arnold.

"Yes sir."

"Well, it's about time a real carpenter showed up." He smiled. "There's the foreman over there. He'll give you the work."

"Thanks Arnold," Philip said, shaking his hand again. "Great to see you."

Philip was hired immediately and began to work helping demolish the old sheds and putting the lumber into disorganized piles. The workers were allowed to take some of the lumber for a small price, and Philip made arrangements to buy two loads of usable heavy lumber for four dollars, to be delivered to Cedarhurst Street. When they arrived, he cleaned out his garage, cleaned up each piece of lumber, removing nails as needed, and placed them neatly in the garage. He cut rafters from the thick and wide floor boards, enough to span a 26x28 foot house. He planned on using the rest of these pieces for ceiling beams. The heavier timber he set aside for floor beams, but realized he needed much more to complete the house. He acquired the requisite lumber for doors, trim, walls, and such, in piecemeal fashion, and before too long had everything he needed to start building his own house.

He received help digging the hole for the foundation, and once dug, began mixing concrete. It was very hard work for just one man, and to his immense gratitude Antoinette joined in helping to mix and pour the concrete into the proper forms. Halfway up the forms ended. Money was tight and Philip did not have enough to continue the work. Fortunately, a man named Ralph Colantuono owed him money and Philip struck a deal – Ralph would pay in cement blocks. Ralph was happy to pay his debt with his labor and before long the foundation was laid. Philip happily spent his days working at Belmont Lake State Park and on his new home, but events would conspire to prevent him from moving in until 1930, following the birth of Philip and Antoinette's fourth child, Anna, the only one of their children to be born in a hospital. In the meanwhile, Philip grew ever grateful for Mr. Belmont – a man he never knew – for unknowingly providing the lumber for his new home, and to Arnold Elliott, who had become a dear friend, a mentor, and who would later save his life.

. . . . .

October of 1929 brought about catastrophe. Philip was once again without work, the job at Belmont Park having been lost due to a tightening state budget. Philip was a hard-working and skilled carpenter, but he had not yet made a name for himself, and when government funds began to run low, projects like that at Belmont grew scarce. Men with bigger reputations found work before people like Philip. Fortunately he found work with Old Man Cullen, for whom Philip had worked in the past. Cullen wanted a second story added to his original room and addition. He hired Philip for two months, for $44 per week, which was enough money to pay for all the necessities in his own home for the winter.

Philip showed up to work at the Cullen residence the morning of Wednesday, October 30, 1929. He was greeted in usual fashion by Mr. Cullen, but Philip noticed that Cullen's face was a little ashen.

"What's wrong?" Philip asked.

Cullen picked up the newspaper and showed him the front page. The headline of the *New York Times* read, "Stocks Collapse in 16,410,030-Share Day, But Rally at Close Cheers Brokers; Bankers Optimistic, to Continue Aid."

"What does this mean?" Philip asked. He was a carpenter, a peasant from Sicily, not a stockbroker or investor. He understood that the news wasn't good, but he had no idea of the magnitude of the disaster that had happened the day before.

"It means that the economy is in big trouble," Cullen replied.

. . . . .

The world of Wall Street was completely unlike the world of North Great River, Long Island. On Wall Street, men in fine suits and shiny leather shoes traded stocks and bonds and dealt with millions of dollars of people's, and companies', equity. In North Great River, Philip labored with his hands in dirty pants and sweaty shirts, a man just trying to build a home for he, his wife, and three children.

On October 24, the stock market had experienced a significant dip in value. Opening at 305.85, the market fell 11% immediately in heavy trading. Wall Street bankers bought shares to prop up the market, and their efforts succeeded, and by day's end the market had lost just 2% of its value. Friday was a positive day, as the market gained 1% to 302.22. Saturday's low volume trading wiped out that gain, and then on Monday, the Dow fell some 13% to close at 260.64. Then Black Tuesday came. On October 29, 1929, the Dow lost 13% as panicked investors sold more than 16 million shares. Wall Street bankers had no ability to stop, or even stem, the tide.

The Roaring Twenties were a time of such economic boom thanks, in part, to the ability of investors to buy stocks "on margin", a new practice that allowed people to borrow money from their brokers, and only put down 10-20% of the value of the stock they were buying. But as the market began to fall, brokers called in these loans. The great scramble began, as people rushed to their banks to take out the money they needed to pay their debts to their brokers. This created a run on the banks, and banks found themselves in an impossible situation.

Some people are under the impression that when they deposit money in the bank, the money just sits there in their own special vault. What banks actually do is keep a certain amount of money in their vault, and take the rest and invest it, earning interest. The assumption is that they will keep enough on hand to handle normal deposits and withdrawals, but no bank has enough money on hand for all its clients to withdraw all their money at the same time.

In the wake of the Stock Market Crash of 1929, as brokers called in their margins, people went to their banks to withdraw the necessary money. But so many people did this that they overwhelmed the banks, and the banks did not have enough money to give the people *their* money. Moreover, the investments the banks themselves made floundered in the crash, so selling their stock for cash to give their clients was exceedingly difficult. As a result, banks began to fail. In 1929, 650 banks failed across the United States. In 1930, more than 1,300 banks failed. In December 1931, New York's Bank of the United States collapsed, at the time the largest bank failure in American history.

· · · · ·

The 1930s saw an unprecedented economic disaster for the United States and most of the rest of the world. In the U.S., wages fell 42%, and unemployment rose 25%. The U.S. economy shrunk by half, and world trade fell 65%. On Long Island, Philip, his family, and his friends experienced the impact of the Great Depression. Famine became a real thing in parts of the country that had never experienced lack. People too proud to do menial tasks – believing themselves above such work – found themselves doing anything to earn scraps. Bread lines came into existence. People were out of work. Crime rose as people grew more desperate.

New York Governor Franklin D. Roosevelt had witnessed first-hand the devastating effects of the Depression on Long Island. He toured the island to see what has happening, and on one occasion, he stopped by the Belmont State Park. It was there that Philip caught his first – and only – in-person glance at the future President.

In 1930, the city of Long Beach cut back employment and let numerous people go because "there was no work for them to do, nor was there money enough in the city treasury to pay them." There was a significant increase in appeals for assistance in Hempstead, as more and more people fell into unemployment and could not meet daily expenses. In Glen Cove and Islip, there were calls for the state government to provide assistance.

Governor Roosevelt swiftly moved to help. He created a fund to provide money for the completion of the Northern State Parkway, a project that employed thousands of men. He started a work relief program. In July 1931, he inspected road construction at Jones Beach, Valley Stream, and Little Neck, even helping some with the construction work. He pledged to launch a project to link the Grand Central-Northern Parkway with the projected Triborough Bridge as well as a connector linking Brooklyn with the Southern State Parkway.

But the state realized that these funds and projects were not enough. Long Islanders organized and called for the federal government to step in. Rev. Francis Healy of St. Joseph's Church in Garden City called on the Hoover Administration to set up federal government work programs, to provide jobs for the people. Roosevelt would run for President, and win, based on his platform formed in large part by his experience as New

York's governor, attempting to come to grips with the worst economic crisis the United States had ever faced.

. . . . .

Bremerhaven, Germany, was home to one Amandus Frederick Ulrich, a young man who took spent three years in apprenticeship, as required by the carpenter's guild at that time. Ulrich married, had two children, and then, after his wife passed away, decided to leave Germany for the United States. He settled in Islip, got naturalized, and became an American citizen. Fred was an expert drinker, but developed a propensity for tremors. He struggled with English, but his jovial disposition and hard-working spirit enabled him to find work on Long Island, and he found himself in Islip.

In Islip, Fred remarried and took to drinking with his friends. He sent many of them into heart palpitations every time he came near a saw, as his hands shook so much he seemed to have a case of palsy. Philip met Fred in Belmont Park in 1929, building the new house for the assistant chief engineer. When work ended, Fred and Philip found themselves out of work. Arnold Elliott was kept on because he had done some cabinet work for the chief engineer during his time off, at no pay.

While Arnold continued to work for the state, Fred and Philip enjoyed the Depression-era status of unemployed. They scraped for work, found little bits here and there, but found the struggle was real. Despite it all, both men were able to keep their families fed, a blessing that they never took for granted.

In the beginning of 1931, Philip and Fred were hired to build a boiler room with two rooms on top of it on Concourse West, Brightwaters, New York. The site was less than a mile from the Bay Shore Yacht and Motor Club, an organization with a storied history but which had predictably seen membership shrink as the Depression impacted even the wealthy. The site sat right on the bank of the Brightwaters Canal, and neither Philip nor Fred anticipated the constant battle they would face from seeping waters from the channel. Putting their collective heads together, they developed an ingenious solution by waterproofing the basement with concrete slurry poured in forms. Their innovation earned them praise and a ten dollar bonus each from the owner.

In 1932, after several more months of scrounging for more work once the Brightwaters job was completed, Philip was rehired by the Belmont

Lake State Park in Babylon. In the time Philip was gone, the site had undergone significant changes. Numerous buildings had been taken down or changed. A new carpenter's shop had been made, converted from an old stable. It housed numerous work benches and heavy wood-working machinery. The original mansion near the squash court had disappeared along with the court itself. Two French cannon that had been there for years remained, pointing off towards the lake. There were new office buildings, housing the administration for all the state parks on Long Island.

The main building was to be made in exquisite detail. Philip marveled at the plan for the walls, to be finished in wide clapboards broken by spaced paneling and topped by solid-looking roof eaves. One large wing was to be a conference room, complete with a kitchen and huge maple conference tables. Arnold oversaw the creation of every single piece of furniture for the entire site.

Philip was brought to the carpenter's shop. He was tasked with assisting Arnold with the milling, assembling, and finishing of every door, window, table, and bench for the project. Philip used a foot-operated mortiser, a heavy cast-iron table saw, a drill press, and other machines like a band saw and small jointer that he would become all too familiar with over the years. Much of the work was still done by hand, as skillful carpenters worked with classic carpenter's tools to create the wooden projects.

The machines helped the work get done much quicker, and with incredible precision, but there were significant drawbacks. Namely, they were dangerous. Today's table saws, for example, come with numerous safety features to prevent – or at least reduce the risk of – injury. The table saw Philip used would never pass a modern safety inspection. Today's carpenters, if they want to make an angled cut, turn a crank and the blade tilts until it reaches the desired angle. When Philip wanted an angled cut, he turned a crank and the entire table top of the saw tilted. Holding pieces of wood at sometimes steep angles is a recipe for injury. Moreover, today's table saws feature safety guards around the blade. The heavy saw in this shop had no such guard; the blade hung open and naked, being kept on its pin by a reverse-threaded nut, so when the blade turned, the nut tightened.

It was in this shop that Philip became the first carpenter to suffer a mechanical injury. He nicked his left middle finger on a saw, resulting in a permanently split nail. It could have been worse, as it was for Fred Ulrich, who should have never been near a saw in the first place with his trembling hands. He managed to lose four fingers of his left hand in one particularly disastrous incident. Arnold, a master craftsman, got stabbed in the abdomen by a strip of plywood that his partner George Reulius accidently let slip, the saw grabbing the wood and shooting it back at more than a hundred miles an hour into Arnold's midsection. Arnold was rushed to the hospital where they removed most, but not all, of the splinters of wood. He had to live with those for ten years before he would undergo another procedure to remove the rest.

. . . . .

The early 30s were a difficult time for Philip, as they were for many Americans. His extended family was not exempt from the challenges the Depression brought, though not every challenge was because of the worsening economic conditions. Philip's sister Giovannina had become mentally deranged and was admitted to a state institution in New Jersey. She would remain there until 1943, when she passed away.

Philip's other sister Lina had nine total children, and Lina was drawn more and more into her religious affiliations and convictions. She was elected by her church to be a missionary and paid for her to take the gospel to Arizona, California, and even Italy.

Biagio took odd jobs, barely enough to pay for food and household needs. Philip's sister Maria took care of her father and their home, each suffering from a lack of medical care. Maria became ill at one point and required hospitalization, and Biagio was left alone, lonely and suffering. Philip managed to scrape a few extra dollars and give them to his father. He earned $5 per day, which wasn't bad, but his family of six needed that much and more. Yet they found a way, and the reality was that Philip and his family, owning their own land and home, making some money here and there, fared better than most, as many were unemployed and many more who were employed by various government agencies could only earn $3.20 per day.

It did not escape Philip's notice, however, that those who fared the best were the bootleggers who avoided arrest. These men flouted the law, escaped the police, and tried to bribe lawyers, judges, and law enforcement officers. When the 21st Amendment repealed the 18th and

Prohibition ended in 1932, these bootleggers turned to even worse pursuits, including selling drugs and engaging in white slavery.

. . . . .

He was born Filippo Vampatella, but he became Philip Vampatella. He was naturalized as Philip Vamptell. But he was also known by another name during the 30s: Philip Vantino. Despite a large Italian population on Long Island, many employers had difficulty with a ten-letter ethnic name, and so, like his descendants to this day, he regularly found his name misspelled, even on official documents. He grew frustrated at the constant errors people fell under trying to pronounce and spell his last name. The frustration boiled over until he decided at one point to simply change his last name – not officially but for public use – to something easier: Vantino. He couldn't figure out why it worked so well, and why people adapted to it so much more easily than to Vampatella, but he didn't care. In 1962 he would sign an affidavit for State of New York that he used various names throughout his life, but they were all the same person.

. . . . .

Philip barely made enough to survive, but survive they did. He ended up taking on many odd jobs on the side, as he was able, to earn extra money. Every penny helped, and Philip, if nothing else, was a hard worker. In the winter of 1933, engineers had let water out of Belmont Lake Park, draining it to be cleaned. Men – many of whom had never used a shovel before but in the Depression, men would do anything for work – scraped the muck, leveling high spots, filling in holes, and dragging dead trees from its muddy bottom. They worked through the bitter cold, hands freezing, faces numb to the cold thanks to the biting winter winds. Artisans, artists, former white collar workers, all found themselves doing the kind of labor they never imagined they would be forced to do in order to survive. They earned their minimum $3.20 a day, not enough for any luxuries, and barely enough to put food on the table, but with enough scrimping and tightening of the belt in every way, these men and their families got through. Some, however, did not get through, as the working conditions made many sick, even to the point of death.

Arnold brought some of these men into his carpenter's shop. Philip took in Jim Sutton, his neighbor, and Jim served the shop by sweeping the floors clean of wood chips, shavings, and sawdust, while Philip and the other carpenters built tables, chairs, doors, and whatever else was needed. The shop was enlarged to add more work benches. They brought in a new machine, a shaper, for the milling of large moldings the architects had drawn up.

Federal dollars began to flow from the Roosevelt Administration. FDR, having won election in 1932, began implementing his New Deal, and some funds made their way to Long Island. The park system found itself the beneficiary of new and improved carpenter and machine shops, and more workers as the increased budget would allow. The new carpenter shop had new machinery too, much to the carpenters' delight. Philip and Arnold grinned as they looked upon two new table saws, a good shaper, a new thickness planer, an eight-foot jointer, a four-foot lathe, and a heavy duty mortiser to add to the old, light one from the previous shop. The band saw was brought over from the old shop, and a single end tenoner went in later to add to the collection. Two new rows of work benches completed the ensemble, and each man received a new personal tool kit. At the northwest end of the shop stood a large lumber shed. Philip credited the existence of this shop to Arnold's original cabinet work done for the chief engineer. Arnold was appointed foreman of the new shop, and he selected Philip as his assistant.

Chapter 18 – Dreams

Belmont Lake State Park typically saw visitors during the pleasant summer months. But in the winter of 1934 a cold stretch froze the lake, making it suitable for ice skating. The park would be opened for winter recreation. Then the snow came, covering the lake with half a foot of thick white powder. It was a beautiful sight, but it ruined the prospects for those looking to put their skates to good use. The park authorities decided that the smart course of action necessitated clearing the snow, once again opening the lake up for skaters. But who to do the work? They turned to the men in the carpenter's shop, among others, for help. Every able-bodied man employed by the park was called in to shovel snow off the lake. It was an enormous task, one that the men resented. They were hired to be carpenters and machinists, not snow shovelers. But the work was to be done, and they were the men to do it. And so they did.

The men grumpily shuffled out to the lake and used shovels, wooden snow pushers, and brooms to clear off the lake for the skaters. Philip groused with every shovel of the thick, heavy snow. The wind bit and the cold froze him to the bone. Every breath filled his lungs with the frigid air. Despite the cold, he quickly worked up a serious sweat and by the time the day was done, Philip was a sweaty, freezing, coughing mess. His physical constitution took a hit, and that opened the door for something much more serious in the months to come.

In March, Philip agreed to help a friend dig a foundation for an addition to be put on his home. It was a damp, chilly day, and Philip worked hour upon hour shoveling dirt and gravel, sweating profusely through his sopping wet shirt. At dark, he went home, ate a cold dinner, and went to bed coughing. Morning came and he felt no better, coughing some more, but Philip trudged off to work anyway.

A couple of weeks later, Philip's Model A, which had been giving him fits, required some repair. Philip parked it in his garage and slid under the car, laying on the cold, damp concrete floor, and went to work. Four hours later, the job complete, he went inside, ate a cold supper, and went to bed. His cough got worse.

The next day he went to work as usual, but he knew something was wrong. He lasted half a day and when lunchtime came, he decided to go home. His first conversation was with Antoinette, and then his second was with Dr. Garbin, who took his payment of four dollars, diagnosed him with "grippe" – a common term for the flu – and promptly went on vacation, leaving Dr. Carmen in charge of Philip's care.

Dr. Carmen came by to check on Philip and was horrified. He immediately called for an ambulance and before long, Philip found himself in the hospital. The diagnosis came back this time not as the flu, but as empyema. Pleural empyema typically comes on the heels of pneumonia, as bacteria settles on the lungs. The bacteria cause pus to form in the area between the lungs and the inner surface of the chest wall, an area called the "pleural space". Because this resides outside the lungs, it cannot be coughed out. Today, antibiotics are sufficient, but in 1934, surgery was required. Philip had developed a case of pneumonia, had gotten a bacterial infection in his lungs, was misdiagnosed as having the flu, and then finally the bacterial buildup resulted in pleural empyema.

By this point, Dr. Garbin had returned, and he and Dr. Carmen conferred. Philip needed the pus removed, but it would be a costly procedure. And, like most people at this point in time, Philip could not afford it. They weighed their options. Philip did not have much hope – he needed the surgery, but could not afford it, and the doctors did not seem to be interested in giving their services away for free. He thought that perhaps this was the beginning of the end.

Arnold Elliott came to the rescue.

He sat down with the doctors and Philip and listened to the situation – both with respect to Philip's health and his financial condition. He agreed that the condition sounded grave. He also agreed that Philip didn't have the money to pay for the surgey that could save his life.

"Doc," he said after a moment's thought. "I'll tell you what. I will make sure the money's there for this procedure."

"How so?" asked Dr. Garben.

"Well whatever Philip doesn't have, I'll cover the rest."

"You're guaranteeing payment?" Dr. Carman asked with a raised eyebrow.

"Fully."

The doctors conferred and agreed. Arnold then contacted his family doctor, a surgeon with the last name of Schlimbaum, and enlisted him to perform the surgery. In addition, he arranged for a special team of nurses to provide round-the-clock care for Philip as he recovered.

Dr. Schlimbaum performed the surgery – cutting through Philip's back, he was able to access the infection and remove it – and Philip slept in the hospital. And slept and slept and slept.

. . . . .

The first thing Philip heard was the voice of Dr. Schlimbaum. He opened his eyes to see the doctor grinning at him. Philip felt anything but happy.

"You owe me fifty dollars," the doctor said.

"It hurts."

"It isn't so much," Dr. Schlimbaum said, making reference to the bill. "It would be more if Arnold wasn't such a good friend of ours."

Philip wasn't interested in the bill. His back was in agony.

"Please, doctor! My back hurts!"

"Oh!" cried the doctor. He spoke a few words to the nurse and left. Moments later Philip felt a stabbing in his back from the needle, the pain diminished, and he fell back to sleep.

. . . . .

The project was quite extensive. A large crew of men worked under his direction. The men worked hard; the men sang while they worked at floating a long section of prefabricated tunnel into the sea. The tunnel would reach across the Atlantic; it would be anchored to the bottom and float a hundred feet below the surface of the sea where no storm would affect it, like it was with submarines. It would be double-decked, each deck for two-way traffic for cars and trains. It would reach South Hampton, branch off to Bordeaux, to Lisbon; it would enter the straight and lead to Velencia, to Marseilles, to Genoa, to Naples, and maybe to Scoglitti. Well, maybe Palermo. But Scoglitti was closer to Vittoria and closer to Biscari, his birthplace.

That was close planning toward the intangible but Philip gave terse and explicit orders, orders that were executed quickly and dexterously by his singing crew.

"Tell the super in the machine shop," he'd shout, "tell him clear and loud to make the anchor chains and the tunnel sections from elastic steel. Tell him to make allowances for the rise and fall of the tides. Tell him to allow for the drag of the Gulf Stream and the drift of the continents. Tell him I apologize for having called him a son of a bitch when I wasn't sure who he was."

He supervised the work with skill and care for hours and years. Then the pain returned.

"You're certainly having a time of it. Did you finish your job?" he was asked.

"Pretty near." A confused moment. "What job? Ouch!"

. . . . .

An intern inserted a rubber tube in his arm. The tube connected to a drip bag hanging from the metal pole standing next to the bed. Philip needed nourishment, but this was the only way he could be fed.

"Tell Antoinette not to worry. I'm busy right now, but I'll be home very soon."

Feliciano Tartaglia looked down at him and grinned. He held in his hand a blade.

"Hey, what's that?" Philip asked, concerned.

"Safety razor. How do you feel?" he asked.

"Never better," Philip replied sarcastically.

Feliciano turned the blade and Philip flinched. "Ouch!"

"I didn't cut you," Feliciano said.

"No, ouch in the back."

Feliciano started shaving Philip's face clean from days' worth of firm stubble.

"Boy, your face is fat on this side. What have you got in your mouth?" he asked, his hand working in an upward stroke.

"I think my teeth hurt. But my back hurts more."

Out of the shadows the nurse appeared and stuck a needle in his arm. The pain lessened, and Philip drifted off to sleep again.

. . . . .

He labored strenuously to the top of a mountain. A castle was on top of it, a walled sort of fort with crenellations on top and lookout turrets at the corners. This was his home. He would go up there and rest for a while. A large line of people waited at the main gate. They waited to be let in. Inside the fort it was snowing — great big green flakes, all of fifty dollar denominations.

He wished he had one for Doctor Schlimbaum. All the people trying to get in looked like Doctor Schlimbaum. He had to get in too, to get fifty dollars. He panted on and up, tiredly. One more desperate try and he was inside.

The money fall had ended. It carpeted the ground deep and wide to the foot of each wall and a little beyond, as far as the horizon. In a circle of clear ground an assortment of peculiar looking creatures were busy holding down men and working on them in a frightening way. They weighted them to the ground, immobilizing them. A different type of being flitted about with dainty little wings, wearing seraphic smiles. They stuffed handfuls of money into the mouths of the prostrated men, while a large and dark one on top of each man rammed the money down his gullet with a broomstick.

"What is this?" asked Philip in horror.

"We are feeding them what they like best," replied a dark one. "Note how nicely we do our work. We don't spill a bit or even touch one another. We seldom get together to enjoy fun like this. The groups of each of our kind belongs to a different region.

"We never tell. But people have different names for us. The names they use for my kind are never nice. They blame us for every bad thing that happens to them."

"Where do you come from?" Philip asked.

"You may find out later, but not now. I can tell you that the flitters and us come from different places and we are supposed to hate each other like mad. Most of the time we do. Not now though; we are having too much fun together feeding greedy people. I mean people who have enough and want more. By the way, what are you doing here?"

"I don't know. I thought this was my place."

"Oh, I beg your pardon."

Philip blinked, and the creatures vanished.

. . . . .

Philip's swollen cheek hurt. Dr. Garben punched small holes in his cheek and inserted rubber tubing in each hole.

"Hope he doesn't sneeze," said the doctor. "This ought to fix the pus in his gums." He watched the patient fof a few moments, then turned and spoke to the nurse.

"If he gets noisy again," he said, "give him another shot of sedative." And he walked away.

An 18-year old boy was wheeled into Philip's room, the victim of a terrific car wreck when his Model A hit a truck head-on. Apparently the Model A was in worse shape than the boy, which Philip found difficult to believe.

A police officer walked over to Philip and in a stern voice said, "Serves you right for having driven like a maniac." He had the wrong bed and the wrong patient, so Philip told him to get lost. He said the same thing to the priest who tried to give him the rite of extreme unction for what seemed like the fourteenth time. To Philip it seemed that the priest was growing impatient at Philip's unwillingness to die.

The pain returned, and as the nurse's sedative took effect, Philip begged someone to tell Antoinette not to worry, that he'd be ok. A hand touched his but he drifted off to sleep before realizing that it was hers.

. . . . .

This time he succeeded in traveling faster than light. When well he had often thought such a feat might be accomplished by some astronautic-minded genius. Now he was doing it himself in his own space ship at many times 186,000 miles per second. He knew he was traveling rather fast; he read the speedometer close to the windshield wiper button on the dashboard.

He arrived at a strange place. He applied his brakes and came to a full stop on a dusty rural road. The scene was vaguely familiar to him, for he had seen activity on farms before. Two men, a horse, and a cow were busy plowing and sowing.

Here the two men were yoked to the plow. The horse behind the plow spurred them on with whip and invectives. The men toiled on all fours, the horse followed on his hind feet. The horse was clad in some kind of garb, possibly his overalls. The cow, also walking on her hind legs, followed wearing eye glasses and a sarong. She carried a large burlap bag from which she extracted seeds and, bending low, she planted them, one at a time, in the furrow left by the plow.

Horse and cow spoke to each other in their own language, but Philip had no difficulty in understanding them.

"Hey, pa," said the cow to the horse. "Look at the togged out stray there. He walks on two legs and he's coming this way. Wonder where he came from."

The horse stopped his plow, walked to the intruder, spoke softly to him, tried to put a halter on him. Philip was scared; he moved back a little at a time.

"Lay off me, you dumb horse," he yelled. "You can't capture me! I am a free American citizen!"

"Hey ma," called the horse to the cow. "A talking human! What do you know about that?"

"Must be a freak. Let's lasso him and take him to the zoo."

"Gimme the rope," said the horse.

He made a loop at the end of the rope and twirled it expertly cowboy-fashion, while he chased the fleeing Philip. It was no trouble for the horse to lasso him. Fast as he ran, Philip could not move an inch. His feet were glued to the ground. The horse trussed him hand and foot. The cow prepared to sit on him.

"Better not, ma. We want him alive so that our mustang and longhorn professors can study him at the university. Besides, he looks too scrawny to barbecue. Now let us eat."

Cow and horse sat on the grass, opened a huge lunch basket, and proceeded to eat. The basket was well filled with their lunch.

Out of the basket came out nicely roasted human arms and legs. The two attacked them with relish.

"Oh, woe is me!" moaned Philip.

He drifted out of sleep back to consciousness. The hazy light of the hospital appeared.

. . . . .

Visitors came by to see Philip.

Ben was by this time ten years old, and he was afraid. He had never seen his father in any kind of condition like this before. Antoinette brought him into the hospital to see his father, so Ben cleaned up and put on his best suit. They made their way to Philip's room and the two of them stood at Philip's bedside. It took a few moments, but Philip finally recognized his son.

"The next time you come for a visit here, son, clean up!" he said.

Ben looked at his father, then up at his mother, very confused.

Fritz' eldest daughter Fanny also came to visit Philip, and she came bearing a gift. She was trying her hand – largely unsuccessfully – at a flower garden. Unfortunately, not much grew in her little flower bed, but for one tulip. She held it out to him and he broke into a big, warm grin.

He was moved by her love and generosity, and in the time that followed he treasured it as one of the finest gifts he had ever received.

The chief engineer from the park came to visit Philip, but Philip had no interest in seeing him. At this point in time, with the economy being what it was, Philip held a grudge against people who lived comfortable lives without concern for those that worked under them. Philip would later come to realize that the engineer had actually come to pay him a visit out of genuine concern for his well-being, but at the time, he believed that the only purpose the engineer's visit served was to make sure that Philip had a good excuse for not showing up to work. Philip later grew ashamed of his irrational reaction to the engineer, but he nonetheless believed that inside the human heart was a capacity for self-centeredness, and that, he thought, is what drove him to this reaction.

. . . . .

On May 15, Arnold came to the hospital to take Philip home. In the preceding days, Philip had tried to sneak out of the hospital. But it was on the third floor and plummeting to his death did not seem like a good idea. On one occasion he tried to leave because the young man who had been in the terrible car accident was in his last throes of life, and Philip could hear the sounds of death. He heard the wailing, the moaning, the struggle for life, and then....silence.

"How many people do they kill in this hospital every day?" Philip wondered aloud.

"About forty," came the reply from the far end of the ward.

With that, Philip tried to open the window but hands restrained him and a needle put him back to sleep.

Arnold gathered Philip's things and led his friend to his car that waited in the parking lot. He arrived on Cedarhurst Street and noticed that the house looked a little more worn that he remembered. Biagio had planted maple trees some time before and they were stretching to the sun, their leaves about to bloom from the buds. Philip considered the fact that life was beginning afresh in the spring, and he thanked God for his own life, which very possibly could not have continued, given the condition he was in.

The trees, the sun, the birds, the budding flowers, and even his old Model A seemed to welcome him home. It had been a month since he was first taken to the hospital, and his children, wife, neighbors, sister, father, and even his dog, seemed overjoyed at his return.

Philip was weak and tired, but very happy. He was home.

Chapter 19 – Recovery

Philip, on more than one occasion, credited his friend Arnold for saving his life. It was Arnold who had given assurance to the doctors and the hospital that the money would be there for Philip's surgery. When Philip returned home, he saw just how Arnold had come up with the money for that, and to help Philip in the ensuing months. He had roused their fellow park employees into action, asking – and getting – much-needed contributions through direct giving, as well as by holding raffles of various sorts. Even though it was the Great Depression, and money was scarce for most people, Arnold had managed to raise enough to cover all of Philip's hospital expenses. Moreover, people had contributed food and other necessities to Antoinette and Philip, who would still be several weeks away from returning to work.

Beyond their fellow employees, neighborhood friends chipped in as well. The local grocer and baker each extended credit to Philip and Antoinette. The milkman provided them with milk and even gave financially. The American Legion and Red Cross contributed. It was more than Philip could fathom, as he had no inkling that he had this many friends. He was truly grateful.

Meanwhile, Antoinette's brother Martin had agreed to move from New Haven to live with Antoinette and the children, acting as a sort of substitute father during Philip's time in the hospital. Just 16 years of age, young and uncertain, Martin had courage and took the mantle of leadership in a way that surprised and inspired everyone. He grew in confidence and skill and in the end, never moved back to New Haven. Instead, he became a great success on Long Island.

. . . . .

When Philip was fully recovered, he resumed work at Belmont. In the interim time, he thought much about how fortunate he was. He remembered his mother's death in Sicily, and the severe lack of medical care on his home island. He often wondered how likely it would have been had he gotten sick still in Sicily, and the more he thought about it, the more he concluded that his chances of survival were minimal. But he was not in Sicily; he was in the United States, which afforded him the opportunity to receive timely health care, and so his life was spared. As much as he loved his native Italy, he was grateful he was living in America.

North of the carpenter's shop at Belmont, a new machine shop had been built. Machines of all kinds were transported from their former home across the lake, and in Philip's eyes, some of the most capable men in the trade worked there. He had much respect for these men, and Philip thought that if the nation was in better financial straits, the machinists at Belmont could make quite a living. But here, in the 1930s, they had to scrape by plying their considerable skills for minimal pay, just enough to survive.

The workers at the carpenter's shop had, even in the Depression, and endless supply of work. They were responsible for benches, tables, chairs, and a host of other things necessary for a park, but not just for Belmont. Jones Beach had its own shop, but nothing the size or scope of the Belmont shop, and so Belmont provided items for many other parks on the island. Even the Jones Beach park needed Belmont workers to shape and mill literally miles of lumber for boardwalks, toll booths, and residential homes of the park officers.

Lumber of various types was used for different projects. Philip had the privilege of working with many species of wood that he had been completely ignorant of before this time. For example, one bar he worked on was made of solid teak, a wood from east Asia. The wood was soapy and gritty at the same time, and did a number on the chisels men used to shape it. Yet, much to Philip's astonishment, it somehow it yielded easily to sand paper. Philip was learning about various wood species and their properties, and how easily they could be shaped and milled, what tools worked best on them, and how strong they were.

Philip received a liberal education not only in various wood species, but in machines as well. Arnold proved a tremendous mentor to Philip, teaching him how to use machines of all types. Under Arnold's tutelage, Philip grew skilled at balancing, shaping, setting up, and operating woodworking equipment, and the more he learned, the more an idea began to crystalize in his mind. He thought that one day he might like to have some machines in his own garage and try to earn extra money on his own. He did not have the financial wherewithal to do anything like that at the time, but he filed it away for future reference.

. . . . .

When Philip was a boy, his mother Angela ran the home. Sicilian culture had defined the roles of husband and wife, and if they had children, fathers and mothers, in traditional fashion. The father was responsible for earning the money and working a trade (farmer, blacksmith, carpenter, etc.), while the mother was responsible for cooking, cleaning, and tending to the children. Of course, Sicilian culture was not unique in this way during Philip's childhood. When he arrived in the United States, married Antoinette, and began having children, these roles continued in traditional Italian fashion.

Following Angela's death and their return to the United States, Biagio earned money while his daughter Maria ran their home. For Philip and Antoinette, it was the same. Philip had the task of finding work to earn whatever he could to pay for what they needed, while Antoinette cooked and cleaned and took care of the children. Being in the United States did not alter Sicilian culture to the point where traditional gender roles were changed.

When Philip was home convalescing from his illness, he got a much more up-close and personal look at what Antoinette did every day. It was a completely eye-opening experience for him. A typical morning was filled with the hustle and bustle of getting the kids off to school.

Antoinette would rouse the children from their slumber, first with a quiet voice and then, inevitably, when the first call went unheeded, with a much more commanding voice.

"Children, get out of bed NOW!" she would say, her voice echoing through the house. That would produce some groans and rustling of covers as Angelina, Ben, Marie, and Anna slowly would rise, feet hitting the floor, shuffling off to the morning routine, still half-asleep and barely functioning. Antoinette would give direction and the children would work their way through the bathroom line, fussing at one another, of course – "Hurry up, I gotta go!" – and then into the kitchen for breakfast.

Antoinette would have their things mostly ready, but after a bowl of oatmeal was inhaled, the children would inevitably discover that they only had one shoe, and could not locate the other.

"Where's my shoe?" Marie would yell across the house.

"I can't find my book," Ben would shout.

"Someone help me with my hair," Angelina would beg.

Even little Anna, getting ready for kindergarten, would be in on the act. She needed more oversight, of course, and Antoinette managed all four of them in these minutes of chaos.

"Hurry up, the bus is here!" she would yell, and the three older kids would finish buttoning their shirts or fixing their collars or collecting their last belongings and dash out the door. Ever patient, the bus driver would wait until all three of them had boarded before giving Antoinette a wave and drive off to the next stop.

Philip did not help with any of this, for two reasons. First, he was still recovering from his illness, and even though he was gaining strength day by day, he was not yet in condition to be a full participant in the household. Second, it was just not his job, as he envisioned it, to prepare the children for their day of school. Antoinette was the mother, and this was her duty. She assumed as much also, and therefore it went unquestioned in the home that Antoinette took care of their children as they went off to school. At no point was there any discussion that perhaps Philip should give her any assistance.

The bus was a relatively new invention at this point. Philip had never, of course, had such a thing growing up in Sicily. He had always walked to school, and he grieved the school bus coming to pick up his children. He had always thought that the walk to and from school was an experience all by itself, something not to be missed. On the bus, the students rode in comfort but missed out on the sounds and smells of life – birds chirping, raindrops falling on your head, the smell of freshly-cut grass or of lilacs, lungs filling with clean, fresh air, the gentle breeze blowing through your hair, and small animals darting in and out of the bushes. All of that was missed when riding the bus to school, and Philip, though he had to accept that was how things were as society changed, never liked that reality.

Philip didn't deviate from his role in the family, but his time recovering did give him a greater appreciation for what Antoinette did. Once the children were off to school, Antoinette took a few moments to herself, and then began her day's work. She always had washing or mending to do. The house always needed cleaning. She had to go to the market to get food for the day. She had organizing and food preparation to get after. She had to arrange doctor's appointments for the children, keep unwanted door-to-door salesmen away, and visit with the neighbors whenever possible. Of course, when the children returned home, she had to make sure that they got their homework done, dinner was eaten and cleaned up, and the kids were put to bed.

She was a whirlwind of activity, day after day, and Philip was in awe of what she was able to do in order to keep their home and family running. Though his role would not change, he had a new respect for her and for women in general, seeing up close the truth of the phrase, "A woman's work is never done."

. . . . .

Philip was nearly fully healed, but Biagio was getting sick. He had spent time with odd jobs, earning enough to get by, with additional help from Philip from time to time. He had developed a case of stomach ulcers, but didn't complain and didn't give in to the pain. He just kept at work making what he could. But in reality, the pain was worsening with each passing week and month. He put up a good front, and passed himself off as buoyant as possible, but deep down he felt ready to die. His beloved Angela had been dead many years, and Biagio didn't think he would be too far from joining her. When they began, Philip was still sick and his daughter Maria was in the hospital, so he was left to himself alone in misery.

Biagio's doctor evaluated him and told him to "take it easy, don't worry, stick to your diet." He prescribed pain killers to take the edge off, and said that if these didn't do the trick, surgery might be required. That did not sit well with Biagio, who was deathly afraid of surgery. So he took his medication, worked when he could, and when he wasn't working, he lay in bed, occasionally hemorrhaging from the ulcers. He kept this to himself but he knew his condition was worsening.

In 1937, Maria returned from the hospital and resumed her role in Biagio's household. Philip would stop by every pay day to leave a few precious dollars with them. It was difficult for Philip to take from his own immediate family, but he could not bear to see his father and sister in such dire straits. They were getting by. Barely.

. . . . .

In the spring, Antoinette's belly began to show. She was pregnant again, and Philip began to worry about his own finances. Another mouth to feed. More clothes to buy. And the Depression was long from being over. He had to figure out a way to bring in more income.

He recalled his thoughts from a while back, and decided to bring his friends Arnold and Fred into his confidence as he laid out a plan.

"We sure could use some more money," he told them.

"Yes, we all can. But how do we get it?" Fred asked.

"Well, what do you think about buying some used woodworking machinery and setting it up in my garage so we could do some building on our own?"

"So setting up our own business?" Arnold asked, rubbing his chin.

"Yes."

"What would we build?" he asked.

"Anything people need. Cabinets. Furniture. Benches. Windowsills. Anything people need built, we can handle it," Philip explained.

"Have you calculated the cost?" Arnold asked.

"Yes," Philip replied, and laid out all the figures. It would be a substantial outlay, with only the hope of getting it back.

"I don't know," Fred said. "Going into business ourselves, with times being what they are....seems risky."

"It's definitely a risk," Philip agreed. "But I think we can make it work."

Fred and Arnold looked at each other. They understood implicitly that if the machinery were to be installed in Philip's garage, with his electricity bill being impacted, that the machines would be his to own. They understood and were fine with that arrangement.

"Ok," Arnold said. "I'm in."

"Me too," replied Fred. "Let's get to work."

They spent the next few months preparing the garage and laying out a sketch of how the workshop would take shape. They saved their money and secured enough for a down payment on the machines, and managed to get a loan for the rest. They had to get the electric company to extend the line out to the garage - $40 in cash for an extra pole to carry the wires over the distance. When all the machines were purchased and set up, they admired their little operation. In the small space they had a cast iron table saw, a three-foot band saw, a cut-off saw, a small jointer, a mortiser, a 14-foot work bench, some clamps, a shaper, and a grinder. They had agreed to buy lumber and other materials as needed. When they were ready to open, they had paid off a third of the cost. The rest would have to come as they found work. With any luck, they'd soon be in business.

They began to look for orders.

. . . . .

On November 12, 1937, the family of six became a family of seven, as their fifth child was born. Irene, the fourth daughter, entered the world. She was seven years younger than her next-oldest sibling, Anna, and the age gap made her the darling of the family. The others fawned over her and took turns watching her and playing with her. She received as much love and attention as any baby could possibly ever want.

. . . . .

Martin, meanwhile, continued to live in their home. He found work with the Works Progress Administration, and contributed five dollars a week to the family coffers. As he got older, he began to look for companionship, and found some in Angelina Capuano, who came from a large family. He made many friends as well, and on one occasion, one of his friends gifted him a chicken. This led to Martin dreaming of chicken farming, and he decided to build a chicken's roost.

Unfortunately, the chicken refused to lay any eggs. Martin's dream of chicken farming was close to dying before it even got off the ground, and he considered having the chicken for dinner. He approached the roost with a knife in his hand but quickly discovered that he did not have the nerve to kill it. He asked Philip to do the honors, but Philip similarly did not have the stomach to slay the poor bird. The hen, as it were, lived on, even if his chicken farm never materialized.

Martin and Angelina fell in love and got married, but it all happened so fast that Mr. Capuano was furious at how this relationship materialized and was consummated. He did not realize how fine a man Martin would turn out to be for his beloved daughter, how hard-working and diligent a provider he would be. He was not without flaws, but Martin was a good man and a good provider.

Somehow, everyone was getting by in the Great Depression.

Chapter 20 – Long Island Express

On September 9, 1938, a storm began to develop off the western coast of Africa, in the waters just a few miles from Dakar, the city that would become the capital of Senegal after it gained independence from France in 1960. The storm was first categorized as a tropical depression as it moved south of the Cape Verde Islands, and was analyzed by ships monitoring the weather. It actually began as a tropical disturbance, as water vapor from the warm waters condensed to form clouds, releasing heat into the atmosphere. As the warm air was pulled upward, a cycle of evaporation and condensation began, with the wind slowly moving around a center point, in a counter-clockwise direction. It would quickly develop into a cluster of thunderstorm clouds.

As the column of clouds built by this system grew higher into the atmosphere, the air at the top became unstable. Warm air rose while the cooler air at the top fell, and winds began to circulate more strongly and spread outward from the center, causing pressure at the surface to drop. More thunderstorms resulted, and the wind began to whip more violently, reaching speeds of 25 to 38 miles an hour.

On September 10, the storm moved westward, away from the coast of Africa, heading out into the open Atlantic. Winds picked up speeds, to the point of reaching greater than 39 miles an hour. The system had become a tropical storm, and continued moving west. The counterclockwise winds known as the Coriolis effect – they move clockwise in the southern hemisphere – brought warm water north and cooler water south.

From September 11-15, the tropical storm continued almost exactly due west, heading for the Caribbean. Then on September 16, the winds whipping around the eye grew greater than 74 miles an hour, and it became a category 1 hurricane. That lasted for one day and on September 17, it quickly became a category 2 hurricane, as sustained winds reached 100 miles an hour. The storm was rapidly growing, fed by the warm water and air being pulled in from the south.

Later on the 17th, as the storm grew in intensity, it reached winds greater than 111 miles and hour, and it grew to a category 3 hurricane. It began a slight turn west northwest and appeared headed for the northern Caribbean or even the southern United States. Tracking these storms without satellites was nearly impossible, so few people took notice.

On September 18, 19, and 20, it increased in intensity even more, reaching category 4 status, with sustained winds of 130 miles an hour or greater, and it was headed directly for the eastern shore of Florida. By the afternoon of September 20, as the storm approached east of the Bahamas, it was a full-blown category 5 hurricane, with sustained winds of greater than 157 miles an hour. It was a monster, bearing straight down on Florida.

The storm hit a deep trough over Appalachia, turned northward and began to run along the coast of the Eastern United States, in virtually a straight line due north. Florida, the Carolinas, and the mid-Atlantic states were spared its wrath as it turned north. Meanwhile, a high-pressure system centered north of Bermuda, keeping the hurricane from escaping eastward out to sea, and creating a channel for the storm to run due north.

This channel launched the storm northward at frightening speed. This rapid movement north meant that the winds on the eastern side of the eye were much faster – and more deadly – than typical hurricanes of similar strength. It weakened on the 21st as it reached the coast of Cape Hatteras, but was moving north at an astonishing 50 miles an hour. Its velocity northward was so great that it did not even have time to weaken from the cooler waters off the coast of New Jersey or New York.

At 9:00 am on September 21, Charles Pierce – a 28-year old novice meteorologist taking the place of two veteran weathermen that day –

analyzed the data. He concluded that the storm would be forced by systems on either side of the storm to move northward into New England, and not out to sea. At 10:00 am, the U.S. Weather Bureau downgraded the hurricane to a tropical storm, and no information was sent on to the New York office.

At noon, Pierce presented his conclusions to the U.S. Weather Bureau, but he was overruled by seasoned veteran Charles Mitchell. E.B. Rideout, a Boston meteorologist, told his radio audience that the storm would hit New England, an announcement that was met with sneers from his colleagues. Still a category 3 hurricane, with winds between 110-130 miles an hour, the storm slammed into the southern coast of Long Island.

Ironically, on the morning of September 21, the *New York Times* ran an editorial praising the U.S. Weather Service for doing such a great job informing Americans about the potentially dangerous storm that was approaching from the east and south. They did not know just how far off the weather service was.

. . . . .

Meanwhile, fishermen off the southern coast of Long Island were aware that something was happening. Their barometers went crazy, dropping rapidly as the storm approached. They could tell that a big coastal storm was coming, and the wiser ones hauled in their traps and nets. They pulled into harbor and docked, checking the weather forecast, which simply told them that there were cloudy skies and gusty conditions. Nevertheless, some decided to let their children out for school.

. . . . .

Philip, Arnold, and Fred had managed to secure small jobs here and there, and their little shop was constantly humming with activity. At the end of the summer, they managed to secure a contract to build several dozen road signs for a road building company. The signs were to be made for the Wantagh Parkway, a new road connecting the Northern and Southern Parkways. The specifications and designs for the sign were, to Philip's mind, fancy and stringent, but he understood that such things were to be expected from a state project. They had to order lumber, tempered Masonite, reflecting buttons, paint, screws, bolts, and several other materials in order to complete the project. The signs called for western cedar wood, a durable stock that had to be ordered from British

Columbia, where it grew in abundance. Bronze carriage bolts and lag screws had to be made specific for this job, and were ordered directly from a manufacturer in Connecticut.

Every piece of lumber had to be treated with preservatives under pressure before assembling. A barrel of hard tar did the trick, applied to the bottom three feet of each post that would go into the ground. The shop was filled with materials, as the partners put out more than two thousand dollars' worth of outlay. When all was ready, they began to work.

They came home from their regular jobs and immediately went to Philip's shop, working well into each and every night to make the signs according to the strictest specifications to meet the state of New York's satisfaction. Piles of sawdust formed. Scrap lumber sat in a heap. The shop quickly became overcrowded, and they agreed that the only suitable solution was to move the finished signs outside. They carried the signs outside and stacked them neatly into large piles, placed on long timbers resting on saw horses. The work continued in early and mid September.

On September 21, the three men enjoyed a rare vacation day from Belmont. The men met early to continue the work at Philip's shop, but the skies grew ominous with dark clouds. Fred said it looked like a storm was coming, and he decided to go home and prepare. Arnold and Philip stayed and continued to work as the day went on, machines humming inside as the wind picked up outside.

The little garage began to shake with the increasing force of the wind. Whenever a machine was off, they could hear the wind beginning to howl outside. A little garage he had built for his Model A – his old garage having been turned into the shop – was starting to wobble, so Philip rushed over and braced it with some diagonal furrow strips. He looked up at the sky and saw a familiar pattern. He recalled the winds from the terrible storm when he was a boy back in Sicily. *Coda di drago*, he thought, for the second time in his life. Then he went back into the shop to continue his work.

The winds increased, coming in from the east due to the leading edge of the storm that moved in a counterclockwise direction. The little building shook but Philip and Arnold continued working – that is, until the power went out. With no electricity, there was little for them to do on the signs. Philip did a little work by hand while Arnold sat down, took out a sandwich, and ate his lunch.

. . . . .

The "Long Island Express", as New Yorkers would later call the storm, made landfall first near Bellport, just 17 miles east of Great River, as a category three hurricane, with a maximum sustained wind of 120 miles and hour. It hit land moving at 47 miles an hour, extremely fast for a storm this size. It drove into land with such force that seismographs 3,000 miles away in Sitka, Alaska, registered the shock as an earthquake. Without satellite pictures and modern meteorological technology, people in the Northeast were taken almost completely by surprise.

The storm slammed into towns all along Long Island's southern coast, ripping down power lines and uprooting trees. Buildings were torn apart, cars were flipped over, and the rain and wind brought the ocean deep inland. The eastern end of the island suffered the most, as the counterclockwise motion of the storm brought more ferocious winds to the east. Otis Bradley, a six year old living in Quogue, 34 miles east of Great River, would later recall, as the water poured inland, "We watched as the ocean came in. We climbed up to the next floor, and the next floor, and the next floor, and eventually onto the roof."

. . . . .

Philip and Arnold felt the garage sway under the ferocious winds that had picked up as the hurricane made landfall. The east gable of the shop began to buckle. It was well-braced by stacked lumber and the very heavy cast iron band saw, so they weren't worried about that wall giving way. A few shingles snapped off the roof, but as Philip looked out the window to see his makeshift new garage topple over from the force of the wind. Glancing the other way, he saw that his house was holding up, much to his relief. Antoinette and the children were frightened, and huddled together in the corner of the house where they thought it would be safe.

The storm abated. They thought the worst was over. They were wrong.

. . . . .

Arthur Raynor of Westhampton, who was just 18 at the time, had always been told that whatever else Long Island may be, it was a place free from the worry of natural disasters. There were simply no blizzards, tornadoes, hurricanes, earthquakes, or floods — it was as safe a place as one could imagine.

Arthur and his friend John were out in John's new Chevy. Around 3:30 in the afternoon, the storm hit Westhampton with full fury. They were driving down the hill at Oneck Lake when three feet of water blasted across the road in front of the car, sending twigs, branches, and debris into their path. They stopped, got out, and inspected the scene. It was ocean water, which to them seemed odd. They knew a way to Arthur's house, but Beaver Dam Creek was in-between them and home. John suggested they chance it and he figured his car was tall and sturdy enough, so they pressed forward. Suddenly they found the engine submersed in water, choking the carburetor's life out. They had to go on foot, but as soon as they opened the doors, water came pouring in. Pine trees fell all around them. They managed to push the car out of the water and up the hill far enough to escape further water surges and the engine, clear of water, fired up again. They turned around and finally found safe haven elsewhere.

. . . . .

Frederic de Foster was not as lucky as Philip and his family. A 54-year old man returning from work in New York City as a vice president and trust officer of the Fulton Trust Company, he was on the train when the storm hit. The train was stuck and would not go, so he got out, still in Manhattan, and decided to take his car instead. Trying to navigate his way home, the winds rocked his car, and tossed lighter vehicles aside. Tree limbs and signs littered the streets. Rain poured down in thick sheets, making it nearly impossible to see where he was going. Stopping was not an option, but going forward was practically fruitless as well. But he pressed on.

His commute from the city normally took a mere 15 minutes. On this afternoon, in the worst driving conditions imaginable, it took Frederic two full hours. He had to navigate downed power lines and poles, trees that were torn apart and had blocked roads, abandoned vehicles scattered and thrown everywhere, signs, wood, and other debris that he nearly smashed into every minute. Frederic endured the two most stressful hours of his life, just trying to get home through a category three hurricane, and upon arriving at his house, entered, closed the door, and then fell dead from exhaustion.

.....

The eye of the storm passed through Great River, and the storm continued its march north. The winds picked up again, this time coming from the west, as the southern half of the storm hit the shoreline. The west end of Philip's shop began to shake, but heavy timbers in the shop served to shore up the wall. In the house, Antoinette and the children huddled in a new corner, one that felt safer than the previous one. The glass rattled, the house shook, the rains lashed against their home on Cedarhurst Street, and they held on for dear life.

.....

In Westhampton, which was devastated by the storm, two members of the Burghard household, along with their friends the Dalins, sought higher ground and shelter from the intense winds and rain. They abandoned their home and struggled through 120 mile an hour winds, heavy rains, flying debris, and a surging ocean, and made it to another home, on higher ground. People were simply unaware of what was hitting Long Island.

.....

In Westhampton Beach, 160 summer homes were destroyed by the storm. Seven bodies had been washed ashore, and at least 30 people were missing. On Fire Island, entire summer communities were obliterated. In Kismet, all the buildings were destroyed. At Saltaire, 100 vacationers were marooned, with up to 1,000 cottages swept into the Great South Bay, and the pier was completely washed away. Ten new inlets were created by the surging waters, including the famous Shinnecock Inlet in Southampton on the eastern end of the island, which cut the island in two, and the town of Montauk, at the extreme eastern end of Long Island, at one point temporarily became an island unto itself, completely surrounded by the rising waters.

.....

For hours, the Coast Guardsmen rode up and down the beaches of Westhampton, telling people to leave and seek safety, but those that lived or vacationed on the shore were not worried, having seen rain and winds come in from the ocean before. Some had even seen storms strong enough to take down a house. What they were not ready for was a storm that took down everything. In some communities in Easthampton, every single home – along with the Coast Guard station itself – was washed away, as the incoming surge, which rose as high as 10-12 feet in some places, loosened the buildings from their moorings, and then were swept out to sea as the surge went back out again.

The destruction in Westhampton was so great that at midnight, the fire alarm went off in Patchogue, some 20 miles to the west, summoning all the available men in town. They were asked to assist the town of Westhampton in searching the beach for bodies and to aid anyone who had lost their home.

. . . . .

The Long Island Express ripped right through the 23-mile wide island, leaving a trail of devastation in its wake. But it was not finished yet. Minutes later it crashed into the southern coast of Connecticut and Rhode Island.

. . . . .

The storm, having passed through Long Island and turned its wrath on New England, abated in Great River. Philip left his shop and went into the house, and found his wife and children huddled up, Antoinette's arms wrapped around each one like a mother hen protecting her chicks. Philip found kerosene lamps and candles, and inspected his property. The house and shop suffered damage to their respective roofs, with missing shingles having been launched by the 120 mile-an-hour winds as far as a half-mile away. The signs they had painstakingly made for the state of New York had been scattered by the winds, being thrown about the neighborhood. They took hours to retrieve them and to their pleasant surprise discovered that, all things considered, they were in excellent shape but for some scratches.

They would not know for several days just how bad the storm really was. They knew they were lucky; they just didn't realize yet how lucky.

. . . . .

The storm rained death and destruction over Long Island – mainly the eastern portion. Thousands of homes, cottages, and other buildings were destroyed or swept into the sea. Approximately 116 people were killed on the island. The Hamptons alone suffered $6.2 million in damages, an enormous figure in 1938. That was just Long Island. The storm changed the shoreline of southeastern Connecticut and devastated Connecticut and Rhode Island before hitting Massachusetts. The upscale Watch Hill section of Rhode Island was wiped out. New London, Connecticut, nearly 70 fires raged throughout the city due to short-circuiting caused by the storm, as 100 mile an hour winds whipped the flames into an inferno. Hartford flooded like never before. Providence was hit with a tidal wave some 100 feet high, which smashed the docks in the city and drowned dozens of unsuspecting people in shops, sidewalks, and even in their own cars. Providence fell into total darkness from a massive power outage as the city was swept under 13 feet of water. In Milton, Massachusetts, the Blue Hill Observatory recorded a gust of 186 miles an hour.

Incredibly, the storm passed through northern New England and swept into Canada, causing even more damage. The final tally from the Long Island Express was unfathomable: 700 dead, and 700 more injured. 9,000 homes and buildings were destroyed, and an estimated 75,000 were damaged. Nearly 3,000 ships and boats were sunk or wrecked. Railroads and farms were wiped out. An estimated two billion trees were lost on Long Island and in New England, and some 35% of New England forestland was impacted. The entire Long Island fishing industry was obliterated, and it would take years to rebuild. The storm caused some $18 million in damages, which is more than $6 billion in 2019 dollars, and was by far the worst storm ever recorded in either Long Island or New England history.

. . . . .

The devastation wrought by the storm required months and years of effort to clean up and rebuild. The state of New York brought in thousands of workers to help clear debris from roads, harbors, and railroad tracks. Bell Systems alone brought in more than 2,700 men to repair downed power lines. This work effectively ended the Depression for thousands of families, as these men who desperately wanted work suddenly found it in abundance.

. . . . .

When power was restored in Great River, Philip, Arnold, and Fred completed the order for the signs, and each man received $132 from New York. Nearly all of it went to pay for the machinery in the shop.

Chapter 21 – World War

The *New York Times* headline on September 21, 1938, said nothing about the hurricane that was racing up the east coast. By the time some people would even be able to sit down at their tables reading the *Times*, the storm would already have barreled into Long Island, beginning its destructive wrath. But that morning the *Times* printed and distributed some 800,000 copies with the main headline reading, "Britain, France Give Prague Hours to Submit on the Peril of Immediate German Attack; Czechs are Declared Determined to Resist". The world was not focused on a storm most prognosticators thought would quickly move harmlessly out to sea; it was focused on the imperial designs of Adolf Hitler.

The 1919 Treaty of Versailles that followed the Great War (soon to be known as World War I) was a wonderful example of how to treat defeated nations harshly. The terms of the treaty were brutal on Germany. Among others, they included the surrender of all German colonies, the return of Alsace-Lorraine, a prized piece of real estate, to France, severe limitations on German armed forces, including what kinds of ships they could build for their navy, and an astounding 132 billion German marks (roughly the equivalent of $400 billion in 2019) – a staggering figure that threw Germany into economic chaos.

The rise of Adolf Hitler is a complex one with many factors, but historians generally point to the Treaty of Versailles as being a key contributor. Hitler was an enlisted man in the German army during the first World War, and joined what would become the National Socialist German Workers' Party (Nazi Party). He, like the other members of the party, strongly believed that the Treaty of Versailles was far too harsh and unfair, and resented France and England. He opposed Russian Marxism and the democratic government of the Weimar Republic, and advocated for a strong sense of German nationalism and Aryan supremacy.

During the 1920s, Hitler rose to power within the Nazi party, thanks to his dynamic public speaking ability, his vision for Germany which resonated with party members, the publication of Mein Kampf, and a willingness to engage in violence to achieve his goals. By the 1930s, the Nazi party became the largest political force in the Reichstag, and in 1933, the Nazis assumed control of Germany's governing body. In January of 1933, President Paul Von Hindenburg appointed Hitler to be chancellor, and in March, the Reichstag passed the Enabling Act, granting Hitler dictatorial power over Germany.

But Hitler was not content with ruling Germany. For decades, many Germans believed in a policy of Lebensraum, or "living space". That is, a growing German nation needed room to grow, room to breathe. The only way to get that space, of course, was to acquire more territory and claim it for the German people. Lebensraum, accompanied by the sense of Aryan superiority, meant that in any acquired territories that had a non-Aryan population, those non-Aryans would be subject to expulsion or termination; hence the establishment of the horrific concentration camps which killed millions.

Hitler's policy did not require war, but of course he realized that war with France, England, and even Soviet Russia was inevitable. He expanded the German military well beyond the boundaries of the Treaty of Versailles, but British Prime Minister Chamberlain did not want war, and so allowed Hitler to rearm Germany without consequence. Naturally, that encouraged Hitler, who rightly believed that Chamberlain would give him a very wide berth.

He took every advantage, and in 1938 began pressuring neighboring Czechoslovakia into ceding the Sudetenland, a small parcel of territory in which a high percentage of ethnic Germans lived. These ethnic Germans wanted to be part of their ethnic homeland, and so supported the transfer of ownership of the Sudetenland from Czechoslovakia to Germany. Hitler gave the Czechs a list of demands that he knew they could not meet.

The Czechs, of course, were not interested in this arrangement, as they would have received nothing in return. But they did not have the military means of preventing Germany from simply taking the territory they wanted, and everyone knew it. Germany kept applying the pressure, and as the hurricane swept over Long Island and New England, British and French ambassadors told Czech President Edvard Beneš that they would have to either accept Germany's demands or face the German army alone. They were simply not willing to go to war over the Sudetenland or Czechoslovakia.

On September 22, the Czech government resigned, and Chamberlain met with Hitler again. Hitler demanded that Germany be able to occupy the Sudetenland by October 1, and on September 23, the new Czech government headed up by new Prime Minister Jan Syrovy, began mobilization of its small, but proud, army. Two days later they rejected Hitler's latest demands, saying that they were "an ultimatum given to a defeated nation, not a sovereign one."

On September 27, Chamberlain gave a speech in which he announced that Britain had no intention of defending tiny Czechsolovakia. He said, "However much we may sympathize with a small nation confronted by a big and powerful neighbor, we cannot in all circumstances undertake to involve the whole British Empire in a war simply on her account. If we have to fight it must be on larger issues than that." A meeting was arranged between Germany, France, England, and Italy to settle the Sudetenland crisis. The Czechs, of course, were not invited.

By this time, the Sudetenland was not enough for Hitler. He wanted Czechslovakia dissolved and the land divided up among other nations – Germany most prominently. Chamberlain opposed this, and Hitler accused Britain of interfering with German "self-determination". War seemed inevitable, as Chamberlain could not grant Germany's wishes for all of Czechoslovakia. Playing the role of peacemaker – or so he thought – Chamberlain agreed that in order to prevent war, the Syrovy government needed to cede the Sudetenland to Germany, which would, per the treaty, guarantee the integrity of the rest of Czechoslovakia. The four powers signed what would be known as the Munich Pact on

September 30. Chamberlain was hailed in Britain and around the world as a great peacemaker, declaring that he had assured "peace in our time".

He would never fathom just how wrong he would be.

. . . . .

Tensions in Europe continued to rise as Germany occupied the Sudetenland. As demanded by Hitler, the Czechs had to leave their military equipment that was in that territory to the Germans, which strengthened Germany and weakened Czechoslovakia. Hitler knew by this point that Chamberlain and the allies had no stomach for war, and he realized that German expansion could continue. He preferred expansion without war, as it was less costly, but if it required war, that was fine too.

. . . . .

Biagio had already been through one great European war, and he hated every minute of it. He detested bloodshed. He detested the way that governments used men as pawns. He detested what war did to communities, to families, to civilization. He understood first hand what men could do to each other, and as the tensions in Europe rose, partly due to Italy and its own fascist head of state, Benito Mussolini, who had become allied with Hitler, he felt sick to his stomach. He could see history repeating itself, and he was powerless to stop it.

But for Biagio, the sickness he felt was mostly due to his ulcers, which grew worse and worse. When 1939 rolled around, he experienced a terrible bout of bleeding, the hemorrhaging being so bad that it frightened him into getting surgery – which was about the last thing he wanted. The doctors performed the procedure, but the damage had been done. Years of ulcers had gone unchecked, as Biagio simply wished them away and took pain killers to make him forget they were there. He was too weak by this point, his health compromised too much by the ulcers and by his age – he was 70 at this point. He remained in the hospital following the surgery, recuperating from the operation. He lasted for three days, but on June 18, 1939, Philip's father Biagio passed away. His hard life of toil was over.

He missed the start of the Second World War by less than three months.

. . . . .

Germany had annexed Austria early in 1938 during the Anschluss, and the Sudetenland from Czechoslovakia in the fall of the same year. By the time 1939 came about, Hitler's eyes had turned to an even bigger prize: Poland. He had acquired two territories without a shot being fired, but he knew the Western allies would not tolerate Poland being brought into the Nazi fold. So he prepared for war. He knew that the Soviet Union would engage, so in order to head them off, he negotiated a non-aggression pact with Stalin in August, thus securing his eastern front from Red Army attack. The pact called for a division of Poland, with each power taking roughly half.

The Polish army in 1939 contained relics from a time gone by: cavalry. Nearly 10% of all Polish army units were on horse, some of which were equipped with, of all things, lances. On September 1, the German Wehrmacht rolled into Poland. The blitzkrieg attack overwhelmed Polish forces all across a wide front and in just a few days advanced 140 miles, threatening Warsaw, the Polish capital. Polish leaders hoped to bring in forces from the east but just at that moment, the Soviet Union, holding up their end of their agreement with Hitler, launched an all-out attack on Poland's eastern front. Within days, the Polish government fled the country, Warsaw was in German hands, and once again Poland was occupied by its stronger neighbors.

Meanwhile, England and France, who had pledged their support to Poland, sat by and did nothing. They declared war on Germany, but even though Germany kept only 23 divisions on their western front, due to the forces committed to the attack on Poland, France – which had every opportunity to attack – held back, even though it had four times the forces along the border (between France and England the allies could have thrown 110 fresh divisions into the attack) and could easily have overwhelmed the German army. Hitler rightly surmised that he could attack Poland with impunity, betting that France and England would not stop him. He was correct in that assessment.

For the next eight months, until April 1940, Britain, France, and Germany engaged in what became known as a "phony war" – the allies had declared war on Germany, and Germany on the allies, yet aside from some action between France and Germany in the days immediately following Germany's conquest of Poland, nobody fired a shot at one another. They simply mobilized, organized, and prepared for the inevitable.

. . . . .

    The Vampatella household also mobilized, organized, and prepared for the inevitable. But in this case, it wasn't for war. It was for a new arrival. On March 31, 1940, the sixth – and final – child born to Philip and Antoinette made his debut. Little Philip Victor was born at home, small and quiet. Antoinette was near forty and the pregnancy and delivery took quite the toll on her; she and Philip agreed that this would be the last child they would have.

    Fifteen year old Ben was very proud of his younger brother, and promptly bestowed on him the nickname of "Flip". Nicknames are funny in that very few people get to pick their own nickname; almost always, they are given by a friend, family member, or co-worker, often to the dismay of the person receiving the nickname. But if they stick, they stick. "Flip" stuck like glue, and would retain this moniker the rest of his life.

    Philip was overjoyed at having another boy. He loved his four daughters, but they would not pass on the family name. It meant the world to Philip to have another son who could bear his name to the next generation.

. . . . .

    The European powers fought their way across Europe in 1940 and 1941. Germany launched an attack through Belgium into France in April and May of 1940. The French, who along with the British failed in their opportunity to kill the war in its cradle in the fall of 1939, got steamrolled by the panzers of the Wehrmacht, who rolled through King Leopold's Belgian defenses right into France. Just one month after invading France, Nazi troops occupied the French capital of Paris, on June 14, 1940. France, threatened with extinction, signed an armistice with Hitler eight days later. German troops would occupy France, and a puppet French government would be set up with its capital at Vichy. Images of Hitler on the Champs-Élysées, in front of the Eiffel Tower, and the Arc de Triomphe, shocked the world. The mighty French, which presumed to have the best army in Europe, was crushed in four weeks by Hitler's troops. The Nazi flag hung in Paris. Britain, for the time being, was on its own.

. . . . .

Hitler knew he had to conquer England in order to achieve complete victory in Europe. But how to do it? The small island nation boasted the best navy in the world and even though Germany could field capable ships and sailors, it knew it was no match for the Royal Navy. Getting across the small channel separating the French coast from southern England was a monumental task, especially with the Royal Navy and Royal Air Force standing guard. Hitler knew he had to deal with England, and the Luftwaffe – the German Air Corps – was called upon to do the job.

The Germans had a chance to effectively end Britain's war effort in late May to early June, 1940. After overrunning France and Belgium, they pursued a host of fleeing British troops all the way to Dunkirk, a tiny town on the northern coast of France. Trapped against the channel with no way out, the British forces prepared for annihilation or capture. Hitler had panzer divisions poised to strike, but Herman Göring, the supreme commander of the Luftwaffe, convinced Hitler that his planes and pilots could destroy the British forces. While the panzers and infantry waited outside the city, German planes bombed and strafed the British for days on end. Meanwhile, England had summoned thousands of ships – military vessels, fishing boats, pleasure yachts – anything and everything that would float, whether military or civilian, were called upon to rescue the trapped soldiers. In one of the most remarkable military operations in history, some 338,000 British and other allied troops were successfully evacuated, in the face of intense fire from German planes. These troops would keep Britain in the war, and serve as the backbone of a new British army that would return to these same shores four years later.

The Luftwaffe had failed at Dunkirk, but Hitler still had confidence in Göring and his air corps. For two months, German planes dropped bombs on British military installations, bases, ships, bridges, rail lines, and factories. The Royal Air Force fought gamely defending the home island. Despite losing more planes, and at a higher rate, than the Luftwaffe (the RAF suffered 21% losses compared with 16% for the Luftwaffe), the British held on and Germany never managed to gain air superiority.

Switching tactics, the Germans began bombing London indiscriminately, hoping to destroy British morale. Prime Minister Winston Churchill had delivered his famous speech in the wake of Dunkirk, telling the British, "Even though large tracts of Europe and many old and famous States have fallen or may fall into the grip of the

Gestapo and all the odious apparatus of Nazi rule, we shall not flag or fail. We shall go on to the end, we shall fight in France, we shall fight on the seas and oceans, we shall fight with growing confidence and growing strength in the air, we shall defend our Island, whatever the cost may be, we shall fight on the beaches, we shall fight on the landing grounds, we shall fight in the fields and in the streets, we shall fight in the hills; we shall never surrender, and even if, which I do not for a moment believe, this Island or a large part of it were subjugated and starving, then our Empire beyond the seas, armed and guarded by the British Fleet, would carry on the struggle, until, in God's good time, the New World, with all its power and might, steps forth to the rescue and the liberation of the old."

Britain stayed true to Churchill's words. Again and again German planes and even the new V-2 rocket rained destruction down on London, the British held fast. After two months of effort, Hitler finally abandoned the idea of invading Britain. And so he turned his attention east.

. . . . .

The non-aggression pact between Germany and the Soviet Union held. The Soviets had focused on fighting Finland – a traditional Russian enemy. But when Germany could not subdue Britain, it shored up the western defenses, and Hitler's gaze wandered east. He knew that the alliance with the Soviets was temporary, and he knew that Germany could not rule Europe unless the mighty and massive Soviets were dealt with.

On June 22, 1941, Hitler launched the greatest assault ever seen in human history, called Operation Barbarossa. He hurled three million men, 600,000 vehicles, and 650,000 horses (in non-combat roles, unlike the Poles) across a massive 1,800 mile front. The Soviets, taken completely by surprise, were thrown back. Entire armies were encircled and either captured or destroyed, and the Red Army fell back against the onrushing Wehrmacht.

Meanwhile, across the globe Japan had imperial designs of its own, and had invaded its traditional enemy, China. For four years the two nations battled in Manchuria, fighting to establish control of the eastern rim of Asia, and its wealth of resources. Japan knew that it needed oil, coal, and precious metals that were not found on its home island, and so sought to acquire them by military conquest. Like Germany, Japan did not want to fight a two-front war, and while Hitler had the Soviets lurking in the east as they crushed the west, Emperor Hirohito knew that the United States lurked to their east, as they fought China in the west.

. . . . .

Philip, with another mouth to feed, needed more money. His job at the park continued, but the pay was insufficient. He, Arnold, and Fred made extra money on the side in Philip's little shop, but that too was insufficient. He asked his superintendent for a raise. The super did not show an interest in helping Philip acquire a raise, being occupied with his own job.

Weeks and months went by and no raise came. Philip had had enough. He told his boss he was leaving.

"You have another job?" the super asked.

"No."

"How you gonna feed your family?"

"The Lord provides. You always say that," Philip replied sardonically.

The superintendent could not understand why Philip, who showed such promise and who definitely needed the work, would quit, just like that. To Philip, it was a matter of principle, and so he left Belmont. He left not without any regrets, however. He had become friends with so many men at the shop, and saying goodbye was extremely difficult.

In May 1941, Philip walked away from Belmont. But he did not yet have a replacement job, and his family wondered what was next. They all, of course, enjoyed the pastime of eating, and without a job, no money meant no food, which meant no eating. That prospect was not encouraging.

Philip tried working for Grumman, which had moved its headquarters from Farmingdale to Bethpage. The man in charge told him there was no opening. He was lying, but there was nothing Philip could do. He next tried Republic Aviation, which had occupied Grumman's old building. He received a polite "no". He drove to Upton where work of all kinds was being done, but he ran into a brick wall of nepotism, kick-backs, and the union – which Philip was not a part – and no job could be found there either.

Back in Bay Shore, Philip managed to secure work with the Kirkup family, who owned a lumberyard and a woodworking shop. Over the years, the Kirkup shop had some of the finest carpenters, turning out some of the finest work, in the entire area. They hired Philip for one, maybe two weeks, as was their policy. They paid him a dollar an hour, which was more than the Parks did, but not enough for his needs. He did not envision a long future there, but a job was a job, and he would end up working there for a full year.

. . . . .

The day that would live in infamy arrived. On December 7, 1941, Japan launched a surprise attack on Pearl Harbor, wiping out most of the U.S. Pacific fleet, and neutering America's ability to wage naval warfare in the Pacific. Japan had a free hand to continue its conquest of east Asia without threat from the United States. In response, the U.S. declared war on Japan. Germany, which had become allied with Japan, declared war on the U.S., which in turn declared war on Germany. The sleeping giant had been awakened from its slumber, and the United States suddenly was at war both in Europe and in Asia. Much had to be done before the U.S. could actually engage in battle.

. . . . .

Philip was playing penne-ante poker with some of his friends, the radio on in the background. Cards were dealt, coins were won and lost, and jokes were made. Suddenly, the radio crackled with the news that Japan had attacked and obliterated the U.S. fleet at Pearl Harbor. The game stopped. The men began talking excitedly, asking questions and giving answers to each other. None knew what was really going on, of course, but they reacted like most of the American population upon hearing the news. The only conclusion they could all agree on was that Japan had thrust the United States – which had so far stayed out of both the European and Asian conflicts – into war. Every American, they believed, now had the duty to get into the war and support the United States.

Young Joe Gagliano, one of Philip's good friends, quit his job and joined the Air Force and became a bombardier. Philip encouraged other young men in the neighborhood to sing up for military service. These boys had such respect for Philip that they rushed to recruiting stations. Philip himself – far too old to join the army – volunteered with the aircraft spotting patrol in Islip and took on the role of air warden.

It was all hands on deck as the U.S. entered World War II.

Chapter 22 – Arkansas

The single propeller biplane flew at a robust top speed of 72 miles an hour, circling 4,000 feet over the German lines. Looking down, pilot Lionel Charlton realized that that the British Expeditionary Force was in trouble. The German troops under General Alexander von Kluck had nearly encircled the men of the B.E.F., contrary to the intelligence that mounted cavalry had reported. Charlton swung round and headed back to base, landed, and explained the situation to the generals on the ground, and so on August 22, 1914, the British began to withdraw from Mons. The lives of 100,000 men were spared thanks to the actions of Charlton. Thus began the era of air power in battle.

Originally, military leaders and governments across Europe did not want airplanes used in battle, for fear of them bombing undefended cities and civilian populations. Their use was restricted to reconnaissance missions like the one Charlton flew. But men being men, eventually airplanes became weaponized. Machine guns were mounted and air-to-air combat began. Moreover, planes were equipped with bombs, which were dropped on enemy troops. War on land, as it had become at sea with the invention and use of U-boats, had become three-dimensional.

Companies quickly realized the potential, and began applying for government contracts to build planes for the military. In the United

States, one of those companies was Grumman. Leroy Grumman had worked for the Loening Aircraft Engineering Corporation, but launched his own company on January 2, 1930. They applied for contracts with the U.S. Navy, and the first aircraft Grumman made for the military was the FF-1, a biplane with retractable landing gear, a special feature that allowed the plane to fly faster with less drag.

Grumman would eventually make many famous airframes for the military. During World War 2, they produced the F4F Wildcat and the F6F Hellcat. In the 1960s, they produced the A6 Intruder and the E-2 Hawkeye, a radar-guidance plane. In the 1970s, they made the EA-6B Prowler and the famous F-14 Tomcat. They also were heavily involved in the U.S. Space Program, producing the famous Apollo Lunar Module and making parts for the space shuttle program.

Grumman's main location was in Bethpage on Long Island, 21 miles from Philip's house in Great River, and at one point it was Long Island's largest corporate employer. Its dependable products engendered Grumman to the U.S. military, which sought their designs and aircraft for decades.

. . . . .

Arnold Elliott was a man of principle, and there were problems at the Belmont Park. Particularly, the management of the park had developed a terrible little habit of irresponsible spending on non-essential projects for themselves at a time when resources were at a premium. As Arnold saw it, the park had begun to look like an independent state, completely isolated and unconcerned with the fate of the rest of the nation; thus, wasteful spending occurred mindlessly – a grave offense to a responsible man like Arnold. Not a man to take irresponsibility lightly, Arnold presented himself before his supervisor, issued his complaint, and promptly found himself unemployed.

Fortunately, Arnold quickly found new work at Grumman. At that time Grumman was building new plants across Long Island, but he discovered that the company was willing to spread out its projects to any other available shop that wanted the work. Arnold's boss at Grumman, Ralph Clark, oversaw a carpenter's shop, a plumbing department, an electrical department, a paint shop, and a labor squad. When Arnold realized that Grumman was interested in giving private shops some work, he approached Ralph, who came over to check on the little shop on Cedarhurst Street.

He met Philip and liked what he saw. He arranged for Philip's immediate hiring, and assigned Philip's garage as an official Grumman shop. Arnold and Philip loved the arrangement, as it meant half the commute for Arnold and a 20 foot commute for Philip. Each man received an extra hour of pay for every week they worked for Grumman out of this shop.

In May 1942, Philip began employment for Grumman, earning more than $67 a week, enough to support his family better and even save some money.

. . . . .

Flip was three years old in 1943, and he made daily trips out to the shop to visit Philip and Arnold. He watched in wonder as the two men hammered and sawed and built whatever it was that Grumman needed them to build. He would bang on the door loudly until, over the din of the machines growling at work, his father would let him in. Flip would never return to the house until Philip or Arnold had let him in.

He would enter and watch and play in the shop while Philip and Arnold worked. He would never forget to say, "See you again, daddy. See you again, Mister Elliott."

Philip beamed with pride at young Flip and saw a lot of promise in him. He always wanted to learn and asked many questions of Philip, Arnold, Antoinette, and his siblings. Occasionally Flip would bruise or cut himself playing, but Philip noticed that Flip never cried. He simply took whatever help they offered, and went about his business.

. . . . .

Philip was also very proud of his older son, Ben. After finishing high school, Ben enlisted in the United States Navy. By this point, the U.S. was fully engaged in two separate theaters in World War II – fighting the Axis powers in Africa and Europe, and the Japanese in the Pacific. 1942 had seen turning points in both theaters, with the defeat of Germany at Stalingrad and the Japanese defeat at Midway. But both enemies were still strong and capable and much was still to be done to bring them to heel.

Ben and Philip celebrated Ben's enlistment by smoking together for the first time. Philip had abstained for ten months but this occasion was the perfect time to resume the rather unhealthy habit to which he had grown accustomed. Antoinette wept as Ben left for boot camp, and with Ben gone, both parents resumed their normal duties. When boot camp was over, Ben was assigned by the U.S. Navy to the *USS Arkansas*.

. . . . .

In 1910, the U.S. Navy contracted with the New York Shipbuilding Construction company to build the latest Wyoming-class dreadnought battleship. Construction was completed in 1912, and just seven months before the *SS Napoli* brought Philip and Biagio across the Atlantic, the U.S. Navy commissioned the ship as the *USS Arkansas*. 562 feet long and displacing 27,243 long tons at full combat load, the *Arkansas* was heavily armed and heavily armored. It possessed 12 twelve-inch guns and 21 five-inch guns, was able to cruise at more than 20 knots, and could launch shells more than 20 miles. Home to more than a thousand men, the *Arkansas* was a ferocious combat platform.

It participated in action in World War I and served as the flagship for the Commander, Battleship Force, in the Atlantic Fleet during the 1920s. During that time, it was modified and modernized with heavier armor and greater displacement. By the time World War 2 came about, the *Arkansas*, though still a worthy vessel, was outdated by newer ships carrying 14 and 16 inch guns. Nevertheless, the *Arkansas* engaged in convoys, protecting merchant ships ferrying men, equipment, and supplies to the European theater.

Ben was assigned to the first battery, feeding powder into a twelve-inch gun. The *Arkansas* could fire nine shells every minute, over and over, launching 2,100 pound projectiles into enemy bunkers, troop formations, fortifications, or other ships. By the time the *Arkansas* got into action in World War 2, the old doctrine of heavy guns blasting away at each other at sea was hopelessly out of date. The invention of the aircraft carrier meant that small planes could deliver devastating blows to these massive ships, and navy warfare soon would feature entire battle groups engaged without even being able to see each other. Planes ruled the seas. But that did not mean that there wasn't a role for these behemoths. Navy doctrine changed, and the battleships began to serve in support capacity, bombarding the enemy on land prior to, and during, land invasions. For hours and even days, ships like the *Arkansas* would batter enemy fortifications, sever communication lines, and demoralize enemy troops, softening the ground for the marines and army troops that were being brought onshore.

. . . . .

Shortly after Ben's enlistment, Philip's sister Giovannina passed away in New Jersey. Philip mourned, as Giovannina was beloved, and Philip regretted that he had not looked out for her more as her older brother. He attended her funeral, saddened by the loss, and thinking back on her life with both fondness and guilt, and he wept.

. . . . .

Philip's oldest daughter, Angelina, was working at Republic Aviation, a place Philip did not think best for her, knowing the ruffian types that populated such plants. But she could handle herself and had made many acquaintances along the way. She would occasionally bring a boy home to meet Philip, Antoinette, and the family, and there were plenty more that were interested. She had grown tall and beautiful and Philip kept a close eye on her.

One day she bumped into a young man with a crooked smile and a sly look in his eyes. They struck up a conversation and quickly hit it off. The boy's name was Frank Skrocki, from Port Chester. His mother had passed away years before, and his father lived until recently before he met Angelina – his unfortunate death occurring when he was hit by a car at night.

Frank's father was Polish, and had been captured by the Russians and pressed into their service. He served as a mounted soldier, but he did not want to be in the Czar's army, and constantly looked for a way to escape. One day he succeeded, and fled into Poland, eventually finding passage across the Atlantic to the United States, where he married and started a family, safe from the Czars.

Frank enlisted in the U.S. Army during World War II, and served in Patton's Third Army, driving a Sherman tank. In one engagement, as he blasted away at German panzers, a German infantryman managed to climb onto his tank and drop a grenade down the hatch. It exploded and killed the entire crew but Frank, who survived, was put back together with bolts and screws, and sent back to the United States. He could not walk without a limp, but he was presentable enough for Angelina.

. . . . .

The Soviet Union battled Nazi Germany over two years, from 1942 to 1943, receiving several hammer blows from the Wehrmacht, surviving them, and returning them in kind. By the time 1944 came about, the Red Army was moving forward, pushing German troops backward across eastern Europe. But Germany was far from a defeated foe, and the Soviets had expended tens of millions of men in the effort.

Winston Churchill and Franklin Roosevelt understood that Josef Stalin was a convenient wartime ally against Hitler, but he was not a man to be trusted. Perhaps the last thing they wanted was to see the Swastika raised all over Europe; but the second-to-last thing they wanted was to see the hammer and sickle raised there instead. They knew that they would have to create a second front to relieve pressure on the Soviets, and ultimately take ground, liberate France, and establish a presence in Europe, not leaving the continent to the communists.

On June 6, 1944, the greatest amphibious invasion in human history was launched against the coast of Normandy, in northern France. Over the course of the day the Allies would land some 156,000 men. But first, they had to secure the beaches.

The previous night, elements from U.S. and British airborne units landed behind German lines, were scattered, but began their missions to cut off communication and secure key intersections in France. Meanwhile, a force made up of mostly American, British, and Canadian units gathered on ships and began their journey across the English Channel. While they loaded into their Higgins boats, American battleships pounded German defenses all along the beach, attempting to knock out fortifications, pillboxes, heavy guns, tanks, and supply lines. Among the ships launching one-ton shells into German positions was the *USS Arkansas*. Ben loaded powder in his twelve-inch gun over and over as the *Arkansas*, firing her guns in anger for the first time in her history, sent hundreds upon hundreds of huge explosives into German targets, hoping to help clear the way for the infantry landing on the beaches. For hours the *Arkansas* rained destruction on Omaha beach in Operation Overlord.

Ben and his shipmates loaded the big guns over and over in a ferocious expenditure of arms. When the "cease fire" command came, it was found that the forward section of the wooden cover over the steel decking of the

Arkansas was torn up, not from enemy fire but from concussions caused by her own guns.

The evening of June 6, Ben left the turret, found a tarp on a section of the deck, crawled under it, and went to sleep, resting his head on a sea bag, which he used for a pillow. In the morning when he woke, he discovered that the sea bag was actually the body of a dead sailor.

. . . . .

The invasion was a success, and the Allies had opened the western front. German troops began moving backward as Allied armies began the march to Berlin.

On June 25, the *Arkansas* bombarded German positions near the French port of Cherbourg, in support of the American attack there. She fell under German fire, and though there were many close calls – one time the Germans had the *Arkansas* bracketed – there were no hits. The next day the Allies took Cherbourg, and the port was open to Allied troops and supplies.

A week later, after a quick refit and resupply in Northern Ireland, the *Arkansas* set sail for the Mediterranean, as Allied forces launched another attack, this time on the southern coast of France in Operation Dragoon. Tens of thousands of men landed, the beaches having been prepared by an armada led by the *Arkansas* and six cruisers. Yet another front was opened as Allied forces slowly began to crush the Wehrmacht.

Following the successful invasion of southern France, the *Arkansas* sailed to the United States, arriving in Boston on September 14, for another refit and resupply. In Boston, the men were granted leave, and Ben caught a train from Boston down to New Haven, where Philip and Antoinette had driven to meet him. It was a wonderful family reunion.

. . . . .

Two months after picking his son Ben up in New Haven, Philip left Grumman. The company had moved into new plants and had stopped using most of the small shops it had employed until then – Philip's included. Philip was giving the opportunity to continue to work with Grumman, only it had to be in the new, windowless shop of plant number three. He declined, and tried his hand at being a fully independent builder. Unfortunately, work did not come fast enough to satisfy his needs, and in the spring of 1945, he landed a job at Republic Aviation, who put him to work in the experimental department. The work was fine; the night shift to which they assigned him was not, and so a month later, he was back in his own shop.

He discovered that owning an independent business came with both pros and cons. He had a short commute, he was his own boss, and he could work when he wanted to. But he had to hustle to find jobs, and customers – with whom he never had to deal while working for Belmont, Grumman, or even Republic Aviation – were often difficult to deal with. His ulcers, which had begun some years earlier, were gaining on him.

. . . . .

Task Force 54 was a fearsome collection of U.S. Navy warships. It was comprised of six battleships, four cruisers, and sixteen destroyers. In January 1945, the *Arkansas*, which had made its way from the Atlantic to California, departed for Pearl Harbor, which had been rebuilt following the Japanese attack three years prior. From there, the *Arkansas* sailed for the Ulithi atoll in the southeastern Pacific, some 1,300 miles east of Manila, in preparation for the attack on Japan.

On February 16, the Task Force, not yet at Ulithi, was stationed off Iwo Jima, a small but strategic island that was a critical part of General MacArthur's "island hopping" campaign. It was close enough for U.S. fighters and bombers to raid Japan directly. Both MacArthur and the Japanese were well aware of this, and both sides fought with great intensity to gain control of the island. The island finally was secured after great bloodshed – some 6,800 American and 18,917 Japanese fighting men died in the battle – and the *Arkansas* continued her journey to the Ulithi atoll. From there, on March 21, the battle group sailed for Okinawa, and four days later the *Arkansas* sat a mile off shore. On March 25, the U.S. Marines landed on Okinawa's beaches, with the *Arkansas* slamming away at Japanese strong points.

Ben and his mates loaded and reloaded shell after shell, along with the massive packs of gun powder needed to launch them, over a period of 46 days, providing support for the men fighting to capture Okinawa. The ship and its crew fired 2,646 twelve-inch shells, 3,240 five-inch shells, and 2,835 rounds of anti-aircraft shells. Ben was below decks, and could not see the frightening and unforgettable image of Japanese kamikazes diving in suicidal attacks on the *Arkansas*. The Japanese, in desperation, tried numerous kamikaze attacks on the ships, including the *Arkansas*, but none struck her. At the cost of 12,520 men lost, the Americans emerged victorious. The end was in sight for Imperial Japan.

Remarkably, Ben and the *Arkansas* were directly involved in four of the biggest battles in the entire war: D-Day, southern France, Iwo Jima, and Okinawa. The *Arkansas*, despite being old and antiquated, had acquitted herself incredibly well.

. . . . .

The Soviets pressed in on Berlin from the east, and the Allies from the west. With Hitler trapped in an underground bunker, he committed suicide along with his love, Eva Braun. The Germans surrendered on May 8, 1945, and the battle in Europe was over.

Japan held out longer, despite the U.S. being right on their doorstep. Once Hitler was defeated, the Soviets declared war on Japan and joined the fray in the Pacific. Japan still would not give up. On August 6, the incredible power of the atom was unleashed on Hiroshima as Little Boy unleashed the power of 16 kilotons of TNT, vaporizing people and destroying the city. Three days later, another atomic bomb – Fat Boy – was dropped on Nagasaki. Even more powerful than Little Boy, the second bomb produced a 22 kiloton blast. Combined, the atomic bombs obliterated two whole cities and killed 120,000 people instantly, and many tens of thousands more due to radiation. On August 14 (in the U.S., August 15 in Japan), faced with total destruction, the Emperor surrendered, and the war in the Pacific was over. On September 2 the formal surrender took place aboard the *USS Missouri*.

. . . . .

The family had hoped to see Ben on Christmas in 1945, now that the war was over. The *Arkansas* had finished her job, her service covered in glory. Antoinette had convinced herself that he would make it home by then, and spruced the house up for his arrival. Typically, they would have cut their own tree down, but this year, being special, they bought one, and when it was delivered, they all saw the problem right away. It was too big to get in the door. Flip suggested that daddy look at it, and Philip went for a saw.

Antoinette was aghast – the tree was perfect and should not be cut.

"Not the tree!" she said in agony.

"No," Philip replied, smiling. "The door." He took measurements of the doorway and of the room inside and made some quick mental calculations.

"Might have to cut the ceiling a bit and maybe part of the roof," he added.

Antoinette was on the verge of tears. The only options left were to cut the doorway and ceiling, trim the tree, or exchange it for a smaller one. Grieving for the loss, she agreed to have Philip trim the tree. Once the job was complete, Philp told her he was proud of having accomplished a blivy.

"What's that?" she asked.

"It's not in the dictionary but in the good old Dixie lingo, a blivy is putting ten gallons of julep in a five gallon jug." He smiled and kissed her gently. "But I've done it for you." Antoinette smiled sheepishly and prepared the tree for Ben's arrival.

But Ben did not make it for Christmas. Demobilization took longer than they hoped

The *Arkansas* made its journey back to the United States, making port in Seattle. Ben was discharged on March 6, 1946, and he joined thousands of other servicemen on a crowded train heading east. Days later, he finally arrived in Great River, and the entire family enjoyed a most joyous reunion. Ben told war stories, drank with Philip, and admired Philip's new white dentures.

. . . . .

In August, the family prepared for Angelina and Frank's wedding. Philip recalled that it is a thrilling thing for a young woman to get ready for her own nuptials, quite a headache for her smiling mother, and a nightmare for her laughing father, as he sees the dollars leave his wallet by the droves.

There was plenty of fuss and noise about all things wedding-related: dresses, veils, shoes, gloves, tiaras, rings, orange blossoms, traveling clothes, churches, priests, and honeymoons. On September 8, Angelina was given to Frank, and the two of them settled in Port Chester.

Much the same as Antoinette had experienced upon marrying Philip, Angelina began to miss her mother, and Frank, the ever loving and dutiful husband, would take her to visit once a week. Over time, the trips grew less frequent as both mother and daughter adjusted to married life.

. . . . .

The *USS Arkansas* had one last mission to accomplish. The atomic age having been ushered in by the Manhattan Project and the two bombs that forced Japan to surrender, it rushed forward with breathtaking speed. Once men knew how to harness the power of the atom, they quickly sought to make bigger and more destructive weapons using this power. The military and government wanted to know how such weapons would work in the air, underground, and in the water. Tests were done in Nevada and in the Pacific. One such test was done on the Bikini Atoll in the Pacific, part of the Marshall Islands.

Bikini had been cleared of all people, and the military had brought in numerous old ships to be part of the experimental detonation. The *Arkansas*, retired from active duty, was one of the ships to be destroyed in the Bikini nuclear test. She sat on calm waters when the blast came out of the depths. A huge geyser of hot water exploded upward from the submerged blast. A vast cloud of smoke and steam engulfed the unfortunate ships, and they experienced a power unlike anything before. No amount of enemy shells, no torpedoes or even kamikazes could unleash the power that had just detonated below the surface. The *Arkansas* was lifted like a toy out of the water and dropped, and when the blast was over, the *Arkansas* was no more. What was left of her settled to the bottom of the ocean, where it remains to this day.

. . . . .

Ben's adjustment to civilian life was relatively seamless, all things considered. He tried his hand at a few occupations, to no avail, but finally discovered where his gifts lay. He had run into a former schoolmate named John Carpentieri. John was building a new chimney, laying bricks while Ben engaged him in conversation during a visit. Ben was intrigued, not only by the bricklaying, but by the fact that John was…working. Was this the same John who had never wanted to work, but only wanted to play? Well, people grow up, and John had grown responsible. Marriage had burdened him with the need to actually earn money and do house projects to make his bride happy. As he lay course after course of brick, Ben watched and learned. He asked John if he could try. John laughed and said of course.

Ben progressed rapidly in his abilities, so much so that he amazed John, Philip and Antoinette, and even his friends. In a few short months he got so good with bricks and mortar that people with masonry needs began to seek him out. Ben's post-military career had gotten off to a smashing start.

That's not all the success Ben had following the war. He had met Hermine Zika, a daughter of Austrian parents living in America, but who had been raised by her grandmother in Vienna after her parents had a falling out. Her brother Rudolph, who was born in Austria, was conscripted into Hitler's army and sent south into Italy. Hermine survived the war and when it was over, had received passage to the United States, the place of her birth.

She was old enough to work, and had a job with one of Ben's sisters in a ceramics factory in Islip. She was soon introduced to Ben, and a romance between the two resulted in a wedding in St. Patrick's church in Bay Shore in 1948. By the time Ben had met John building his chimney, Ben and Hermine (who would become known as "Minnie") had been married and produced a son, also named Biagio.

· · · · ·

Minnie's grandmother in Vienna had become ill and Minnie and Ben decided it was best for her to go stay with her grandmother for a while. She made the trip, discovered that her grandmother was on the mend, stayed a little while, and returned back home. A year later, their second son, Jimmy, was born. Ben was doing wonderfully as a mason, and Minnie was excelling as a mother. Years later a half-sister, Michele, would be introduced to the family.

· · · · ·

Steve Rapuano, at the age of 64, moved into the old chicken coop behind Philip's house. It was by then, of course, no longer a chicken coop, but rather a small dwelling that Philip had finished shortly before. He struggled with his health thanks to his prodigious drinking habit, which brought about dim eyes, a halted gait, and a far-too-large belly. Steve was grateful for his daughter and son-in-law for granting him a place to stay – it was, of course, the reverse of when he had put Philip up decades before.

Drinking was Steve's only passion and solace, and Antoinette and Philip let him be until he would become wobbly and obstreperous. At that point the bad language came out and Philip would have to settle him down. In his sober periods, Steve proved himself quite helpful around the house. He tended the plants in the summer, helped keep Philip's shop clean year-round, and did little odd jobs that needed to be done. He wished to do his part around the home.

For all Steve's faults, he was a nice man with an attractive personality that Philip always gravitated towards. Steve was likable – even lovable – when he was sober, anyway, and his winning smile and sense of humor engendered himself to people. He loved children, and they loved him back. He had many silly moments, like the time he stepped on a rake and the handle lurched up to smack him in the face.

Steve's stay with Philip lasted nearly ten years.

. . . . .

Philip's fourth child, Anna, had graduated from high school and had grown into a beautiful young woman. After trying her hand in a sewing shop, she began to work at the ceramics factory, where she met Minnie, and subsequently, introduced her to her brother Ben.

One day at a soda shop, she met a man named Charles Golden. Fritz (Feliciano) Tartaglia had a daughter named Marion, who introduced Charles and Anna to one another. Charles was born with the name Charles Titone. His mother remarried to Knute Golden and that marriage allowed her to change her sons' last names as well. Charles and his brother Robert became Charles and Robert Golden. Charles and Knute would have a daughter named Marie not long afterward.

Charles – everyone called him Charlie – was a terrific husband to Anna. He worked hard and was a good provider. He loved Anna with his whole heart and the two of them were unobtrusive and self-effacing, two traits that Philip admired. They never asked for anything, and it did not appear they had many needs, thanks to the way the two of them worked together in building their life as a couple.

In the years following World War II, Philip could boast two sons-in-law and one daughter-in-law. Things were perking up.

Chapter 23 – Internment

Pasquale DeCicco immigrated to the United States from Italy in 1903, and over a six year period, went through the process to become a naturalized American citizen. He rose to prominence in the city of New Haven, serving as acting vice consul of the city's Italian consulate. He enjoyed a wonderful reputation in the city, representing the Italian community in New Haven, and proudly living and working as an American.

When the First World War began, Italy sided with France and England against Germany and Austria-Hungary. When the United States entered the war following a period of neutrality, DeCicco's two beloved nations – his homeland and his adopted country – were allies. But DeCicco, before the U.S. entered the war as it proclaimed in strong terms its neutrality, decided to enlist with Italy, much as Biagio was urging Philip to do. He fought bravely and survived the war, returning to Connecticut when his service was finished.

Forty-two other members of his family, over numerous years, had immigrated as well and had become U.S. citizens. New Haven had a large contingent of Italian-Americans from the DeCicco clan, who loved their native country, but who loved their new citizenship as well, having chosen to make their lives in America.

. . . . .

In 1935, the FBI had begun a secret campaign to identify and investigate individuals the U.S. government feared had ties to communist or Nazi organizations. By 1938, they had comprised a list of 2,500 individuals they considered to either be communists or Nazis, or at least be sympathizers. As the world lurched uneasily towards war, President Franklin Roosevelt placed FBI director J. Edgar Hoover in charge of all counterespionage and counterintelligence, and Congress held meetings discussing the establishment of concentration camps for political extremists and disloyal citizens. The government had a list of some ten million persons that the FBI was monitoring.

At the same time, Hoover initiated the creation of a "custodial detention index", otherwise known as the "ABC lists", which was a master list of civilians the FBI considered to be a threat to some degree or another; these individuals could be arrested and detained in case war broke out, each person being put in one of three levels of perceived danger to the U.S.

The majority of German and Italian citizens on these lists were U.S. citizens.

In 1940, Congress passed the Alien Registration Act, forcing some 4.9 million foreign-born residents who were not yet citizens to be fingerprinted and placed in a national registry. Justification for this came from the Alien Enemy Act of 1798, which gave the President the authority to detain or deport resident alien individuals in time of war. In 1940, however, the Alien Enemy Program, headed by Hoover, also targeted naturalized citizens who were born in enemy countries. Hoover made it clear he was concerned about, as he put it, "the naturalized citizen whose cloak of citizenship is a sham and is dangerous to the nation's security."

The U.S. Navy and Coast Guard began moving against Italian ships. On March 30, 1941, the Coast Guard detained and confiscated some twenty-eight Italian ships, arresting the crews on the charge of attempted sabotage. In December, the Italian luxury liner *Conte Biancamano* was boarded at the Panama Canal, captured, and turned into an American troop ship, re-commissioned the *USS Hermitage*. Its 483 Italian crewmen were taken into custody and detained at Ellis Island. They were then transferred by train to a detention center in Missoula, Montana, where they were held indefinitely.

When Japan attacked Pearl Harbor, the United States responded with a declaration of war against Japan and Germany, but not yet Italy. Nevertheless, the government immediately began arresting men and women of Italian descent under Hoover's program. By the time the U.S. declared war on Italy on December 11, 147 other Italians were already in custody by U.S. officials. Often there was no more evidence against these people other than the fact that they were of Italian descent; they had committed no crimes, and had never indicated any hostility of any kind against the United States.

U.S. Attorney General Francis Biddle had explained to Roosevelt his plan for internment, after New York Mayor Fiorella LaGuardia had warned Biddle, "You're not going to do what you did to the Japanese. The Italians of the East Coast will form into a revolutionary army and we will march on Washington."

Undeterred, Biddle explained his plan to Roosevelt, who replied in an approving tone, "And you're going to intern all of them?"

"Well, not quite," replied Biddle.

"I don't care about the Italians," continued Roosevelt. "They are a lot of opera singers, but the Germans are different; they may be dangerous."

. . . . .

Frank DiCara was 14 years old, living in an Italian neighborhood in Baltimore called Highlandtown. He heard the news that Japan had bombed Pearl Harbor, and knew that the U.S. was thrust into the now global conflict. His parents had arrived from Sicily in the early 1910s, and to them, the news was particularly horrifying. The DiCaras understood that in an instant, their beloved homeland was the enemy of the nation to which they had since pledged their citizenship, decades ago. They realized that they couldn't even talk about their native Sicily without risking treason.

The next few years were dark for the DiCara family, all of whom were American citizens. Wherever they went, they faced hostility and prejudice. People shunned them. They were called the traditional Italian slurs – "*dago*", "*wop*", and "*guinea*". These were terms Frank had heard before, of course, as by the 1920s, the U.S. generally expressed the view that Italians were a separate race from Anglo-Americans, lesser people of color with strange customs, dark skin, and an unhealthy attachment to alcohol and crime. But it was worse, of course, once war broke out.

He feared going into certain parts of the city, concerned for his own safety, just for being of Italian descent. Frank, of course, was born in the U.S., and had never personally even visited Italy. His parents had been American citizens for more than twice as long as they lived in Italy. But none of that mattered. Italy – the nation of their heritage – was the enemy of the U.S., and so the DiCaras were looked upon with scorn and derision.

Immediately following Pearl Harbor, the government arrested 10 Italians in Baltimore. Two months later, officials entered the DiCara home and confiscated their short wave radio. Agents from the FBI routinely made surveillance visits to Highlandtown, as all Italians were now under suspicion, whether they were U.S. citizens or not.

They faced regular harassment from neighbors and from the police. They felt, like many Italians, that they had to prove their love for America, and as a result, Italians served in the U.S. military in World War II at a higher rate than any other nationality. Frank served in the U.S. Army, fighting in the Pacific theater, while his two brothers saw combat in Europe.

. . . . .

President Roosevelt's famous 1942 Executive Order 9066 established a host of concentration camps all along the west coast of the U.S. Some 120,000 Japanese-Americans were uprooted from their homes and taken to these camps, a grave injustice that can be read about in most American history books. What is virtually never talked about in those same history books is that EO 9066 also called for the forced relocation of some 10,000 Italian-Americans, many to the very same camps where the Japanese-Americans were held, and restricted the movement of some 600,000 more Italians in the U.S.

. . . . .

On April 24, 1942, Pasquale DeCicco heard a knock on the door. He opened it to find FBI agents standing there. Within moments, Pasquale was under arrest and taken into custody. His crime? He was Italian. He was also 63 years old and had been by that time a pillar in the community. He was taken to Boston where he was fingerprinted, photographed, and held for three months. From there he was transferred to a detention center on Ellis Island.

No hearing was scheduled, and Pasquale was taken to an immigration facility at Fort Meade, Maryland. On July 31, he was declared to be an "enemy alien" of the United States. His service for Italy in World War I – despite being an American ally in that war – was held against him. He wrote numerous letters pleading his loyalty to the U.S., to no avail. He was charged with no crime, and no evidence of him being any sort of enemy was ever brought against him. He was nonetheless held captive until December 1943, months after Italy's surrender to the Allies. During his incarceration, he lost 32 pounds.

. . . . .

EO 9066 gave the FBI and law enforcement license to not only arrest and imprison Italians with no evidence other than that they were Italian (the same was true of Japanese-Americans and German-Americans as well), but also to seize homes and businesses run by Italians. Earl Warren, who would later become a Chief Justice of the U.S. Supreme Court, was at the time the Attorney General of California, and he was vigilant and relentless in registering "enemy aliens" for detention.

. . . . .

Joe DiMaggio was perhaps the most famous baseball player in America when World War II broke out. He played centerfield for the great New York Yankees, was the American League's Most Valuable Player, and had set a record by getting hits in 56 consecutive games. He was a national icon by every definition of the word. He was a first generation American, as his parents had immigrated to the United States, but were not citizens. When the U.S. got involved in the war, DiMaggio enlisted in the U.S. military, sacrificing several years in the prime of his life in order to serve his country. It would have been difficult to find a more loyal American.

Joe's father Giuseppe owned a restaurant on Fisherman's Wharf in San Francisco. California was particularly aggressive in enforcing EO 9066, and officials cracked down on any and every "enemy alien" in their jurisdiction. Italians were restricted from the coast and barred from any port or harbor. Giuseppe, though not arrested and taken to a camp, found that his livelihood was destroyed, the fishing industry – largely operated by Italians – was nearly wiped out. Giuseppe was unable to even show up to run his restaurant. He could not find new employment due to his "enemy alien" status.

He would only be able to return many months later, joking that he had to look after "Joe's restaurant".

. . . . .

Josie Patania's brothers were fishermen off the coast of Gloucester, Massachusetts. Carmelo, Angelo, and Vincent discovered one day that the government had commandeered their fishing vessel, with the purpose of turning it into a patrol boat. They forcibly removed Josie's father from the boat and he managed to find work in the local spinach plant. Carmelo, Angelo, and Vincent did what many young Italian men did; enlisted in the U.S. military. Vincent would fight in Normandy and Carmelo in the Philippines.

Frank Firicano likewise fished off the eastern Massachusetts coast. Convoys routinely sailed from Boston harbor, and officials set up a vigorous security system for any and all boats coming in and out. Firicano had to have a password every day in order to leave or return. He had to go to a Customs House to get clearance and a pass, and then go through a Coast Guard inspection barge off Deer Island, where his boat was searched for contraband that he might be bringing the enemy. He was not allowed to use his radio except in case of extreme emergency.

. . . . .

In Pittsburg, California, some 2,000 Italians were ordered to leave. Many were fishermen, and their boats were impounded and confiscated. They had no other trade, and many lost their homes. At no point were they told of their "crime". They were simply relocated for being "enemy aliens", which meant nothing more than that they were Italian.

Popular opera singer Ezio Pinza was arrested on March 12, 1942, removed from his home, and was for a time imprisoned on Ellis Island. In May, California Assemblyman Jack Tenny targeted Italians for disloyalty and for "treasonous" actions; San Francisco mayor Angelo Rossi was accused of giving a Fascist salute.

. . . . .

Nino Guttadauro was an American citizen who had years earlier worked as an accountant for the Italian consulate in San Francisco. His name landed on the FBI lists when J. Edgar Hoover wrote of him that, "It is recommended that this individual (Guttadauro) be considered for custodial detention in the event of an actual emergency." Of course, the FBI had no evidence of any wrongdoing by Nino, nor had he shown any signs of treason; yet his past employment was enough to put him on the list.

Eleven months later, in August 1942, he was handed a custodial detention card and ordered to leave his home. The U.S. assistant attorney general had actually written a letter in support of Nino, saying that there was no evidence against him. The FBI did not listen, and he was required to show up at a special hearing. He arrived at the Whitcomb Hotel on September 8 for his hearing, and was promptly told that he would not be able to learn who his accusers were, nor receive any information as to the nature of the accusation itself. Moreover, he was denied any legal counsel.

Nino had served the U.S. honorably in World War I, but that service counted for nothing at his hearing. He was declared a threat to public safety in California, and officers barred him from traveling to or living in roughly half of the United States. The government pressed to remove his citizenship, and for the next three years fought off investigations and interrogations, hounded by the government every step of the way. He moved his family to Salt Lake City, where he went to work as a grocery clerk.

. . . . .

Thousands of Italian families were uprooted and decimated. Italian businesses were destroyed. The wave of anti-Italian sentiment swept the nation, and the government violated the civil rights of thousands of its citizens – and hundreds of thousands of non-citizens who had been living and working peaceably in the U.S. for years – simply on the grounds that they were Italian.

All the while, Italians signed up to fight for America at a higher percentage than any other ethnic group in the country.

. . . . .

Prominent Italian politicians began to push back, led by LaGuardia. Finally, on Columbus Day of 1942, EO 9066 was rescinded verbally (though not legally). President Roosevelt, knowing he needed the support of Italian-Americans if the U.S. was to successfully invade Italy (which was in the works), delivered a speech recognizing Italian-Americans as patriotic citizens, and the "enemy alien" status was removed, though for many of those who were interned, it would still be months or even years before they were allowed to go home. Columbus Day, because of Roosevelt's speech and the resulting freedom that came with it which began that day, became imbued with special significance for Italian-Americans, as it became the turning point in how the nation perceived people of Italian descent.

For decades, Italians were considered lesser people. Associated with organized crime, strange religious and cultural practices, bootlegging, and other vices, Italians were considered to be people of color barely a step above African-Americans. The government itself, from racist statements made by Teddy Roosevelt and Woodrow Wilson, to laws passed in the 1920s designed specifically to restrict Italian immigration, to EO 9066, embarked on a decades-long campaign of persecuting Italian-Americans and treating them with prejudice. And this, despite Italian-Americans making some of the most remarkable contributions in American society over that time period.

Italian-Americans called the awful EO 9066 chapter in American history *una storia segreta* – the secret story, or secret history. History books routinely discussed the horrendous treatment Japanese-Americans received during World War II, but never mentioned similar treatment doled out to Italians in the U.S. Remarkably, EO 9066 was still on the books as a law until 1976, when President Gerald Ford officially and legally rescinded the order. In 2000, Congress passed a bill that ordered a full review of the treatment of Italian-Americans during World War II, and the report was issued two months after the 9/11 attacks. It affirmed the idea that the behavior of the U.S. government towards Italians living in America was wrong, and formally apologized for its grave error.

In 2010, the California legislature passed a resolution apologizing for the American mistreatment of Italians living in the state during the war, making note of the various restrictions and offenses, as well as the destruction of family business and enterprise.

. . . . .

Frank DiCara was grateful for the government report and apologies, but the memory of mistreatment for him and for so many that still live long after those terrible events took place, lived on.

"My nephew always says, 'Uncle Frank, remember when you four were all in the service and they came and took the shortwave radio out of the house?' I say, 'Yeah, I remember.'"

Chapter 24 – Passeggiata

The sun drew low in the sky and in the town of Biscari, and the townsfolk emerged from their homes after a day of work. Biagio and Angela, newly married and enjoying life alone as a couple, put on some of their nicer clothes – which, to be fair, were still quite modest – and joined hundreds of others in town in a leisurely stroll. The town's few streetlamps were lit, but there was still some light from the fading sun, enough to see the warm faces of people they knew. They walked slowly, hand in hand, taking in the sights and sounds of the town and its people.

The warm Mediterranean air, pushed by a soft breeze, wafted through their hair. They walked down the street and encountered some friends – Giovanni and Isabella Caprese – and chatted. Biagio released Angela's hand, and she took her friend's. Biagio said to Giovanni, "*Andiamo a fare qualche vasca,*" which meant "let's do some laps", and Giovanni clapped his friend on the back as the two men took up positions in front of their wives.

Biagio and Giovanni talked about goings on in the world and at their work. Angela and Isabella talked about the latest town happenings – Angela had no need to really know all this but Isabella liked to share and, well, it was the custom for women to gossip as they walked. For the people of Biscari, this leisurely stroll was not just a way to get a little exercise, it was a social engagement. They passed numerous eligible young ladies showing off their smiles and best clothing, hoping that an eligible young man would notice. Their social saunter was being repeated in virtually every town all over Italy.

It was known as the *passeggiata*, a word that has no direct translation into English, but it comes from the root word *passeggiare*, which means "to walk". But *passeggiata* is not just any old walk. It is a leisurely stroll, but even the word "stroll", while probably the most accurate translation, lacks the power and resonance that *passeggiata* has in Italian culture. The *passeggiata* is a social event, where people all over town come to the town center or seafront and walk casually, chit-chatting about all sorts of things, presenting themselves in their finer clothing, and enjoying pleasant human interaction with friends and family.

Biagio loved the *passeggiata*, and he loved it so much that he developed his entire life's philosophy around the idea. He called the entire span of life, from the cradle to the grave, a *passeggiata*, or *The Passeggiata* – the ultimate walk. It was to him a stroll in one direction, not looking back or going back, only forward. To Biagio, it was crucial for each individual to make the stroll of life, their own *passeggiata*, with care, as it only comes once and is never to be repeated. Without taking care, one might fall into a snare or pit that life often presented to a person.

Biagio understood that there would be sunshine and rain, joy and sadness, love and resentment, thrill and agony, success and failure, elation and frustration – every possible emotion a human could have – but regardless of the season of life one was in, their *passeggiata* always moved inexorably forward.

Biagio was a simple man. Not simple-minded; goodness no, anything but that. But he had simple tastes and a simple philosophy of life that expressed itself in a handful of truisms that he passed on to Philip. True wealth, for example, lay not in the relative material abundance one might possess, but rather in the number and quality of friends he might enjoy. The physical needs a man might have were few: food, clothing, shelter, and learning. Anything beyond that was cupidity – excess and tendency towards greed. These were traits that Biagio despised, and taught Philip to despise as well. For Philip, then, his modest home and modest belongings were more than sufficient, because he had wonderful friends and a family that would make any man proud. He was grateful beyond measure.

. . . . .

Over the course of his life, Philip remembered and wrote down a handful of sayings Biagio had often repeated, which served as life lessons, which helped shape a philosophy.

"Because there is so much of the sad in it, the world seems to hold little happiness. Because of the cost of ugliness covering our world, it is difficult for morals to see the beauty it is endowed with. Many people are prone to notice the hurts more than the favors they receive in their lives. Complaint in varied nuances is a profitable habit for connivers, but by degrees it loses favorable response, the practitioners of this game usually become isolated and forgotten. They have failed to find beauty in honesty. There is comfort and much beauty in self-denial, stoicism, charity, forgiveness, cleanliness, love for God and man, thankfulness for God's favors in the simplest sign of friendship, in another day to live and bask in its sun."

Philip took from these words the idea that it's easy to complain and focus on the offenses and hurts one might receive in life. The reality is, everyone receives many offenses and hurts in life, and for Biagio – and subsequently, his son and pupil Philip – some people practically make a living being offended and dwelling on the harm they've experienced. Instead of living in these offenses, life is much more beautiful if we focus on the simple blessings of life that come our way.

"If a man were to hate the world seven days a week it would be a tragedy. If he hated it one hundred percent on Monday, sixty percent on Wednesday, forty percent on Friday morning, and a half of one percent at 11:30 Friday night, chances are he would hate nobody on Saturday and love everybody on Sunday. That would be not only beautiful, it would be acceptable in the eyes of God."

For Biagio, even a little love went a long way. Recall the story of his forgiving the man who tried to steal figs from his tree back in Biscari. Biagio lived out his philosophy as consistently as he could, and that made an impression on Philip his whole life.

"If a man committed a crime and asked to be punished for it, I believe it would be beautiful; some lawyer might have to learn a different profession for his daily bread and that would be beautiful."

Biagio taught Philip the value of personal responsibility. If a man did something wrong, it was important that he own up to it. Biagio considered it immoral for a man to commit a wrong and then to try to find a way out of it, especially by skillful manipulation of the law. If every man was responsible for his own actions, the world would be a much better place.

"Were the final words '...and may God have mercy on your soul' followed by the words 'for men cannot have mercy on your body and your mind', not only it would ennoble the society of man, it would be beautiful. How much more beauty there would be in life if no one were to utter those words, nor anyone be compelled to hear them!"

For Biagio and Philip, compassion, love, and forgiveness were essential components to human morality, and formed the cornerstones of a worldview that shaped their decision-making. They were not flawless men, of course, but they both understood the value of family, of friends, and of loving and forgiving others. This is not to say that neither man harbored no bitterness or resentment in their hearts. Both had little patience for wicked men. At one point Philip would say of Stalin that in the 1950s, he did the only decent thing in his life: he died. Nevertheless, the simple virtues of relationship: love, kindness, gratitude, and forgiveness – these were hallmarks of Biagio and Philip.

Biagio's *passeggiata* was his own to live. But as a philosophy, he passed it down to Philip. When Philip wrote his memoirs and put them into book form, he titled it *Passeggiata*.

. . . . .

Biagio had his own life and philosophy, but it was not divorced from Sicilian tradition. One of those traditional views that he passed on to Philip was the importance of the family name. Vampatella is, like *passeggiata*, a word without a direct translation. It is really a unique mix of two terms that when put together, produce a rough meaning of "little fire". Like most Italians, Biagio believed it was important for the family name to carry on. As Italians follow the tradition of the wife taking on the family name of the husband, having a son was therefore a matter of great importance. Having two sons was a gift from God and insurance for the name's legacy.

Accordingly, Philip's son Ben was of tremendous importance for Philip. After three more daughters – each of whom blessed Philip immensely – the birth of his sixth child, Flip, had Philip beaming with pride, and exhaling with relief that the family name now had two possible routes.

Philip had always imagined the Vampatella family name flourishing in generations past in Sicily, but wars, plagues, famine, poverty, and an abundance of girls being born had, Philip theorized, reduced the family name down to a scant few. Philip was the oldest son of Biagio, but his other brothers had all died in infancy, so it was up to Philip to pass along the family name. He had, in his mind, a sacred duty to have at least one son. Ben's birth secured that, but Flip's...ah, well, now *that* was something. Having not one but *two* sons that could possibly have progeny? Philip was ecstatic.

Despite his elation at having two sons, Philip was wary of Ben's entering the Navy. After all, many young men died in war, and death seemed indiscriminate. If a shell struck the *Arkansas*, it would only be a matter of luck – good or bad – whether a sailor lived or died. Every piece of news Philip got from Ben was good news – it meant his eldest son was alive. When he returned home from the war fully healthy, Philip thanked God – yet another blessing he would not be remiss in noting.

. . . . .

The community in which Philip, Antoinette, and the children lived was filled with Italian-Americans. In most of those homes, Italian was the predominant language, especially if the family was of recent immigrant status. This made sense, as Italian was the mother tongue, and every generation living under the same roof would be raised in whatever Italian dialect was spoken there.

Philip, however, had another perspective. In the Vampatella home, they spoke English. Philip reasoned that he had moved to America, had become an American, and English was the language of America. He took great pride in learning English – everything from grammar to lexicon to the subtleties and nuances that every language possessed. English is not a Romance language like Italian, and so Philip, from the very first moment he set foot on Ellis Island, worked very hard making sense of it, and, frankly, struggled a great deal in his English education. But his work had paid off, and he had become fluent in English, albeit with a Sicilian accent. In his home, even though his children would naturally learn English simply by living in an American neighborhood and going to American schools, wanted his home to be English-speaking. It was, as he viewed it, not a turning away from his Italian heritage, but rather a full embracing of his adopted American one. And so all six of his children, though they picked up some Italian here and there, spoke English exclusively. Their children, in turn, never learned Italian, at least in *their* homes; any such learning would have to come in school.

Philip was proud of his family and family name. He was proud to be an Italian. But he was proud to be an American, and an American he would be. For Philip, the idea of being an Italian-American was not something he considered. He thought that one could remain connected to one's heritage while still fully embracing being an American. If he had ever used the term "Italian-American", the emphasis was on "American".

Philip's own *passeggiata* had led him from Sicily to Long Island. Who knew where it would go from there, but all he knew was that his own stroll through life meant that he was, above any other national identity, an American.

Chapter 25 – Fifties

In the years following the Second World War, Philip's older children were busy adding to the next generation. Ben's oldest, Biagio (Ben Jr.) was born, with Jimmy soon to follow. Meanwhile, Angelina had her first child, Mary Frances, in 1947. Philip was the proud grandfather of three little ones, and meanwhile, his own younger children were growing fast.

Flip was nine years in 1949, and was the apple of his parents' eyes. He was lively, eager to learn, eager to help out in whatever was needed, and quick to shower other members of the family with affection. He was five when his big brother Ben returned from the war, and in Flip's eyes, nobody could be more impressive than his strapping older brother. He was to Flip, everything a young boy could want in a hero.

At school, Flip was very popular with his classmates, children both older and younger than him, his teachers, and adults of all sorts. He worked hard, asked question after question out of sheer curiosity, and always pursued extra assignments in school. He was respectful, thirsty for knowledge, and eager for fun, sports, and work.

Flip slept in the same bed that Philip had made for him upon his birth, located through his first ten years in Philip and Antoinette's bedroom. At ten, he achieved independence and was moved into his own room on the second floor of their small home. Every night he fell asleep quickly, the result of great expenditure of energy at all Flip's activities – school, work, and play.

His work ethic and eagerness to learn prompted Philip to take notice of Flip's potential. Never before had any Vampatella attended college, and though that prospect was still a long ways off, Philip made himself a promise that if Flip showed that kind of potential and interest, he would find a way to make it happen.

. . . . .

In 1951, war broke out again. Korea had, like much of the world, experienced an influx of communism. China had experienced civil war over several decades, but the government was unified under Chiang Kai-Shek, who garnered assistance from the Soviet communists. Japan loomed as a threat, and Chiang tried to modernize China and prepare them for the war with Japan that began in 1937. Though China had vastly larger numbers, it was inferior to the Japanese in every conceivable military way, and Chiang was forced to ally with the United States. When World War II ended, the civil war in China resumed, and Chiang was exiled to Taiwan, where he spent the remainder of his days leading an "independent" (not according to the People's Republic of China) Taiwan. Meanwhile, the communists under Mao Zedong took control of China and began to export communism around the region.

China was not the only nation exporting communism. The Soviet Union sought to expand its influence anywhere and everywhere. Japan had seized control of Korea in 1910, and with their defeat at the hands of the allies in 1945, the United States and the communists both sought to influence the Korean peninsula. At the Cairo conference in 1943, China, Great Britain, and the United States all decided that "in due course Korea shall become free and independent."

When the Soviets declared war on Japan three days after the Hiroshima bomb, the Red Army began moving into the Korean peninsula. Several attempts to hold elections failed, and a "temporary" two-Korea solution was established at the 38th parallel, the location where Japan had surrendered. The Soviets installed a communist government in the north under Kim Il-sung, while the United States established a democratic government in the south under Syngman Rhee. In 1948, the Soviets withdrew their troops from the peninsula, and a year later, the United States followed suit.

Il-sung immediately began supporting the Chinese communists in their civil war against Chiang, providing material and manpower. A link was developing between communist China and communist North Korea. When the Chinese communists won and exiled Chiang to Taiwan, they honored the support of North Korea, and pledged their support in turn to North Korea in the event of war with the south.

The North Koreans sought the support of Stalin as well, and by 1950, he believed that the time was right for war with the democratic south. From Stalin's perspective, he saw this as a golden opportunity. The communists had gained control of China, U.S. troops were out of Korea, and the Soviet Union had even detonated its own atomic device, providing them with something of an equal footing with the United States. In April 1950, Stalin gave his full support to a war, with the condition being that Mao was to provide reinforcements if needed.

War began, and the North Korean troops rolled through Seoul and decimated the already small South Korean army. The United States, as part of a United Nations mission, stepped in to defend the democratic south. President Truman understood the wider implications of this war in Korea, despite the Korean peninsula itself not being of big strategic value for the United States. He saw intervention in Korea as part of a global strategy of containment of communism. He said, "Communism was acting in Korea, just as Hitler, Mussolini and the Japanese had ten, fifteen, and twenty years earlier. I felt certain that if South Korea was allowed to fall, Communist leaders would be emboldened to override nations closer to our own shores. If the Communists were permitted to force their way into the Republic of Korea without opposition from the free world, no small nation would have the courage to resist threat and aggression by stronger Communist neighbors."

Once again, just six years after defeating fascism in Europe and the Japanese empire in Asia, the United States was at war, this time with the communists in Korea.

General MacArthur's forces were thrown back by powerful Korean units, backed by the Chinese. Before long, the American military was backed down to a tiny portion of the peninsula, by Pusan, in desperate need for relief. That relief would come, and the U.S. army, after landing forces behind North Korean lines, began to push north again, taking lost ground. The U.S. sent hundreds of thousands of men and machines to Korea to combat the communist threat.

. . . . .

Philip had no worry that his sons would be called to serve in Korea. Ben had done his duty on the *Arkansas* in WWII, and Flip was too young. But Philip believed he had a duty to help the war effort, so he agreed to go back to work for Grumman, occupying space in the wood shop of the experimental department in plant 5. He had vowed never to work in the windowless shop, but his patriotic duty won out, and before long he grew accustomed to the work space.

By May 1953, with the war looking more and more like a hard-fought draw, with the 38th parallel being the dividing line between a split nation – North Korea above the line, and South Korea below – Philip once again found himself in the hospital. He had fallen unconscious at the toilet bowl, surrounded by large splatters of hemorrhaged blood, caused by his ulcers that had grown more numerous and intense in nature. The doctor rushed him to the hospital, and his recovery took several months. By August, he was back at work, feeling fully healthy.

. . . . .

"Swagger Ed" worked at Grumman with Philip, and joined in a car pool to and from the plant. He was a man whose main passion in life seemed to be to argue. It did not matter the subject – he took a contrary position on anything and everything. He was a a post commander of a military organization, and believed that his status made him an authority on nearly every subject imaginable.

"Now show me in the pages of history," he said regularly. On one occasion he said this, and Jim, a fellow rider replied, "Look between pages 63 and 64." The next day Ed returned with a big grin.

"I didn't find anything between pages 63 and 64," he announced triumphantly. Philip and Jim looked at each other and laughed.

"Next time, split the sheet edgewise – you'll find what you're looking for," Jim said sarcastically.

It took a moment, but Ed finally got the joke.

Ed was not merely a self-proclaimed authority on most everything, he was also a poet of smut. Nearly everything he discussed had to have some connection to pornography. Philip surmised that Ed's education, stemmed in the lower grammar grades, had not risen with age. Ed was a cynic, full of arrogance, flippant, and had total disregard for the feelings of others.

He was, however, skilled at his work. His father was a machinist and had taught Ed how to read rules and scales, how to do trigonometry, how to use the various machines, and even taught him the properties of various metals. Ed's skill was valuable to Grumman, even if his personality was not. Despite his father's patient teaching, Ed never failed to take the opportunity to call his father a "bum" for having failed to give Ed a Christmas present during the Depression. Among other character traits, it appeared Ed was thankless.

He also was slow to realize that other people were not complete morons, but rather individuals with some common sense and intelligence. On one ride, Philip engaged him in conversation about the moon.

"The distance from the earth to the moon is about 240,000 miles," Philip remarked.

"Now tell me another lie," sneered Ed.

Philip paused, grinned, and replied, "You are a gentleman."

The look on Ed's face told it all.

. . . . .

Ten thousand engineers at Grumman flooded the workshops of the different plants with their various ideas. Each man thought of new ways to design aircraft and aircraft parts to maximize flight characteristics, technology, safety, durability, and reliability. Grumman was proud to produce some of the finest aircraft the U.S. military possessed.

Philip was proud to work with such skilled people, all working towards the same goal – to produce excellent planes that would allow U.S. fliers to maximize their chances of returning home alive, and to dispense maximum damage on their missions, in support of U.S. soldiers. Grumman, for two wars now, had served the American military with distinction.

But for Philip, it was more than just the quality of product that Grumman put out. It was the way Grumman treated their employees. All possible opportunity was given to each individual. A man only received his walking papers when he failed entirely to prove himself after an abundance of tries. The leaders of the company, Mr. Grumman and Mr. Swirbul, were held in high esteem. Swirbul was the one mostly in contact with the employees, regardless of their rank or station at the company.

He worked hard and long hours for his company and for his employees. The welfare of both was his constant driving interest. He had worked hard at developing Grumman, and his philosophy was to make a superior product, while at the same time developing superior employees, and the way to do that was to treat them well, treat them with respect, and give them the tools they need to succeed.

When Mr. Swirbul passed away, his body was laid in the Oakwood cemetery in Bay Shore, not far from where Biagio would eventually be buried. His death was, in Philip's estimation, a terrible loss for not just Grumman, but the world.

. . . . .

The Korean War had ended, and the country once again returned to a peacetime footing. Philip's youngest daughter Irene graduated from high school, and secured a job at the Central Islip State Hospital as a stenographer. His daughter Marie had planned a marriage with a good-looking widowed playboy but she called it off when she had seen one too many of his antics. She quit her sewing machine job and, upon visiting her sister Angelina in Greenwich, got a computer job with a publishing house. She lived and worked there until Angelina and her three children – Mary Frances, Frank Jr., and Annette – moved back to Great River in the little hen coop - turned living quarters behind Philip's house.

Ben had two sons and had decided it was time to build himself a house. Anna and her husband Charles had two boys – Charles Jr. and Robert – and lived in nearby Lindenhurst. Flip was doing well in high school and had won citations for leadership and citizenship, had been inducted into the Honor Society, became class president, and had won an American Legion medal. The "cadet", as Philip called him, was moving towards high school graduation, and Philip began saving money for college.

. . . . .

In December of 1953, Philip flew to Florida to visit Fritz and his wife Julie. A friend picked him up in Jacksonville, who drove him the forty miles to St. Augustine, where Fritz owned land. He had not developed the property and had hoped that Philip would help him with it, and move down to Florida with him. Philip loved the idea, but his American roots ran deep on Long Island. His job was on Long Island. His family was on Long Island. He declined Fritz' offer. Fritz understood.

After a few days, it was time to return to New York, and they had a final meal together. Fritz offered Philip a glass of wine.

"I'm afraid of it," Philip said, refusing politely.

"Don't be silly. Drink it," Fritz urged. "It won't harm you."

Philip had not had a drop of wine since the thirties, when Ulrich had gotten him drunk. In 1946 he had celebrated with his brand new son-in-law by drinking some whiskey, and his ulcers paid a dear price for that dalliance. The ulcers were gone but he did not dare touch alcohol of any kind. Moreover, he had despised Steve Rapuano's excess, and Philip had concluded that alcohol only brought misery.

"I'd rather not," he said.

"Oh come on. A glass of wine with your meals is good for you. If it hurts, you don't drink it the next time."

Philip shrugged and after a moment agreed. "Okay. One glass." Fritz smiled and poured him a glass. Philip put it to his lips and the wine slid down his throat. He had expected a harsh, unforgiving experience, but the wine produced a pleasant warmth. He downed the glass and then asked for another.

When he returned home, he did not tell Antoinette about the two glasses of wine. He began to accept the offers of wine on occasion. It was not something he worried about, but these were the first steps down a dark path for Philip.

· · · · ·

In 1956 Philip bought two acres of land directly across from his home on Cedarhurst Street. He had taken great pains to have a lawyer make sure that the land was clear of any legal snags – a lesson he had learned years before – and discovered that the land was owned by a family spread out from Connecticut to California. He secured legal releases from all of them, and went forward with the purchase, acquiring a clear title from the town.

He surveyed the land and plotted the property into three equal parts. He had planned on putting up three houses, one at a time, but the government – ever helpful – stepped in. Philip described the ever-changing zoning laws as the products of "new wizards just out of high school, with little knowledge of building but with an alert eye towards making assets liable to a higher tax assessment." To that end, they issued new regulations requiring a minimum floor area of 1,000 square feet.

Philip had no choice but to comply, and built the first house better and larger than zoning laws required. On inspection, town officials complimented him on the quality of construction, and he put it up for sale. Months went by and Philip grew nervous. He had spent two years on the project, but by 1958, he needed the money for Flip's pending college costs. Philip received a lowball offer, panicked, and sold anyway, getting less than it was worth, but providing him with money he would need to send his youngest son to college.

During this process, Philip was flummoxed by the vagaries of property taxes and tax law. Why, for example, did this new house impact the tax assessment of his older one? What did one have to do with the other? He grew skeptical of government, and considered town officials to be little more than an elite gang of freeloading thieves. He wondered, moreover, where all that tax money went, as the very streets long under town supervision were in such great disrepair.

Later in life, Philip would look back on his attitude towards local government officials with some shame, realizing that they may not have been evil people after all. But he did have experience with immoral activity by government officials, so that notion did have some merit in his mind. Maybe it was like this everywhere – there were, after all, unscrupulous people in every walk of life. But sometimes he wished that Native Americans would oust the dishonest white man from the land rightfully belonging to them.

. . . . .

Flip graduated from high school in the spring of 1958, and had been accepted to Rutgers University in New Brunswick, New Jersey. Two other boys from East Islip – Roger Wyman and Raymond Smith – joined him in the Rutgers freshman class in the fall of 1958. On a beautiful September morning, the entire family drove the cadet to his dormitory at the top of the Frelinghuysen building at Rutgers. It was a proud moment for Flip, but also for the entire family, as no Vampatella had ever attended college before.

Philip gave Flip a few hundred dollars. Antoinette wept on her departure. This was the second time, after all, that one of her sons would leave her, though these circumstances were quite different from when Ben left to join the Navy. She was slowing down, aging, in physical pain, and sick at heart.

Flip embraced life in college with gusto. He engaged in his Liberal Arts education, figuring he could determine his major over his last two years at school. Though Flip was an eager learner, he discovered that college had much more to offer than just academics. He did not anticipate the hours that non-academic activities would consume, and school became more difficult than he had ever experienced before. Moreover, he was homesick, ate haphazardly, and time management became an issue. He made frequent trips home, secured extra dollars from Philip, and upon returning to Rutgers, found school more difficult with each passing week. He joined Alpha Chi Rho and entered the ranks of a fraternity, which helped provide regular meals, but which also contributed to typical freshman horseplay.

Flip's grades began to drop, but he passed and became a sophomore – now the first Vampatella to make it to his second year of college.

Chapter 26 – Departure

There are about 200 types of cells in the human body. Each type is predetermined by the genetic instructions in a person's DNA. DNA contains billions of lines of code for how to construct a body, and each cell, whether it is a skin cell or bone cell, contains the full DNA program in each person's body. In that code are instructions for how to make specific cells, and to put them in specific places in the body. DNA often contains switches that get turned on and off based on various input a person receives – it could be exposure to sun, types of food, trauma, or any number of other things.

When cells replicate and multiply, normally they do so according to plan. Occasionally, however, mistakes are made. When a piece of DNA is not translated properly from one generation to the next, a genetic mutation occurs. It could be an insertion of a random string of genetic "letters" into the code. It could be a deletion of important segments of DNA. Or it could even be simple changes in "letters" or "words" within the gene. Some of these mutations are harmless. Many of them are quite harmful. Some of them are deadly.

Antoinette did not yet know it, but her cells were mutating, and these mutated cells were spreading.

. . . . .

Steve Rapuano had lived with Philip for some time now, but his health was failing. His years of drinking had caught up with him, and the family could see that his time on earth was slipping away, and in 1959, he breathed his last. The entire family was devastated. Antoinette felt the blow the hardest, and now she was without both her parents. Philip had loved Steve as well and took his death hard. Antoinette's siblings were equally saddened, and Philip and Antoinette's children felt the loss greatly.

Her grief added to her physical woes, which worsened by the day. Pain bothered her more and more, and she went to get her body x-rayed. The pictures showed nothing, and she decided to consult another doctor. The new doctor prescribed medication that did nothing to help Antoinette, much like the first doctor's medication. After several months of no improvement, the new doctor decided that she needed surgery.

Antoinette was deathly afraid of surgery. Philip, who had experienced a life-saving procedure himself years before, tried to convince her that surgery was the best option. His words gave her some courage, but in the years to come, he would regret encouraging her down this path. Three more months went by, and in 1960, she finally agreed to let the doctor take his scalpel to her.

The doctors opened her up in the area where she was feeling the pain, and what they found alarmed them. They had discovered a mass of cells that were not supposed to be there. They were cancer cells, which had mutated and replicated out of control, and had spread in her body. Normal, healthy cells replicate according to a specific timetable as instructed by our genes. Cancer cells not only mutate, but they replicate without such timetables, and they can quickly get out of control. By the time they operated on Antoinette, the cancer had reached a very serious stage of development.

The doctors informed Antoinette and Philip of her condition. It was grave. More surgery would be required, along with other unpleasant forms of treatment. Such a course of action was to be extremely expensive. As Philip would put it, in making a person well physically they kill her financially. Philip had survived and had done well to earn a living, providing for his family, but the cost of doing what it took to make his wife well was an almost impossible burden. What to do? He grew frustrated at the cost of making people well.

They shared the news of Antoinette's cancer with the rest of the family. She was the beloved mother of six, and this news devastated each and every one of them. Her situation was grave, and the six children, Philip, and the grandchildren that were old enough to understand were all crushed by this development. Her operation complete, she fought on, with an amazing will to live. She worried about her family, and struggled to live on to be there for them.

She had fallen into a routine of sorts. She was sent home, lay in bed trying to recover, until the pain got so bad that she had to be taken back to the hospital. Irene spent most of her time at Antoinette's side, praying for her, talking with her, and trying to make her comfortable. Every day, however, the pain increased, and Antoinette's condition worsened. The cancer kept growing.

The months of March, April, and May came and went. She underwent blood transfusions and breathing on oxygen. Her condition worsened. She was in excruciating pain.

Antoinette loved the apple blossoms in the back yard for years. She loved the lilac trees near the old hen coop where Steve had taken up residence. She would take the lilacs and put them in vases on her dining room table. This season, however, the apple blossoms would not feel her gentle caress. The lilacs would bloom, wait in vain for her to trim them and take them into her home, and then…wilt and die.

Day by day her pain increased and the cancer grew, spreading throughout her body, the mutated cells multiplying uncontrollably, taking over, killing her. On May 16, 1960, Antoinette breathed her last and passed from this world to the next, following her mother and father who had passed before. She had fought the good fight, had lived well, but in the end, the cancer had won, and Antoinette was buried.

. . . . .

The four older children – none of whom were children by this point, obviously – were devastated. But among the kids, Antoinette's loss was felt the hardest by Irene and Flip. By the end of Antoinette's life, it was clear that nothing could be done, and Philip, knowing there was nothing that could save her, had prayed not for her survival but for her peaceful passing. When it came, there was relief, and there was grief unlike anything Philip had ever experienced.

Antoinette was the love of his life, the woman who held everything together. Decades before, at their first meeting, she was cool towards him, and Philip often joked with her about that. Then they fell in love and married and had a family and he could not imagine life without her. Yet here he was, facing the dark, bottomless void. Philip had lost his mother decades before, and his father years before, but losing Antoinette was a darker plunge into the depths of anguish. He was angry with God. How could God have done this? How could He have taken Antoinette away?

He knew he was a blessed man, to have lived the life he had, to have the wife and children and friends he had, to give him a skill to bless others with the products of his own hands. He knew he had little reason to complain, but none of that dulled the ache he felt in his heart. It would be a long time before Philip could accept the bitter loss of his beloved Antoinette.

. . . . .

Flip took Antoinette's death very hard. The youngest of six, he was in many ways the family favorite. He loved his mother more than anyone in the world, and try as he might, he could not concentrate on his school work. During her illness, he lost track of assignments, and saw his grades plummet. He somehow managed to get passing grades and qualified to become a junior at Rutgers, but he did not care about his third year. His mother gone, he became somewhat of a shell of his former self. He struggled worse in his third year, dropping out of ROTC, neglecting his work, even paying little attention to his girlfriend.

At the close of his third year, Rutgers informed him that he had not passed and would not be returning for his senior year. The first Vampatella to go to college was no longer a university student.

. . . . .

Flip understood the significance of flunking out of school. To be sure, the circumstances were understandable, but he knew he could have kept at it, and determined in his heart that he would resume work on his college degree at a future point. He promised Philip that he would go back to school and get his degree. For the time being, he needed work. He was not suited for office work – not enough money, too boring and restrictive. He chose the work of a trade laborer. He took on a job wielding a shovel, received decent pay and numerous blisters. The blisters convinced him to look for something else.

His draft card told him he was eligible for induction if he was not in college. Well, he was no longer in college, and did not relish the idea of being drafted, so he chose to enlist instead. This way he at least could have his choice of service branches. He applied for naval aviation. As he took his enlistment physical, they discovered that his sinuses were unfit for flying, and Flip paid for surgery to correct the problem. He passed his next physical and the U.S. Navy accepted his enlistment. At the end of July, 1962, Philip drove Flip to the airport so his son could fly to Pensacola, Florida, for training. Flip was about to earn the nickname "cadet".

. . . . .

Flip's older sister Marie had met Walter Joseph Caddell, nicknamed "Bud", fell in love, and in short order the two of them were wed in April 1961. A member of the Caddell clan performed the service, and Philip gave Marie to Bud. For the first time since her mother's death, Marie was a happy woman.

During the wedding, the priest was sober, Bud was sober, and Philip was sober but very thirsty. At the reception, Philip indulged himself a little too much in satiating his thirst with alcoholic beverages. He looked around the reception room and saw Bridget, Bud's mother, who had been a widow for many years. Philip sat down next to Bridged, flirted with her, and proposed to her. She laughed at him and walked away. He had another drink, went home feeling sorry for himself, and fell asleep.

Three of his daughters had gotten married. One to go. Philip hoped it would go well with Marie and Bud.

Bud had multiple jobs going, repairing vending machines and cars. He did not make much money from these endeavors, and a sizeable portion of his somewhat meager income went to child support from a previous marriage. He had many friends, most of whom were female. Marie's income from her key punching job in Farmingdale paid most of their family's expenses.

When Marie's workday was done, she drove back to her home in East Islip, made Walter dinner, and usually spent the evenings in tears, as Walter almost always came home late or not at all.

. . . . .

Angelina had moved into the chicken coop living quarters in the back yard following Steve Rapuano's death, but it was an inadequate space for her family. Philip sold a parcel of land across the street to her, and Angelina had a builder put up a new home. Her impatience cost her. Philip could have saved her considerable time and money if he had built it in his spare time, but she was in a hurry. Unfortunately, the house cost more than she expected, and took a year before it was ready.

Nonetheless, she was glad for her home, and Philip was glad to have her nearby. Angelina's husband Frank had secured a job with the Winfield door company in Lindenhurst, which helped bring in even more money from just what the government gave him as a military pension. She worked at her sewing trade, and loved to play poker.

. . . . .

Ben, meanwhile, had decided to build his own house on his parcel. He asked a friend to draw up plans for the house. His friend thought big. He drew a plan for a 60x40 building with three bedrooms, a large living room and dining room. The foundation was dug and the footings were put in place. The masons came over to build the foundation with blocks and their arrival coincided with the arrival of a dozen cases of beer. A race began between the men building and drinking. Despite the alcoholic intake, the home was beautifully constructed.

Ben build a frame structure over the foundation and covered the exterior walls with brick. Philip cut and nailed a hip and valley roof over the frames, extending the overhand two feet beyond the brick line. The house was sturdy, big, and beautiful in every way. The home inspector came to the house and determined that the eave overhang was a half-inch too wide and told Ben he needed to cut it back. Ben agreed and the inspector left. Ben never cut back the eave.

Chapter 27 – Here and There

Ben's house was built, Angelina and Frank Skrocki were living next door, and Flip was heading to Florida for training to become a U.S. naval aviator. Philip had served in World War I, his son Ben in World War II, and though no Vampatella served in the armed forces during the Korean War, Philip worked for Grumman, building planes that U.S. fliers would utilize in combat against the communists.

Ah, the communists. They had been spreading like the plague across the globe, beginning in 1917 with the October revolution in Russia. Vladimir Ilyich Ulyanov – otherwise known as Lenin – had successfully revolted against Czar Nicholas II, and established the first communist government in world history. After Lenin died from a stroke in 1924, Josef Stalin, at that point the General Secretary of the Communist Party, emerged from a power struggle as the new leader of the Union of Soviet Socialist Republics (USSR).

Three years earlier, Mao Zedong had established a communist party in China and seized control of the Jiangxi province in 1927, creating the first soviet republic in the world's most populous nation. A year later, Chiang Kai-Shek launched an anti-communist revolt and, after emerging victorious, set up a nationalist government, with Chiang at the helm. Mao continued the fight, however, and China entered into civil war.

The communists spread into eastern Europe and Korea, and had established movements in numerous nations by the time World War II came around. In an alliance of necessity, not of ideology, the communists defeated the fascists in Germany and Italy, as well as the imperial government of Japan. When the war ended, Winston Churchill, accurately assessing the aims of the communists, declared there to be an "iron curtain" dividing the democratic governments of the world from the communists. The Cold War had begun between the Soviet Union and newly established NATO.

Following the communist victory over Chiang in China, and the stalemate in Korea, Stalin passed away and Nikita Khrushchev assumed power in the Soviet Union. Initially, there appeared to be a thawing of communist oppression as Khrushchev denounced Stalin's hard line regime, and in 1956 in Hungary, the people revolted against the communist government. The United States offered moral support, but little else, not wanting to engage militarily. Khrushchev sent Red Army troops in to crush the rebellion.

Three years later, Fidel Castro led a revolution in Cuba, and the United States watched in horror as communism gained a foothold just 90 miles off the coast of Florida. Castro defeated dictator Fulgencio Batista and, upon gaining control of Cuba, set up a communist government with, of course, Castro at the helm. The United States responded with a futile attempt to arm democratic revolutionaries in the 1961 Bay of Pigs invasion, which was a disaster for both Cuba and the United States. It was an embarrassment for the administration of John F. Kennedy.

By the early 1960s, communism had firm control of eastern Europe through the Warsaw Pact, a large part of Asia with the Soviet Union and China leading the way, and east Asia as communism had spread to North Korea. It had also gained traction in the western hemisphere through USSR-backed Castro in Cuba. The democratic west needed to stem the tide, but western leaders did not want direct conflict with the Soviet Union, which was understandable given the nuclear weapons the USSR now had available.

. . . . .

Ho Chi Minh was a man small of stature but large in presence and vision. His tiny nation of Vietnam was part of the French colonial empire, and following World War II, Minh yearned for independence. On

September 2, 1945, he proclaimed the democratic republic of Vietnam to be independent of France. The French, naturally, did not take kindly to this gesture and sent troops to the small southeast Asian country and fought to keep its colonial empire together. The United States sent one billion dollars in support of the French, bearing some 80% of the war's economic burden.

It was all for naught, however, as the Vietnamese defeated French forces in the Battle of Dien Bien Phu, and on May 7, 1954, the French surrendered. During the Geneva Conference to negotiate the terms of peace, Cambodia, Laos, and Vietnam all received independence. However, Vietnam, though independent from France, was not a unified nation. Minh had defeated the French, but had not secured control of the whole of Vietnam, and the nation was divided along the 17th parallel. In typical communist fashion, Minh implemented numerous "reforms" in the north, which consisted of executing tens of thousands of citizens. In the south, Prime Minister Ngo Dinh Diem, who had not signed the Geneva treaty and who was not as popular amongst the general Vietnamese population as Minh, nonetheless secured the support of the United States in his resistance to communism.

The communist north began a campaign to undermine Diem in the south. Large scale dissonance campaigns, political violence, and the formation of the National Liberation Front (otherwise known as the Viet Cong) all contributed to unrest in South Vietnam. By 1961, communist forces were waging – and winning – war all over the globe. The North Vietnamese were creating unrest in the south, the Berlin Wall had gone up, dividing the historic city into communist east and capitalist west, and the Bay of Pigs invasion had been a failure. U.S. President John F. Kennedy faced a dilemma with respect to the Vietnamese crisis. He determined to "draw a line in the sand" in Vietnam, committing the U.S. to stopping the advance of communism.

In October 1962, Cold War tensions mounted to the highest they had ever been. The Soviets shipped nuclear missiles to Cuba, and when the U.S. discovered their presence, a standoff occurred between Kennedy and Khrushchev. The two played a tense poker game from October 16-28, with the Soviet dictator folding at the last minute. The USSR withdrew the missiles and for the moment, the U.S. seemed to have slowed the communist creep.

But on November 1-2, 1963, Diem and his brother Ngo Dinh Nhu were assassinated, throwing South Vietnam into chaos. Three weeks later, the United States, in the midst of the rapidly growing threat of communism, would suffer an even greater loss.

. . . . .

World events impacted the Vampatella family, but Philip still had a life to live while President Kennedy was staring down Fidel Castro, Nikita Khrushchev, and Ho Chi Minh. His heart was broken from the loss of his beloved Antoinette, and he grew lonely, wondering if he would ever remarry. He needed companionship, but beyond that, he knew that he was incapable of shouldering the burden of maintaining a home. He lacked the skills in household tasks such as cooking, cleaning, washing clothes, and even shopping. Moreover, he realized that Irene, the last unmarried daughter living at home, was unable to perform these duties after a long day at work herself.

Philip decided he needed a new wife. His first attempt was with his sister-in-law Rose, whom Antoinette had said he should marry should Antoinette die first. Rose was a widow, was committed to her family and to not moving from New Haven. Nor would she "sleep in the bed once occupied by my sister", and consequently, she said no. Philip was relieved.

A friend found another possible mate, someone his age, a little plump, but who was willing to marry Philip sight unseen. Philip said he wanted to see her first without being seen himself.

"How are we going to do that?" asked his friend who made the suggested union.

"When it gets dark you sit her at the table near that window. Make sure all the lights in the room are on and the window shades are up."

"Won't she see you too?"

"No," Philip explained. "I will be in the dark outside." He demonstrated how this would work and the friend was convinced.

The meeting was arranged but it took about two seconds for Philip to decline the offer. The woman was not "plump". She was, in Philip's eyes, *immense*. Later on, when he met her with no marriage anticipations, he discovered that she had a booming voice and her weight was so much that the floorboards creaked under each step. Not knowing that Philip was the man she was supposed to meet, she told his friend that day, "Too bad

I did not meet that fellow. We could have made a good go of it. I have $5,000 in the bank and he could have all of it. I wish I could meet him."

Philip never let on that he was the man.

Philip's sister Maria offered to help find him a mate. She had in mind a woman involved in her religious organization who she thought might be a good match.

"I don't know if she wants to marry again," Maria told Philip. "But if you don't mind her religion, she is in good shape."

Philip drove with Maria to meet the woman, who was 55 years old and quite good-looking. During the conversation, the woman made it clear that she would never marry again, due to her first marriage being abusive. Philip graciously bowed out, and after two more attempts by Maria to find a mate, she gave up on the prospect.

. . . . .

Loneliness hits people in different ways. Philip once was a teetotaler, but having rediscovered alcohol a few years before, he began to drink more often, and with greater vigor. Some nights he simply fell asleep from drinking. Other nights his imagination ran wild. He was often hung over in the morning, waking with a pounding headache. He knew he was moving quickly towards alcoholism, something he detested but couldn't stop. Amazingly, even as his alcohol consumption increased, his ability to create wood masterpieces did not decline. That was a good thing, as he had two more years until retirement.

The emptiness gnawed at him. There was no one to turn to for comfort, to talk with, to share life with. He did not engage his children in conversation about his troubles, as he did not want to burden them with such matters. More and more, his only comfort became the glass of wine or whiskey or bottle of beer he drank while watching television. He would occasionally write in his journal, slowly going through his memoirs, recalling stories from when he was younger – recording his thoughts that would turn into his autobiographical biography he would title "Passeggiata."

One day his phone rang, and upon answering, discovered a friend calling.

"Hello?"

"Hello Phil. Want to meet a nice lady?" his friend asked.

"Who is she?"

"You don't know her."

"Do you know her?"

"Yes," his friend replied. "She's a fine person. I've known her for a long time."

"Is she fat?" Philip asked, still scarred from his previous experience.

"Not too fat."

"Is she young?"

"Fifty-four. She comes to my shop pretty often, has two children. Both children are married. Lives with her daughter, has been a widow for three years." *Fifty-four years of age*, Philip thought. *Nine years younger than me. That will work.*

"Can you arrange a meeting?"

"Yes."

Two days later, Philip met Kate outside a beauty parlor. On first glance, Philip saw that she was plump and that her legs had varicose veins. His sister Maria had accused him of being too particular. Perhaps she was right. Philip took Kate to a diner to eat and talk. He discovered that Kate did not beat around the bush – she told him she was looking for a nice man to marry. He liked her straightforward approach.

"My husband died three years ago," she said. "We had been divorced for several years before he died. He had left me alone to raise my children by myself. The girl grew up to become a registered nurse, married a doctor, has four children. The boy did his bit in the army, married; he too has four children. The girl and her family live in Port Washington and I live with her. The boy lives in Hicksville. I don't want to live with either one or depend on them for a living and, in fact, I don't want to be a burden on any man I may marry. I can still work to support myself even if I marry again."

Philip listened intently. He wanted to know what kind of person she was, what her character and dispositions were. He enjoyed his time with her and drove her back to her house and met her daughter Rosalie, her son-in-law Anthony, and several grandchildren.

Philip smiled. He was pleased.

. . . . .

Italian families were traditionally very large. In the early 20th century, of course, many children died young from various diseases and maladies. Kate was one of 17 children of the Puccio family, which hailed from

Palermo, Sicily. Her father was a fisherman and he and his wife had immigrated to the United States. She was pregnant at the time, and within hours of arriving in the U.S., Catherine was born. It was 1907.

As was the case with many large families at the time, numerous children passed away. Nine of Kate's siblings died from different ailments, and at 40, her mother died as well. Kate was 16 at the time, married, and suddenly put in charge of the rest of the family. She had the responsibility of cooking and caring for the rest of the children, even as she had a husband of her own.

She was raised in a very traditional Sicilian home, where parents protected their daughters and forbade them to talk to boys. Parents arranged marriages for their children, hoping to find acceptable matches for them. If the parents caught their daughters in any sort of sexual shenanigans, the offending boy would be met with threats, often of the knife and gun variety.

Whatever benefits such a system conferred – and there were indeed some – were counter-balanced by the reality that for young Sicilian girls, marriage was not a choice of love. Of course they could fall in love, but that would usually – if it happened at all – occur after the marriage had already begun. Marriages were selected on the basis of fit, not on the basis of love.

As a 15-year old girl, she discovered a young push-carter who worked near the sweatshop where Kate was employed. Every time he passed by her, she smiled at him. It didn't take long for her to smiles to work their charms, and before long, this young man was smitten.

Unbeknownst to either of these two, a Sicilian named Bernardo Calma had noticed her and smiled at her. Her response was a curled lip of disdain. Bernardo hatched a plan. He pretended he was a friend of the push-cart boy, and with that news, Kate looked at him a little differently. He managed to engage in conversation with her, mostly about the push-cart boy.

One day when Kate exited the sweatshop on her lunch break, Bernardo sauntered over and told Kate he had something he wanted to pass on from his friend the push-cart boy.

"But I need to tell you in private," he said. Kate agreed, and the two entered a taxi waiting around the corner. The cabbie drove through Manhattan and the Bronx as Bernardo talked with her. It took some time for Kate to realize that she had been gone a long time. Bernardo told her they were on their way back to her place of employment.

The cab stopped in front of a house in White Plains, quite a long ways from her sweatshop. She was frightened. He assured her that everything was ok.

"I want you to meet my aunt," he said soothingly.

They got out and went inside the house. The aunt greeted the girl suspiciously, wondering what was going on. Bernardo called her aside, whispered something in her ear, took his leave, and left the house. She promptly peppered Kate with questions, realized that Kate was innocent and not part of any plot, and concluded that her nephew was indeed a rascal.

The situation, however, violated Sicilian norms. Kate had unwittingly been caught up in a plot of Bernardo's making. Sicilian culture called for Bernardo to marry her; if not, he would have to run for the rest of his life out of fear of reprisal for besmirching her reputation. Kate was stuck. She had unwittingly violated Sicilian decorum and she was either to marry Bernardo or be subject to ostracism, exile, or even death. Faced with the alternatives of either becoming a prostitute or marrying Bernardo, she chose to marry.

By the time she met Philip, she had many years of a loveless life, lots of hard work raising children, and a yearning for something better. Thankfully, Bernardo had passed away three years before she had met Philip.

. . . . .

Philip wasn't sure Kate was right for him, but he made a habit of inviting her for conversation, and even occasionally wrote letters to her. Unsure of what the right step was for him, his drinking did not help clarify his thought. He decided to choose what appeared to him to be the lesser of two evils between drowning himself in drink or marrying Kate: he chose to marry Kate.

Kate was deaf in one ear and had diabetes. She spoke loudly, which Philip did not like. But she was also energetic and indefatigable, possessing dignity and character. He found Kate to be like a child ready to welcome any sign of affection, any gesture of tenderness. Philip thought she seemed to reach for a day she had lost, a dream that had never come true. Philip found this quality very attractive, and in June 1961, they set a date for their wedding, a month hence.

Kate wanted a church wedding, and Father Pavone of Our Lady of Fatima in Manor Haven was called to duty. Philip had wanted a civil ceremony but Kate won out, and in July 1961, for the second time in his life, Philip was wed.

. . . . .

Kate discovered that Philip's penchant for reading – a habit begun as a young boy in Sicily – annoyed her. She regarded printed material as rubbish, but for one kind: she loved fashion books and magazines. She loved looking at bridal gowns, which fit her perfectly seeing as though she was an accomplished maker of wedding dresses.

She was not readily accepted into the Vampatella family by Philip's children. They were still grieving the loss of Antoinette, and resented Philip's marriage as if it was some sort of treason. They had a difficult time coming to terms with their mother's death, and made life difficult for Kate. She understood, but couldn't help grumble to Philip about it. She tried to win them over with acts of kindness, but his kids refused to accept them.

Philip began to wonder if he had not made a mistake in marrying Kate. His father Biagio had warned him about accepting the consequences of your mistakes, but Philip, though concerned he may have made one with Kate, did not think it was a grave error. He knew she was a good person, and clung to patience that it would all work out.

. . . . .

On September 14, 1962, Philip retired from Grumman with a pension of nearly $100 per month and better than $120 per month from Social Security. Moreover, he had a thousand dollars in the bank. He had calculated that those funds would be sufficient for him without her needing to work, but Kate was not satisfied. She went to work anyway.

It was a good thing, as Philip's calculations proved to be far from correct. He had a large insurance bill attached to his property. His medical benefits were reduced. Property taxes soared. And his cigarette and alcohol addictions cost far more than he had figured. Kate demonstrated her worth to the family right away as she went back to work, saving as much of her pay as possible.

․․․․․

Flip made it through his initial training – which included some very difficult survival training in the case of enemy capture – and on August 16, 1963 was appointed "a reserve officer in the grade of ensign in the United States Navy." He received a certificate on February 16, 1964 that said that "Philip Victor Vampatella has completed the prescribed course of training and having met successfully the requirements of the course, has been designated a naval aviator."

In Philip's eyes, his son Flip was made of the same mettle as his father Biagio – a gentleman, a man of honor, possessing strong will and character. That was Philip's father and now, he saw, his son.

Flip was assigned to further training in San Diego, and the Miramar Naval base.

․․․․․

Meanwhile, in April 1963, Irene had met Robert (Bob) Jones, a young man in his thirties who worked in a bank in New York City. They fell in love and decided to marry in December 1963. Irene was coming up on 26 years of age and had, like her father Philip, begun to get streaks of gray in her hair. She was a child full of love, joy, and laughter until Antoinette passed away. Now Irene was a full adult, ready to be married and start a family of her own.

Kate undertook the task of making Irene's wedding dress. Kate and Irene poured their heart and soul into this marvelous creation. Irene looked beautiful in it, and Kate was proud to have made it. The date was scheduled during Flip's two weeks of leave, so even though Philip did not relish the idea of another winter wedding, it made the most sense since now the entire family could attend.

On Irene's wedding day, the snow sparkled white and the air was crisp and cold. St. Mary's Church waited and Philip led his youngest daughter down the aisle to Bob, who would shortly become another son to Philip. He lifted the veil, kissed her, pronounced his blessing, and gave her to Bob.

The entire family was indeed there except for Ben, who had suffered a sudden hospitalization. He and their uncle Jim had taken a trip to New Haven to visit relatives, when Ben's nose started to bleed – just a few drops at first, but then a torrent. Jim rushed Ben to the New Haven hospital where a doctor stuffed his nose with gauze. That seemed to do the trick and Ben and Jim headed back to Long Island. In short order, Ben's nose began to bleed again, dripping on his lips and chin, and trickling inside his mouth. Ben spit out some blood and somehow made it all the way home. Ben's doctor recommended hospitalization, and he was at Southside Hospital the day his youngest sister wed Bob.

When the wedding was over, the entire family went to visit Ben in the hospital. Ben was thrilled – and surprised – to see everyone. He kissed Irene and wished her happiness. Their visit not only brightened Ben's heart, it also lifted the spirits of others on the hospital floor, getting to see a young newlywed couple and their family. People forgot for a moment about their own pain and got to share in the family's joy.

. . . . .

A month after Irene's wedding, the family suffered a loss. Marie's husband Bud was driving down the Northern Parkway heading east. His car began to veer right, hit the curb, and rolled down the embankment. Emergency crews arrived at the scene and rushed Bud to the Huntington hospital. He was still alive, but could not move or speak. He had suffered a severed spinal cord and was paralyzed. He was unconscious for a long time and had difficulty breathing. Doctors opened his trachea and inserted a metal grommet to help him breathe. He was fitted in a special bed with cords and weights, his head screwed into a device to keep him stable. He had lost all sense of feeling and all mobility of his limbs, but his mind still worked perfectly.

Marie stood at his side and tended to him. She took every moment she had available to be with him, neglecting her own needs. Her pay decreased as she spent more and more time with her ailing husband. He needed her more than any man ever needed his wife, and she was there for him. He could not help but realized the value of this priceless woman.

Philip was very proud of his daughter. He understood her sacrifice. They moved Bud to a veteran's hospital in Brooklyn, but his condition did not improve. Moreover, they discovered that his veteran's benefits did not allow him to be hospitalized for long, so they had to find another place for him. She finally found St. Charles in Port Jefferson, and they took him in, regardless of Marie's ability to pay.

Bud's cuts and bruises healed. He even began to speak with less difficulty. But he never recovered feeling or movement in his limbs. On November 22, 1964, he passed away.

. . . . .

In early November 1963, Diem was assassinated in South Vietnam. Less than three weeks later, on November 22, one year to the day after Marie's husband died, Lee Harvey Oswald shot President John F. Kennedy in Dallas. Kennedy had been battling communism in Europe, Asia, and North America, and as he passed away, Lyndon Baines Johnson became the President. He would lead the United States, and Philip's son Flip, into war.

Chapter 28 – Flip

The Korean War experience had taught the U.S. armed forces that new, faster fighters were needed, with increased firepower to better deal with enemy aircraft and ground targets. Vought, a company founded in 1917, specialized in aircraft carrier-based planes, and produced thousands of aircraft during World War II. In order to meet the specialized demands following the Korean War, Vought created a new, elite fighter that was capable of dogfighting with other fighters, but also possessed the ability to effectively attack enemy ground forces. Several prototypes made successful tests, the first one occurring on March 25, 1955, flown by John Konrad. On April 4, 1956, what was then known as the F8U-1 flew for the first time off a carrier deck.

The F8 series broke new ground in several areas, from design to speed to thrust capacity. In 1957 John Glenn completed the first supersonic transcontinental flight in an F8U-1P, making the trip from California to New York in a little over three hours and twenty-three minutes. In 1962, the United States Department of Defense decided to standardize military aircraft along Air Force designations, and the F8U-1 became the F-8, and was assigned the name "Crusader". It possessed the capability of firing four heat-seeking Sidewinder missiles and had powerful 20mm cannon, which were its primary weapon. As the last fighters to use guns as its main weapon, the F-8 was nicknamed the "Last of the Gunfighters".

During the Cuban Missile Crisis in 1962, the F-8 flew reconnaissance missions that no other plane at the time could perform. It was film developed from F-8 flights that demonstrated conclusively that Castro was indeed importing and setting up Soviet-made missile launchers capable of hitting the U.S. in mere minutes. New to American military service, the F-8 had already proved extremely valuable. It would really show its stuff over the next ten years in a small, troubled nation in southeast Asia.

. . . . .

Flip had arrived at Miramar in San Diego in 1964 and was spending his days training and his nights enjoying what the beautiful California city had to offer. He had become a Naval aviator, and the plane he had been assigned to was the F-8. The F-8 was incredible powerful, but due to its unique wing design it was difficult to fly; it required extraordinary skill to handle such a challenging bird. As a result, it earned the unfortunate moniker "ensign eliminator" due to it having one of the highest mishap rates in the entire U.S. armed forces.

It was fast and formidable, powered by a single Pratt and Whitney J57 turbojet engine. It was the first fighter to reach 1,000 mph, and due to its more than 18,000 pounds of thrust, had incredible climbing capability. But despite its strengths, its shortcomings were notable, especially the single engine. If one engine fails on an F-18 Hornet, for example, the other engine is capable of flying the plane. If one engine fails on an F-8, the plane is dead.

On April 23, 1964, Flip guided his F-8 through a series of maneuvers, performing a standard training exercise. Suddenly, the engine quit. Flip had no control over the aircraft as it plummeted to earth. He tried to re-ignite the engine, but it would not fire. His descent was rapid, and he quickly had to make a decision. He pulled the handle and the cockpit burst open as the seat lurched upward thanks to the small explosive packs triggered by Flip's jerking of the ejection handle. The explosions caused the seat to ram upward into Flip's lower body, breaking his back. He was launched out of the plane and sent skyward, while his Crusader crashed into the Pacific. His parachute deployed and he landed in the waters off San Diego.

His parachute got tangled, and he struggled freeing himself from the cords. His lift raft had deployed, and he worked to climb into it. His back was in so much pain, however, that he could not get into the raft. Sharks who called these waters home sensed a disturbance and began to swim towards him. He had set off his mayday call before ejecting, and Naval rescue aircraft had immediately taken up a search-and-rescue operation. Unfortunately for Flip, they were off target, and for 45 excruciating minutes, he battled pain and fear, waiting to be found.

Eventually a pilot in a stray plane caught sight of the burst from his flare pistol. The pilot signaled other aircraft and soon Flip was hauled out of the water and taken to the hospital, where he would stay for many weeks. That night Philip received a phone call indicating that his youngest son had a training mishap. He did not know the details, but he knew he had to go see his boy.

. . . . .

Patricia Weth was the third of four daughters born to Arthur and Cecilia Weth, and unbeknownst to Flip, she grew up no more than six miles from his house on Cedarhurst Street, having grown up on Park Avenue in Bay Shore. In nursing school she became friends with another Pat, Pat Gamble. Pat was married to a U.S. Navy sailor named Steve, who was out to sea but was on his way back from his Vietnam tour. He would be arriving in San Diego within a couple of weeks. Pat Mega had her newborn and Patricia and Pat decided to drive cross country to San Diego to meet up with Steve when he returned.

Pat's older sister Jane happened to know Biagio (Benny) Vampatella from Great River, and so Pat knew of the Vampatella family. Benny had told Pat that his younger brother Philip (Flip) was stationed at Miramar. When Patricia and Pat arrived, Pat had the idea that maybe Phil would enjoy a good home-cooked Italian meal, something she was quite proficient at providing.

"Who's Phil?" Patricia had asked.

"He's from Long Island, not far from you," Pat replied. "I know his older brother Benny."

The dinner was set for April 23, and Patricia and her friend Pat waited for Flip to arrive. He was late. They waited longer. He was very late. They waited a little longer until Flip was beyond late, and they gave up. Frustrated at being stood up, they turned on the television to catch the evening news. U.S. Navy operations were always big news in San Diego at the time, and when they flipped the T.V. on, they saw the story of Flip's training accident. They concluded that he did, in fact, have a good excuse for missing their evening out together.

Pat Mega visited Flip in the hospital a few times, and finally was able to convince Patricia to make a visit of her own. She went reluctantly at first, but when she and Flip met, they hit it off instantly, realizing that they had several friends in common back on Long Island. As it turned out, it was somewhat remarkable that the two had never met before. Six weeks after Flip was released from the hospital, he and Patricia were engaged.

. . . . .

Philip and Kate flew out to San Diego on May 5. When they arrived, a young man in civilian clothes greeted them at the airport.

"I'm Richard Adams," he said. "Flip showed me your picture. You are Mr. and Mrs. Vampatella. I have his car at the parking lot and have arranged for a room for you at a lodge near the hospital." He drove them directly to Balboa Naval Hospital and escorted them to Flip's room.

Flip greeted them in a wheelchair. He could stand by this point, and explained that the doctors wanted him to remain in the chair until his back was sufficiently healed. To Philip's amazement, Flip only seemed to be concerned with the loss of his Crusader.

"One and a half million dollars' worth of flying beauty, Dad," he said. "Lost in the drink."

"Yes, but it might have been much more than that," Philip replied. "Planes are not hard to replace."

"I know what you mean, Dad. I tried to find a way to save it, but no time to do it. I had to eject." He paused for a moment, and then continued. "I wish there was a better way of leaving a jet in flight though, than being shot out of it. Just the same, I think I'm very lucky."

They spent some time in San Diego, paying Flip numerous visits. At the end of their stay, Ensign Adams, who was tasked with making them feel as comfortable as possible, gave them a tour of the Miramar air field. There they saw several planes take off and land. He showed them some F-8s, and smiled proudly as if they were his own.

"Aren't they beauties?" he asked. "Aren't they the best the navy has?" Philip smiled, thinking that young Mr. Adams had not seen any of the impressive Grumman designs, but happy that his own son was flying a worthy aircraft.

Adams showed them around and then stopped, pointed at one plane, and raised his voice in amazement.

"Hey, look! Flip's plane number is on this one! What do you know about that?"

Philip knew nothing about airplane designations; he only knew that this meant that his son would fly again, and he smiled.

. . . . .

Flip healed and was assigned to the *U.S.S. Hancock*, an Essex class carrier built during World War II, where she earned four battle stars in combat. The *Hancock* was decommissioned after the war was over, and refitted in the 1950s as an attack carrier. It was the first U.S. naval platform to use steam catapults to launch aircraft. The *Hancock* served admirably in the war, her planes wreaking havoc on Japanese airfields when U.S. forces invaded Okinawa. The *Hancock* served alongside Benny's *U.S.S. Arkansas* during that battle. During the battle, she suffered terrible damage from a kamikaze attack that killed 62 men and wounded 71 others. Yet she was able to fight on in the battle, helping U.S. marines establish a beachhead. When the Japanese formally surrendered aboard the *U.S.S. Missouri* in 1945, planes from the *Hancock* flew overhead.

Following World War II, the *Hancock* was decommissioned in order to be refitted as an attack carrier, a modernization process that cost some $60 million. On February 15, 1954, the *Hancock* was re-commissioned but shortly thereafter underwent another alteration, having an angled deck added on to increase launch capability. On November 15, 1956, she was once again commissioned and retained her configuration as the U.S. got involved in Vietnam. In November 1965, the *Hancock* steamed from the United States to the waters off South Vietnam, complete with a squadron of F-8 Crusaders.

. . . . .

VF-211 was the Navy squadron known as the "Fighting Checkmates". Established first in the mid 1940s, it underwent several iterations before finding a home at the Naval Air Station at Miramar in 1961. The Checkmates would make seven deployments in Vietnam, making bombing runs, taking reconnaissance photographs and, perhaps most importantly, engaging enemy Soviet-made MiG-17 fighters. Because of VF-211's exemplary record, they would become known as the "MiG killers". Flip was assigned to this elite group, having been trained in the powerful F-8 fighter.

He arrived for his first combat tour in 1964 and engaged the enemy's ground forces, dropping bombs and incendiary weapons in support of American soldiers. During this time, he continued to send letters home to Philip, but most of his letters went to Patricia.

Philip often thought of his own military experience as he worried for his youngest son. Flip, he thought, was a navy man. Here Philip was, an ex-army private, surrounded by the United States Navy – his oldest son a gunner on a World War II battleship, and his youngest son a naval aviator flying the fabled F-8 Crusader off an aircraft carrier in Vietnam. He felt silly being a mere army private compared to his two sons, yet he was very proud of both of them. He spent many hours watching news of the war on television. On one occasion in March he saw a news story about the A-6 Intruder, an attack plane made by his fellows at Grumman. A fine plane, Philip was proud of what his company produced, and yet more than anything he longed to see the checkered tails of VF-211, in hopes of seeing anything related to his son. This was a new experience, following the war on television, as World War II was not covered in remotely the same fashion by American media.

. . . . .

The United States space program was a source of endless fascination for Philip. He followed closely the missions of the Gemini program. In March, Gemini 8 prepared for lift off, with Neil Armstrong at the controls. On March 16, the spacecraft lifted off. Philip listened to the radio broadcast with rapt attention.

The Gemini 8 mission was to test whether astronauts could successfully dock two craft in space. Astronauts would also perform a tethered space walk, maneuvering in the vast gravity-free expanse of space outside a spacecraft. Philip was a long, long way from horse and buggy carts and steam powered trains running along the tracks in Sicily.

The countdown to liftoff was underway. Philip took a drink and listened attentively. Just then, with 30 minutes to go, Maria entered the room. Philip angrily sent her away, frustrated with the interruption. Maria stormed off; Philip didn't care but realized that she was not too happy. He turned his attention back to the radio.

The rocket took off and Philip heard excited chatter over the radio. Liftoff was smooth as the rocket arced into the atmosphere. Gemini 8 was on its way to meet the Agena craft with which it was scheduled to dock.

The craft successfully docked with the Agena while in orbit. But then there was a malfunction and the mission had to be cut short. Scheduled originally for three days, the mission terminated and the capsule splashed down in the Pacific at 11:00pm. It turned out that the malfunction was caused by a short-circuit in the wiring of the capsule.

When the broadcast ended, Philip spoke with Maria and apologized. As it happened, Maria was simply trying to bring her brother a slice of pizza she had just made. He was ashamed of himself, but the fact of the matter was, while he loved pizza, he could get that anytime he wanted; space rockets were few and far between.

. . . . .

Flip's first tour of Vietnam ended, and upon returning to the United States, he and Patricia made it official, getting married on June 26, 1965. He began a second tour, which lasted from 1965-66. He was granted leave and Patricia flew out to spend a week together in Hong Kong. When she returned, she spoke with Philip and told him what a grand time they had. Shortly thereafter, Philip received a letter from Flip. He wrote his father about the time he had, and about a naval autobiography written by Daniel Gallery that he had read and sent back home.

"Dear Dad, about four hours ago I very reluctantly put Patty in a plane for home....we have just spent the most enjoyable six days.... Hong Kong was wonderful. It was just great to spend the time with Patty...we saw lots of things...splurged on clothes, shoes, all tailor made...cheap. We went broke saving money. If I can wrangle a cruise to the Mediterranean, I'll have Patty come to Europe....Glad you liked *Eight Bells and All's Well*. Let Ben read it. Gallery's whole book worth book worth the singe sentence, 'I'd rather go through life believing in God and find He does not exist than not believe in Him and meet Him face to face'....We leave in the morning...thirty days, maybe eighty, ninety days on the line. Give my love to everyone...pray that I shall not be afraid of anything...I love you all dearly."

Philip was so proud of his son.

. . . . .

Flip's second tour of duty in Vietnam was marked by a dramatic encounter with the enemy. On June 12, 1966, Flip's squadron leader, Commander Hal Marr recorded the first Crusader kill of an enemy MiG-17. Flip was Marr's wingman for the mission, and the two of them encountered two MiGs. Marr and Flip saw the MiGs split, and they passed by one of them head-on. Marr fired his 20mm cannon and missed, and then tried a Sidewinder missile, which also missed. The MiG had been on afterburner and was low on fuel, so the pilot turned for home when Marr engaged his own afterburner and closed rapidly with the fleeing MiG. Marr fired another Sidewinder – his last – and it clipped the tail of the MiG. In a fiery explosion, the plane crashed to earth, and Marr had his kill. The other MiG escaped and Marr and Flip flew back to the *Hancock*.

Nine days later, Flip was on another mission, this time with his friend Cole Black and another Checkmate F-8 pilot. They were providing fighter escort for a bombing mission. Meanwhile, 45 miles away, Flip's roommate Dick Smith was escorting a photo reconnaissance plane. The reconnaissance plane Smith was escorting was shot down, and the pilot safely ejected, but was now on the ground in enemy territory. Smith began circling and calling for help. Black, leading the F-8 escort mission, ordered the bombers back to the *Hancock* and they sped off to support Smith.

The four F-8 pilots circled over the downed pilot, waiting until the rescue helicopter would arrive. Enemy antiaircraft guns let loose, riddling Flip's F-8 with holes – some 70 in all – and Flip knew he had been hit hard. The engine was performing all right, however, and he still maintained control over the Crusader. However, he was running out of fuel and soon reached "bingo" status – indicating that either he had to leave for the *Hancock* now, or eject in enemy territory. As he flew towards the ocean, he heard the call of "MiGs!" and, despite being nearly out of fuel, he turned back to provide help for his fellow F-8 pilots, who had been jumped by enemy fighters. He entered the fray and saw a MiG on the tail of one of the Crusaders. It was his friend Cole Black.

"F-8, you've got a MiG on your tail!" he radioed. Black attempted to maneuver, but could not shake the MiG. Flip got behind the MiG and got a successful tone with his heat-seeking Sidewinder, indicating that it was locked onto a target, but Flip had no idea whether it was locked onto the enemy MiG, or his friend Cole. He held off from firing, and before he knew it, the MiG had fired into Black's plane, shredding it with shrapnel, and forcing him to eject.

At this point, another MiG had gotten behind Flip, and he had only one alternative – to outrun the North Vietnamese aircraft. The Crusader was built for speed, and, despite being almost out of fuel, he hit the afterburner. The MiG tried to keep up, and managed to fire his own cannon at Flip. Flip's damaged plane couldn't attain top speed and he couldn't outrun the MiG, so he dove for the "deck". Racing at 600 knots, the plane shook violently. Never the easiest aircraft to control even under the best of circumstances, Flip's F-8 was barely avoiding a deadly crash. His helmet banged against the canopy of his cockpit.

Suddenly, Flip turned around and jammed the F-8 forward with every ounce of power it had left, and re-engaged the stunned enemy pilot. Getting within missile range, he fired a Sidewinder, which ran right up the MiG's tailpipe and exploded. Flip had a kill, but at what cost? His fuel was virtually gone, and he eased his F-8 out to sea, radioing desperately for help.

A nearby tanker, dangerously low on fuel itself, radioed back. Flip managed to siphon just enough fuel to make it back to the *Hancock*, enough for just one try at a successful landing. But he took so much from the tanker that the tanker, too, only had enough fuel for one try at a successful landing. Both Flip and the tanker pilot managed to land with their planes virtually empty of fuel – just six minutes' worth left in the tank. Flip owed his life to the tanker pilot, and for his own actions, Flip received the coveted Navy Cross.

. . . . .

Philip was soon contacted by the newspapers, who had word of Flip's heroism before he himself did. Shortly thereafter, he received a letter from Flip, telling him some of the story, and asking Philip to not speak to the press, who were of course making this a big story, and Flip did not want it reported inaccurately. He also did not want his family bothered by intrusive media members.

Philip's oldest son had survived kamikaze attacks off the coast of Okinawa in 1945. Twenty-one years later, his youngest son survived MiG attacks over North Vietnam.

Philip had two very brave, and very fortunate, sons.

Chapter 29 – Endings

Flip left the service, having been honorably discharged after two tours of duty in Vietnam. For a while he continued to serve in the reserves, but then ended his service and flew full time for Pan American Airlines. Everywhere he went, he was treated like royalty, as Pan Am pilots represented not only one of the most famous companies in the world – Pan Am's blue dot was the second-most recognized logo in the world behind the Coca-Cola bottle – but also served as de facto ambassadors of the United States. Often, Americans who found themselves in trouble overseas chose not to go to an American embassy, but rather to Pan Am's local headquarters. As such, Pan Am helped out innumerable Americans abroad in need of assistance.

Part of Flip's perk for being a Pan Am pilot was that his parents got to fly for free. Philip determined that it was time for him to see the old country, and Flip arranged a two-week trip to Italy for Philip and Kate. It had been more than 55 years since Philip had been to Sicily. He and Kate landed in Rome and they first toured the Vatican. Philip had his issues with organized religion, but he was a man who believed in God, and so the Vatican did hold some significance for him.

Philip once wrote in his journal, lamenting the human condition that led to so much war and strife. He wrote, "I wonder why God has so much compassion for mankind. Perhaps He sees some ray of hope in some human souls, souls such as say, my friend Arnold, my father, His son Jesus. Most of the human race is not like that; most of the human race defies Him; most of the human race denies His existence. Let me take my punishment for believing in Him. As a very wise man said, 'I'd rather believe in God and find He doesn't exist, than not believe in Him and then have to face Him.'"

Philip knew God was real, but he was not above a little mischief, even in such a venerable place as St. Peter's Bascilica. While craning his neck upward at the massive golden domed interior, amazed at what man had wrought in the name of God, he felt a little rumbling inside and then passed gas, a mere 20 yards away from the Papal altar. He giggled to himself and made a mental note to share the story back home, as he considered it noteworthy to have broken wind in the heart of Roman Catholicism.

Philip's tour of Rome ended, and he and Kate traveled to his home country in Sicily. There he discovered a world unlike what he imagined. Sicily had always been one of the poorest parts of Italy, and looked nothing like Rome or Milan. But time did not completely stop there either. When Philip had left in 1913, Sicily was populated by peasants working the land, by horse-and-buggy transportation, a few motor vehicles, and some train tracks. Soldiers carried wooden-stocked rifles that fired one shot at a time. People used latrines. By the time he returned, men had explored nature at the atomic level and had traveled in space. Planes took men in the sky and flew twice the speed of sound. Computers filled rooms and did millions of calculations that was not even considered possible by the people of Philip's boyhood.

Electric lights brightened busy city streets. Cars were everywhere. Sicily was not Paris or New York, but it was not the Sicily he remembered. It was home but not *home*, and after just a few days there, he longed to be back in the United States with his family. What was scheduled to be a two-week trip was cut in half, as a somewhat disillusioned Philip took his wife Kate and made his second east-to-west crossing of the Atlantic from Italy to New York, this time in a Pan American airliner instead of a steamship, the trip taking less than 7 hours instead of a week.

He would never go back to Italy again.

. . . . .

The end of the 1960s brought about some blessings and one significant loss for Philip. On the plus side, three new grandchildren were born. In December 1966, Judith was born to Flip and Patricia. In January 1968,

Pat gave birth to their second daughter, Joan. And in December 1969, Pat and Flip's third child – a boy named John – was born. Philip was delighted with his new grandchildren, but as was the case with the birth of his sons Ben and Flip, his new grandson took on special significance – not because he was anything more special than the girls, but because he represented another generation of Vampatella men that could pass on the family name. As was the case with his own sons, this mattered a great deal to Philip. In his youngest son's new son, he saw great potential for the family legacy. Time would tell if that that potential would be realized.

When Judith (everyone simply called her Judy) was born, Flip and Pat were still living in San Diego, and Philip decided to pay them a visit. But Philip was a man of some odd quirks. He flew hours across the country and arrived at their door. Flip was out when he arrived at night. He knocked on the door. Pat opened it and there stood her father-in-law.

"Come in!" she said, gesturing for him to enter their home. He shook his head.

"I can't."

"Why not?"

"Because I have a cold."

"So wait, you flew all the way out here to see us – and your granddaughter especially – but you won't come in?" Pat was incredulous.

It took some effort on her part, but finally she was able to convince him to come in and hold Judy for the first time.

. . . . .

The space program continued to enthrall Philip. He was raised in rural Sicily in a time when technological advances consisted of the telephone and internal combustion engine. By the time 1969 rolled around, scientists had developed penicillin, the atom had been split, and the United States and Soviet Union were racing to put men on the moon.

The moon! Philip could hardly believe it. The Gemini program launched the Apollo program, and NASA's moon program gained considerable steam. There were setbacks, of course, but the nation held firm in its conviction to beat the Soviets in the space race. The massive Saturn V rocket would transport astronauts into space, breaking through the earth's atmosphere, and the Apollo craft would fly several days to the moon, at which time two of the three astronauts on board would descend in the lunar module – the LEM as it was known – and land on the lunar surface.

The crew was chosen for Apollo 11, which was scheduled to be the first mission to land human beings on the moon. Neil Armstrong, Edwin "Buzz" Aldrin, and Michael Collins were assigned to the mission, and on July 16, 1969, the Apollo 11 spacecraft successfully launched through the atmosphere and into space. On July 20, after some 30 orbits around the earth, Armstrong and Aldrin entered the *Eagle* lunar lander and began their descent. Some 530 million people worldwide were transfixed to their televisions as Walter Cronkite and other journalists reported on every movement of the Eagle and its two astronauts. At 8:17pm, the lander successfully touched down on the surface of the moon, and after completing a safety checklist, Armstrong radioed NASA, "Houston, *Tranquility Base* here. The *Eagle* has landed."

In reply, a breathless Charles Duke replied from ground control, "Roger, *Tranquility*, we copy you on the ground. You got a bunch of guys about to turn blue. We're breathing again. Thanks a lot."

As they began preparations for departing *Eagle*, Aldrin radioed, "This is the LM pilot. I'd like to take this opportunity to ask every person listening in, whoever and wherever they may be, to pause for a moment and contemplate the events of the past few hours and to give thanks in his or her own way." Aldrin was an elder in his Presbyterian church, and was planning on taking communion on the moon. But NASA was in the midst of a lawsuit filed by atheist Madalyn Murray O'Hair, who demanded that NASA not broadcast astronauts' religious views and activities while on the mission. Hence his wording to give thanks "in his or her own way."

At 2:56am, on July 21, 1969, Neil Armstrong stepped off the footpad of the *Eagle* and placed his boots on the lunar surface. He declared to the world, "That's one small step for a man, one giant leap for mankind."

Philip now lived in a world where man walked on the moon.

. . . . .

His newest grandson, John, had been born on December 1, 1969, just four and a half months after Armstrong stepped on the moon. This was a cause for celebration, but a pall hung over Philip. His daughter Marie was ill, and it was grave. Philip had seen the devastating effects of cancer on his dear Antoinette, and now his daughter faced the same enemy: ovarian cancer. Marie was a widow and living with her father, who tried to get her the best medical care he could provide, but it was a losing effort. In December, she succumbed to the deadly illness, and Philip had lost his first child. The entire family mourned the loss of Marie, who was a beloved figure to everyone.

. . . . .

In October of 1971, Pat gave birth to another daughter, Jean – giving them four J's – and before long, Irene was pregnant again with their second. The brood of grandchildren was growing and would be completed in July 1972 with the birth of Marie to Irene and Bob, who now had two girls, with their oldest daughter Jennifer having been born in November 1965. Philip now had 14 grandchildren – 8 girls and 6 boys – and he was proud of each and every one of them.

. . . . .

The Vietnam war entered a new phase with the election of Richard Nixon in 1968. Vowing to end the war, Nixon took the approach that it was important to end it from a position of strength. He increased troop levels and the intensity and scale of the fighting grew.

As the 1972 Presidential campaign came around, he found himself embroiled in a very difficult political battle against the Democratic nominee, George McGovern. McGovern was nominated officially at the Democratic National Convention in July, but one month earlier, Nixon operatives engaged in activity that would alter the political landscape forever.

On June 17, 1972, five men broke into Democratic party headquarters at the Watergate Hotel in Washington, and the subsequent investigation led to E. Howard Hunt, an ex-CIA officer who was one of President Nixon's "plumbers" – a man tasked with fixing leaks in the White House. Such leaks were, of course, not literal, but metaphorical – information leaks. Hunt was connected to Charles Colson, who was special counsel to Nixon. Nixon did not order the break in, and it is entirely possible that he never even knew about it. Nonetheless, the storm clouds were brewing, and Nixon's team began to cover up the administration's links to the crime.

Nixon would survive long enough to defeat McGovern in a one-sided election, but two years later, after declaring, "I am not a crook," would resign in disgrace. In 1975, the Vietnam war would come to an end.

. . . . .

When Philip had arrived in the United States, many – perhaps even most – Americans had a negative view of Italians. They were seen as lazy an uneducated. They were considered to be people of color and the lowest class of society. Their language, skin color, and religious traditions offended many white Americans. They were viewed as being apt to commit crimes and many associated Italians with organized crime.

In 1972, Mario Puzo's landmark production, *The Godfather*, made its way to the silver screen. It captured the imagination of a nation, who saw the inner workings of a fictitious Italian mafia family – the Corleones – and fell in love with them. Organized crime, specifically the Italian mafia, was glamorized. It became…fashionable…to think well of mobsters. Mafia life was romanticized.

When the New Orleans lynching occurred, Italian mafia were vilified, and it cost many innocent people their lives. In the 20s, Al Capone was seen as public enemy number one. Following World War I the United States government made laws limiting immigration, especially with Italians in view.

But Americans' view of Italians – though derogatory terms like *"wop"*, *"guinea"*, and *"dago"* were still regularly used – had changed. It had become…cool…to be Italian, especially if you were Sicilian and could reasonably get people to think that just maybe you had connections to the mafia.

Nonetheless, the Italian stereotypes continued, and even though *The Godfather* glamorized Italian organized crime, it nonetheless perpetuated the stereotype that had plagued Italian immigrants for a hundred years and led to so many forms of mistreatment by American citizens and the government itself.

. . . . .

It turns out that cancer has a genetic component. That is, it can run in families. Philip had already lost his dear wife to cancer in 1960, and then, nine years later, his daughter fell to the awful disease. In 1972, it once again entered the family, working its evil on Philip's oldest daughter, Angelina.

A few days before Christmas, fighting for her life against the same exact form of cancer that claimed her sister, Angelina died from ovarian cancer. It was a devastating blow to Philip and the family. The blow was doubly crushing as just a few days later, Jimmy Rapuano – Philip's beloved brother-in-law and friend, and favorite uncle to Philip's children – passed away. Within the span of a handful of days around Christmas, the Vampatella family lost two dear members to death.

Christmas – one of the family's favorite holidays – was tragic.

A few days after Jimmy died, the family gathered together, on December 31. The new year approaching, with the tears still flowing, everyone agreed that 1972 was, by all accounts, a terrible year. Someone cried out, "Screw you, '72!" which became a rallying cry of sorts. The clan agreed that something needed to be done. They wrote 1972 on a paper plate and went outside behind Philip's house. A hole was dug and the plate was thrown into it. They spit on it and defiled it and swore at it and buried it, venting their deep grief and anger at the loss of Angie and Jimmy.

They then agreed that Christmas needed a do-over. In July 1973, the Vampatellas celebrated "Christmas in July", complete with Santa and presents, and an outdoor kiddie pool for the young grandchildren to play in as temperatures reached 90 degrees in Great River.

. . . . .

Ten more years passed. Over that time, Philip and Kate aged, Philip's older children reached their 50s, and his younger children reached their 40s. The older grandchildren grew into adults and started having kids of their own, and Philip became a great grandfather. The younger grandchildren reached the teen years.

Time, as it always does, marched forward inexorably. Undaunted by human activity or world events, the earth continued to spin and orbit the sun, year after year. The Vampatella family endured some hardships and many blessings. Its members loved each other and occasionally fought, as families do. Flip's family moved to Maine and Philip saw him, his wife, and his four children, much less than before. Long Island developed and even little Great River, while still small, became something resembling a town rather than a sparse collection of homes spread out over many square miles.

Richard Nixon resigned in 1974 and Gerald Ford assumed the presidency, only to lose the 1976 election to Georgia governor Jimmy Carter. The Soviets invaded Afghanistan and once again the United States found itself confronting the evils of communism. In response, the U.S. boycotted the 1980 Moscow Olympics. In Iran, the Ayatollah Khomeni took control over the U.S.-backed Shah and 52 American diplomats and citizens were held hostage as Iranian fanatics besieged and took over the American embassy in Tehran. Jimmy Carter, seen as a weak President, lost the 1980 election to Ronald Reagan.

. . . . .

1983 arrived. Philip began the year feeling fine but by late summer, he was not doing well. His head hurt and he didn't know why. But Philip hated going to the doctor, and as a result never got it examined. He just lived with the pain, taking aspirin when he thought of it.

In late September, Philip fell and hurt himself. At first, it was believed that Philip fell because he had been drinking too much. He finally saw a doctor and after numerous tests, they determined that he had a brain tumor, which was pressing against his brain, causing Philip to lose his sense of balance. It had grown so prevalent that it was inoperable. Moreover, the cancer – clearly a Vampatella family trait – had metastasized throughout his body, and it was at this point just a matter of time. Had Philip gone to the doctor for regular physicals and testing, they may have discovered it early enough to treat it effectively, but by this point it was too late. Death was imminent.

On October 13, 1983, another Vampatella succumbed to cancer and Philip went to be with his first wife, Antoinette, and two daughters, Marie and Angie. He was given a military funeral as he had earned from his service in the United States Army back in World War I.

Flip's family traveled from Maine to join the rest of the Vampatella family. They stayed with Pat's older sister Eileen, and the morning of the funeral, Flip and his son John stood in the kitchen of Eileen's house, both of them dressed in a suit and tie. John, just twelve years old and experiencing his first death, saw something in his father for the first time. Tears.

John walked over to his father and hugged him. Then the tears flowed freely as Flip held his son for a long time, the two of them embracing in grief. They were a physically affectionate family, but this was different. Flip cried for many minutes. On the way to the funeral parlor, he tried to lighten the mood with a pun about a hearse, and everyone in the car laughed.

Philip's casket was covered in an American flag and a proper mass was held. The flag was folded up in proper military fashion and handed to Flip. Philip's body was lowered into the ground amidst the weeping of all his family members.

The flag was, in turn, handed to John, who was told, "Grandpa wanted you to have this," and he cried some more.

. . . . .

Philip Vampatella, my grandfather, died at the age of 86, having traveled as a teenager from Sicily to the United States. He managed to work and live and marry and have children. He survived a war and the Great Depression. He fathered six children and sent two of them off to war, both of them surviving hair-raising combat. He lost his wife and two of his children before he himself passed away. He lived a full life and I am here because of him.

And I still have his flag.

Afterword

Following my grandfather's death, things went back to normal for most of us. Having lived in Maine, our family felt the loss less than the others, as the distance meant a lot less time spent not only with my grandfather, but also the rest of the relatives. To this day I am saddened by that fact.

Kate (we called her "Grandma Kate") lived another ten years before passing away, and though in the beginning she found acceptance hard, the family came to love her and she was missed by all. I never personally knew my grandmother Antoinette, and Grandma Kate was the only Vampatella grandmother that I ever knew. The same is true, of course, for my three sisters as well as Jen and Marie. The rest of the cousins, being significantly older than the six youngest of us, knew both Antoinette and, of course, Kate.

As a boy I never understood why I received my grandfather's American flag, but it turns out that he had a soft spot for me. I'm sure much of that had to do with being the youngest boy in the family; that Sicilian culture of wanting to pass on the family name meant that there was disproportionate hope put in having boys in the family. My grandfather loved the New York Yankees, and my father did as well, but growing up in Maine, I embraced their archrivals, the Boston Red Sox.

My grandfather knew this, and every time the Red Sox and Yankees played, while he rooted for the Yankees, he always felt bad for me when the Yankees won, knowing that his youngest grandson would be sad.

The importance of passing on the family name is a real Sicilian phenomenon that took my wife some getting used to. Our name did not survive long in Sicily following my grandfather's immigration to the United States. In fact, my cousin Cathy (Golden) Gallagher and her husband Mark have done considerable research into our family history, even having traveled to Sicily to see where my grandfather grew up. Our name simply is not found anymore anywhere in Italy, that we've been able to discern. Yet the name is distinctly Sicilian. I know this because when I first traveled to Italy (a 2006 trip to Milan for work), the customs agent read my passport and said, "Vampatella....you are from Sicily, yes?" I had to tell him that yes, my grandfather was from Sicily but immigrated to the U.S. in 1913. Then I asked him how he knew where my family was from. He shrugged and simply said, "It's a Sicilian name." I never understood how he knew that, especially if the name is essentially extinct.

When my wife and I first started talking about marriage, my father made it plain to my future bride: male children were expected. This was hard for my wife to digest, not because she didn't want boys, but because it seemed **so** important to my father. This was her introduction to this family name issue. We ended up having four children, and the first two are boys, which relieved quite a bit of pressure off us. We did our job passing on the family name!

For decades, we believed we were the only Vampatella clan on the planet. But a number of years ago we discovered another branch of the family tree. There are Vampatellas in Australia, and we believe they were connected to Biagio's family. We do not know the exact origin, and though we have made contact with the Australian Vampatellas, we do not know exactly how they came to be or how they got to Australia, but we think that branch began through one of Biagio's siblings.

In February 2006, Uncle Benny, still working as a mason at the age of 80 in Nevada, suffered a heart attack while driving to work, careened off the road, and hit a telephone pole, putting him in a coma. He passed a week later. His body was flown back to New York, and I had the honor of performing his memorial service. Three years earlier he had given his life to Jesus Christ and had a powerful testimony of a changed life.

My father gave a moving eulogy – the third time I've seen him cry. The first was at his father's funeral, as I described in the book. The second was when we dropped my oldest sister Judy off at college for the first time. And this was the third. He spoke of his brother thusly: "When I was born, Ben was my brother. When I was a boy, Ben was my hero. When I got older, Ben became my best friend. So in one instant, I lost my brother, my hero, and my best friend." I was practically sobbing when he finished, and I had to follow him and continue leading the service.

That left three of Philip's children alive: Anna, Irene, and my father Philip (Flip). All three of them loved the Yankees and would spend time talking about their games. In 2011 my family took a trip to New York City and I was able to take my two sons, my father, my cousin, and my Aunt Irene to Yankee Stadium. It was an amazing experience seeing my father and his sister enjoy the ballpark. Unfortunately, the Yankees won the game.

Irene and Anna talked baseball every day and were the best of friends. Anna passed away in January of 2012, leaving another huge void in the family. Her husband Charles had died years earlier from a bad heart. My father and Irene are the only two surviving members of the family raised on Cedarhurst Street, following the deaths of their four siblings, their spouses, and Irene's husband Bob.

In the summer of 2018, the Vampatella family got together for the first non-funeral, non-wedding reunion in a very long time. Not everyone could make it, but it was wonderful seeing those that could. One of the most memorable moments was when my cousin Jen played a recording my grandfather had made at the very end of his life. The sound quality – an old cassette recorded in a digital format having been played over the air – was not good, but Jen took the time to transcribe it. My grandfather talked philosophically, as was his wont, and for the first time my children and everyone of their generation heard their great grandfather's voice. It had been a long time – more than 35 years – since I myself had heard his voice. I had forgotten what it sounded like, but when Jen started the recording, it all came back to me. Deep, thick, accented, it was hard to understand him. Her transcription helped a great deal, but honestly, the words weren't even important. It was that I was hearing his voice. I miss my grandpa.

I regret that he didn't speak Italian in his home. I understood why, but because of that choice, my father never learned Italian, and consequently, I never did either. I have picked up some along the way, but I wish I was fluent. He believed strongly that to be American meant speaking the language – English – instead of one's native tongue. Right or wrong, that was his philosophy.

My father, Flip, ended up returning to college more than two decades after dropping out at Rutgers, and in fulfillment of the promise he had made to his father Philip, got his bachelor's degree from the University of Southern Maine. He has told many people over the years that failing out of college was the best thing that ever happened to him, as without that, he never would have joined the Navy, never would have met my mother, and my three sisters and I, along with our own children, would not exist.

During this project I have learned a lot about many aspects of US and world history, as well as my own family's own background. The Italian side of me (my mom is Irish-German) is proud to have this heritage. When I went to Italy for the first time, I discovered an affinity with the country in ways that are hard to describe. Even though I was in northern Italy (Milan), and have yet to visit anywhere in the country south of Rome, I walked the streets, saw Italian words everywhere, and felt…home. It was a very strange sensation, to be perfectly honest. But I felt like I just fit there. Having the last name that I do certainly helped. In 2007 I was able to bring my entire family (six of us total) to Milan, Rome, and Venice. That represented the largest number of Vampatellas in the nation of Italy since Biagio and Philip left in 1913. Not for 94 years had there been this many people in Italy with the last name Vampatella.

I can't wait to go back.

Made in the USA
Coppell, TX
25 August 2022

82023395R00152